Feud in the Icelandic Saga

To Gayle and Ashley

The whole of Icelandic history is miraculous. A number of barbarian
gentlemen leave Norway because the government there is becoming civilized
and interfering; they settle in Iceland because they want to keep what they can
of the unreformed past, the old freedom. It looks like anarchy. But immediately they begin to frame a Social Contract and to make laws in the most
intelligent manner: a colonial agent is sent back to the Mother Country to
study law and present a report. They might have sunk into mere hard work
and ignorance, contending with the difficulties of their new country; they
might have become boors without a history, without a ballad. In fact the
Icelandic settlers took with them the intellect of Norway; they wrote the
history of the kings and the adventures of the gods. The settlement of Iceland
looks like a furious plunge of angry and intemperate chiefs, away from order
into a grim and reckless land of Cockayne. The truth is that those rebels and
their commonwealth were more self-possessed, more clearly conscious of
their own aims, more critical of their own achievements, than any polity on
earth since the fall of Athens. Iceland, though the country is large, has always
been like a city-state in many of its ways; the small population, though widely
scattered, was not broken up, and the tour quarters of Iceland took as much
interest in one another's gossip as the quarters of Florence. In the Sagas,
where nothing is of much importance except individual men, and where all the
chief men are known to one another, a journey from Borg to Eyjafirth is no
more than going past a few houses. The distant corners of the island are near
one another. There is no sense of those impersonal forces, those nameless
multitudes, that make history a different thing from biography in other lands.
All history in Iceland shaped itself as biography or as drama, and there was no
large crowd at the back of the stage.

—W. P. Ker

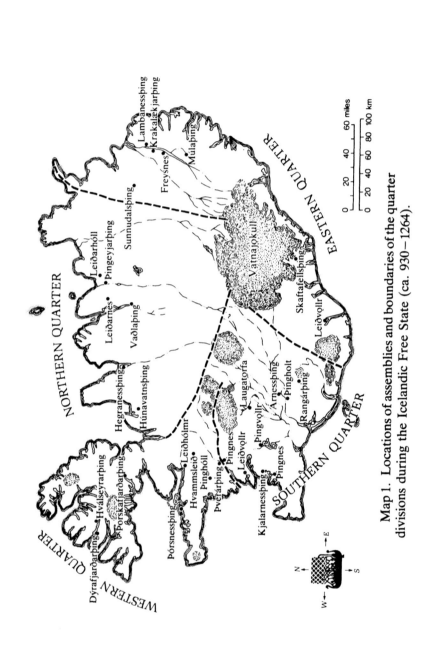

Map 1. Locations of assemblies and boundaries of the quarter divisions during the Icelandic Free State (ca. 930–1264).

Contents

Preface   ix

Acknowledgments   xvii

1   Introduction   1

2   Feud in Saga Narrative: Its Roots in Icelandic Society   24

3   The Syntax of Narrative Elements   47

4   Units of Travel and Information and the Feudeme of Conflict   63

5   The Feudeme of Advocacy   74

6   The Feudeme of Resolution   98

7   Feud Clusters and Feud Chains   114

8   The Importance of Land in Saga Feud   143

9   Two Sets of Feud Chains in *Njáls saga*   161

10   Saga Narrative with Low Cluster Density   191

11 Conclusion

11 Conclusion 205

Appendixes
A. A Brief Account of Legal and Social
   Terms 209
B. Examples of Conflict 222
   Material Sources of Conflict 223
   Nonmaterial Sources of Conflict 234
C. Examples of Advocacy 245
   Brokerage 245
   Self-Advocacy 254
   Goading 256
   Information Passing 257
D. Examples of Resolution 259
   Arbitration 260
   Direct Resolution 265
   Rejected Resolution 272

Index 277

Maps
Map 1. Locations of assemblies and
   boundaries of the quarter divisions vi
Map 2. Locations of some family and
   Sturlunga sagas xiv
Map 3. Eyjafjǫrðr (ca. 1184–1200) 84
Map 4. Journeys of Flosi Þórðarson
   and Kári Sǫlmundarson as
   described in *Njáls saga* 166

Preface

Too often studies of the Icelandic sagas have become embroiled in attempts to prove either the highly literary or the highly oral nature of these medieval narratives. Such argumentation has sapped energy from saga studies which could have been put to more fruitful use. This book is based on the premise that the extant sagas are a written literature of the twelfth and thirteenth centuries, but a literature that maintained a strong link to an earlier narrative tradition. Extant Icelandic works of history, law, science, and literature show that in the thirteenth century Iceland was not only a society that knew and appreciated the importance of writing, but also one that had a long oral tradition of prose and poetry.

Elaborate theories have been proposed to explain the origin of the sagas and to chronicle their supposed literary development, but a simpler and more reasonable explanation has been ignored. It is that the crucial element in the origin of the sagas is not the introduction of writing in the mid-eleventh century or the impact of literary borrowings from the continent in the twelfth and thirteenth centuries, but the subject of the tales themselves, that is, Icelandic feud. This idea led me to undertake an examination of Icelandic feud and of the narrative technique of recounting it. If the Icelanders could develop complex and dependable forms of feud, they could also develop a way of recounting to one another the stories of their feuds before they learned how to write.

The sagamen who composed the Icelandic family sagas used a reliable but unarticulated narrative strategy to develop tales of feud. They combined three core elements—conflict, advocacy, and resolution—and interspersed among them accounts of travel and units of essential or useful information such as genealogies, portents, advice, history of family lands, background to personal and political obligations, and descriptions of settings. The feuds in the sagas do not concern the grandiose affairs of national politics or the fates of princes. Rather, the sagas narrate tales of a conservative, rural, isolated, island society whose members carried on their daily personal business and met regularly in district and national assemblies. Because the roots of the compositional technique of the sagas are deeply set in the cultural traditions of medieval Icelanders, I have included throughout this study background information on Iceland, especially that which concerns the relationship between farmers and chieftains.

In order to illustrate my conclusions, I have drawn examples from a wide variety of sagas, though the list is by no means exhaustive, and at times I have felt that I am only scratching the surface. Perhaps because of my personal fascination with their stories, numerous examples are drawn from *Njáls saga*, considered to be one of the most literary of the sagas, and *Vápnfirðinga saga*, rarely subject to literary criticism because it is so thoroughly steeped in district politics. These and other family sagas have often been characterized as a literature of conflict, but this formulation tells less than half the story, for the sagas are as much, if not more, a literature of resolution. Resolutions of feud were not always lasting. The often temporary nature of settlements is a key aspect of saga story, for violent resolutions were often coupled with later compromises until a suitable settlement was finally arranged. Advocacy, of which the primary type was brokering of support, acted as a link, both inducing and restraining conflicts and resolutions. These three active elements of saga feud—conflict, advocacy, resolution—I have called feudemes, and a large part of this book is devoted to examining how these narrative components combine to form saga prose. After much experimentation, I decided to annotate these narrative elements according to their most simple linear order while at the same time recognizing their rich paradigmatic possibilities.

This preface includes a listing of the family sagas and a map designating the areas of Iceland in which the events of particular sagas took place. Chapter 1 includes a discussion of the types of sagas and closes with nine narrative segments taken from different sagas. These saga selections, referred to throughout the study, illustrate varied aspects of saga feud and narrative. In chapter 2, I provide a sketch of the societal background of feud before turning to an example of a small feud from *Droplaugarsona saga*. Chapter 3 opens with a discussion of narrative terms and then moves on to consider the characteristics of feudemes. Occurrences of units of travel and information and the different types of conflict make up chapter 4; chapter 5 focuses on types of advocacies. Resolution in saga feud is the topic of chapter 6. The process of Icelandic decision making is considered throughout the three chapters on the feudemes. The formation of the basic narrative elements into feud clusters and feud chains is the subject of chapter 7. Chapter 8 expands the discussion to consider the importance of land in saga feud. Two long sets of feud chains from *Njáls saga* are examined in chapter 9. In chapter 10, I consider the categories of sagas whose narratives are constructed somewhat differently from the standard method of narrating most feuds set in Iceland. Chapter 11 provides a brief conclusion and proposes questions for future studies.

The four appendixes are meant to enrich this study by offering useful material that is too lengthy to be included in the text itself. Appendix A gives short definitions of standard Icelandic terms, such as *goði* and *bóndi*, and provides background information about Icelandic institutions and legal procedures. As knowledge of this terminology and material is assumed in the body of the work, Appendix A is a beginning point for those unacquainted with such matters. Appendixes B, C, and D offer, respectively, examples of conflicts, advocacies, and resolutions in various sagas. These appendixes, arranged according to the same categories used in chapters 4, 5, and 6, may be read as adjuncts to those chapters.

The book presents four maps. Of these, the first two are maps of the entire island. Map 1 (frontispiece) shows the locations of assemblies and the boundaries of the quarter divisions. Map 2 shows the locations of some family and Sturlunga sagas as well as of important regions and places mentioned in the sagas. Map 3, of Eyjafjǫrðr, illustrates a specific discussion of chieftains and thingmen in one region, and map 4 charts the travels, described in *Njáls saga*, of Flosi and Kári as each searches for support after the burning of Njáll's farmstead.

A note for nonreaders of Old Norse: The letter þ ("thorn") is pronounced like *th*, as in thought; ð ("eth"), a voiced spirant, is pronounced *th*, as in breathe. The name Þórr would be Thor in English and Óðinn would be Othin (often written Odin in translations). In Icelandic words, the letter *j* is pronounced like *y* in yes. Icelandic names are inflected and I have used the nominative form, except in the titles of sagas, where the person's name is in the genitive case; for example, *Njáls saga* is named after Njáll, *Víga-Glúms saga* is named after Víga-Glúmr, and *Guðmundar saga dýra* is named after Guðmundr dýri.

In this book I refer to the standard editions of the family sagas, the *Íslenzk fornrit* volumes, edited by Icelandic scholars and published in Reykjavík by Hið íslenzka fornritafélag (1933–1968). In planning the *fornrit* edition, the editors took into account the regional nature of the sagas and presented them in geographical order, beginning with volume 2. Volume 1 contains two historical works of national scope, *Íslendingabók*, the Book of the Icelanders, and *Landnámabók*, the Book of Settlements (literally the

Book of the Landtakings). The saga volumes begin with
Egils saga (vol. 2), placed in Borgarfjǫrðr in the Western
Quarter. The succeeding volumes progress clockwise along
the shoreline, gathering together the tales of the coast and
the corresponding inland districts. The majority of the
sagas are arranged according to the local areas where the
major events of the tales took place. In the relatively few
sagas, such as the poets' sagas and the outlaw sagas, in
which the story is not centered on feud in a specific region
but follows the wanderings of a character in Iceland or
abroad, each tale is placed in the area where its hero was
raised. The regional nature of the family sagas is extended
by frequent trips to the annual national assembly, the
Althing, held at Þingvǫllr, the thing plain, in the south-
west. There, individuals from the different parts of the
island joined with one another in legal, social, and economic dealings. Many sagas therefore have both a regional
and a national ambience.

In this book I refer to each saga according to the chapter
number in the *fornrit* edition. Often these same chapter
numbers are retained in saga translations. The family sagas
discussed in this book are taken from the following volumes
of the *Íslenzk fornrit* (*ÍF*).

ÍF 1. *Íslendingabók* and *Landnámabók*, 2 vols., ed.
Jakob Benediktsson, 1968.

ÍF 2. *Egils saga Skalla-Grímssonar*, ed. Sigurður Nordal, 1933.

ÍF 3. *Borgfirðinga sǫgur*, ed. Sigurður Nordal and
Guðni Jónsson, 1938, for *Hœnsa-Þóris saga*,
Gunnlaugs saga ormstungu, Heiðarvíga saga.

ÍF 4. *Eyrbyggja saga*, ed. Einar Ól. Sveinsson and
Matthías Þórðarson, 1935.

ÍF 5. *Laxdœla saga*, ed. Einar Ól. Sveinsson, 1934.

ÍF 6. *Vestfirðinga sǫgur*, ed. Björn K. Þórólfsson
and Guðni Jónsson, 1943, for *Gísla saga
Súrssonar, Fóstbrœðra saga*, and *Hávarðar saga
Ísfirðings*.

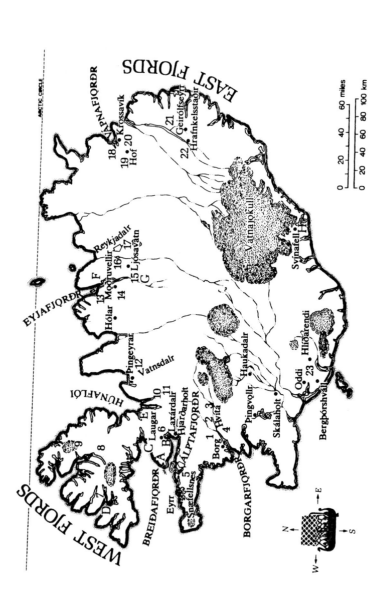

WEST FJORDS

EAST FJORDS

ARCTIC CIRCLE

VATNAJOKULL

EYJAFJORÐR

HÚNAFLÓI

BREIÐAFJORÐR

BORGARFJORÐR

HVALFJORÐR

VAPNAFJORÐR

Krossavík
18
19 • 20
Hof
21
Geirólfsstaðir
22
Hrafnkelsstaðir

Reykjadalr
Móðruvellir
16
15 • Ljósavatn
F
13
Hólar
14
G

Svínafell

Þingeyrar
12
Vatnsdalr

Hlíðarendi
Oddi
23

Bergþórshváll

Laugar
A B • 6
C
Laxárdalr
E
Hjarðarholt
10
11

Borg
Hvítá
1 2 3
4
5
Eyrr
Snæfellsnes
D

Þingvöllr
Skálaholt
Haukadalr

N
E
W
S

0   20   40   60 miles
0 20 40 60 80 100 km

ÍF 7. *Grettis saga Ásmundarsonar*, ed. Guðni Jónsson, 1936, for *Bandamanna saga.*

ÍF 8. *Vatnsdœla saga*, ed. Einar Ól. Sveinsson, 1939, for *Hallfreðar saga* and *Kormáks saga.*

ÍF 9. *Eyfirðinga sǫgur*, ed. Jónas Kristjánsson, 1956, for *Víga-Glúms saga*, and *Valla-Ljóts saga.*

ÍF 10. *Ljósvetninga saga*, ed. Björn Sigfússon, 1940, for *Reykdœla saga.*

ÍF 11. *Austfirðinga sǫgur*, ed. Jón Jóhannesson, 1950, for *Þorsteins saga hvíta*, *Vápnfirðinga saga*, *Hrafnkels saga Freysgoða*, *Droplaugarsona*

Map 2. Locations of family and Sturlunga sagas. When a saga is spread over a wide area, the number (for family sagas) or letter (for the Sturlunga sagas) shows where the major character was raised.

Family sagas: 1—*Egils saga Skalla-Grímssonar*; 2—*Hœnsa-Þóris saga*; 3—*Gunnlaugs saga ormstungu*; 4—*Heiðarvíga saga*; 5—*Eyrbyggja saga*; 6—*Laxdœla saga*; 7—*Gísla saga Súrssonar*; 8—*Fóstbroeðra saga*; 9—*Hávarðar saga Ísfirðings*; 10—*Bandamanna saga*; 11—*Grettis saga Ásmundarsonar*; 12—*Vatnsdœla saga*; 13—*Svarfdœla saga*; 14—*Valla-Ljóts saga*; 15—*Víga-Glúms saga*; 16—*Ljósvetninga saga*; 17—*Reykdœla saga*; 18—*Vápnfirðinga saga*; 19—*Þorsteins þáttr stangarhǫggs*; 20—*Ǫlkofra þáttr*; 21—*Droplaugarsona saga*; 22—*Hrafnkels saga Freysgoða*; 23—*Brennu-Njáls saga.*

Sturlunga sagas: A—*Íslendinga saga* (covers large area of Western, Northern, and Southern Quarters); B—*Sturlu saga*; C—*Geirmundar þáttr heljarskinns*; D—*Hrafns saga Sveinbjarnarsonar*; E—*Þorgils saga ok Hafliða*; F—*Guðmundar saga dýra*; G—*Prestssaga Guðmundar góða*; H—*Svínfellinga saga.*

Frequently used geographical terms; *á* (pl. *ár*) = river; *dalr* = dale; *ey* (pl. gen. *eyja*) = island; *eyrr* (pl. *eyrar*) = gravelly riverbank or small tongue of land running into sea; *fell* = mountain; *fjǫrðr* (pl. *firðir*) = fjord; *holt* = a wood or a rough stony hill or ridge; *hóll* (pl. *hólar*) = a hill or stone heap; *jǫkull* = glacier; *tunga* = tongue of land at the meeting of two rivers; *vatn* = lake; *vǫllr* (pl. *vellir*) = plain.

saga, *Þorsteins þáttr stangarhǫggs*, and *Ǫl-kofra þáttr*.

ÍF 12. *Brennu-Njáls saga*, ed. Einar Ól. Sveinsson, 1954.

Sagas from the Sturlunga compilation are taken from the standard edition, *Sturlunga saga*, ed. Jón Jóhannesson, Magnús Finnbogason, and Kristján Eldjárn, 2 vols. (Reykjavík: Sturlunguútgáfan, 1946). Sagas from volume 1 referred to in this study are *Geirmundar þáttr heljarskinns*, *Þorgils saga ok Hafliða, Sturlu saga, Prestssaga Guðmundar goða. Guðmundar saga dýra. Hrafns saga Sveinbjarnarsonar*, and *Íslendinga saga:* from volume 2, *Svínfellinga saga*.

Map 2 assists the reader in placing major family and Sturlunga sagas in their proper localities in Iceland.

When it seemed appropriate I have translated the names of persons and places. Although I have not been entirely consistent, I hope that the information added will make the book easier for the nonspecialist to read.

Because there is much cross-referencing of chapters in this book as well as referrals to the sagas, I use the abbreviations "chap." to refer to my study and "ch." to refer to chapters in the sagas.

All errors are my own, and I hope that they are few.

J. L. B.

Acknowledgments

THIS STUDY of the sagas has been a long time in preparation. My research began in my student days at Harvard University with a study of *Eyrbyggja saga* under the direction of T. M. Andersson. Our rather tempestuous meetings, tempered by Professor Andersson's good nature, helped me to solidify the position I put forward in this book. Einar Haugen and Kenneth Chapman guided me toward the development of an appropriate method of redefining saga feud and early saw the necessity of taking into consideration the struggles over land and power evident in the sagas. This subject formed the basis of my dissertation which was read by these two scholars. My belief that advocacy is a key concept in saga feud was later strengthened by discussions with the Icelanders Björn Þorsteinsson, Gunnar Karlsson, Vésteinn Ólason, and Helgi Þorláksson. The kindness of these scholars in reading drafts of the manuscript, and their comments and encouragement are heartily appreciated.

During my years as a teaching fellow at Harvard, and ever since, Albert Lord has provided me with a wealth of comparative information and valuable insight into the nature of oral narrative. He has helped me to approach narrative with the medieval audience in mind and to see the sagas not as representations of reality but as reflections of a medieval society's concerns and the forms in which these concerns were manifested. Since the book began to take shape, my UCLA colleague Franz Bäuml, with the precision of a scholar truly devoted to research in the field of medieval literature, has repeatedly encouraged me to forge ahead. His comments and his leaps of thought have aided me in keeping a critical eye on what is present in the sagas rather than in detailing what might make the stories more acceptable to the modern literary critic. I would also like to thank Richard Tomasson, whose interest and scholarship span all of Scandinavia, and Eugen Weber, whose vision of the university helped to make this book possible.

The National Endowment for the Humanities and the Academic Senate at UCLA have assisted me with generous grant support. The Center for Medieval and Renaissance Studies at UCLA kindly granted me two quarters of research time from Rebecca Ziegler, a graduate student whose abilities as a young scholar are outstanding. Nietzchka Keene, another exceptionally promising graduate student, has been a consistently capable research assistant committing long hours to this project and acquiring a thorough knowledge of the family sagas. Grace Stimson's time and energy as editor have made the text far more readable than it would otherwise have been. Her knowledge, wit, and good nature have made the editing of this book an enjoyable, learning process. At the University of California Press James Kubeck provided much necessary and useful assistance, for which I am grateful.

The sources for the epigraphs are as follows:

Dedication page.

W. P. Ker, *The Dark Ages* (New York: Mentor Books, 1958), pp. 200–201.

Chapter 1.

Björn Þorsteinsson, review of *Das alte Island* by Hans Kuhn, *Mediaeval Scandinavia* 5 (1972):186.

Chapter 2.

Heinrich Beck, "Laxdœla saga: A Structural Approach," *Saga-Book* (London: University College, Viking Society for Northern Research, 1977), p. 398.

Lucien Musset, *Les peuples scandinaves au moyen âge* (Paris: Presses Universitaires de France, 1951), p. 212.

Chapter 3.

Einar Ól. Sveinsson, "The Icelandic Family Sagas and the Period in Which Their Authors Lived," *Acta Philologica Scandinavica*, 12, 1–2 (1938):77.

Chapter 4.

W. P. Ker, *Epic and Romance: Essays on Medieval Literature* (London, 1896; New York: Dover, 1957), p. 200.

Chapter 5.

Robert Cook, "The Sagas of the Icelanders as Dramas of the Will," *Proceedings of the First International Saga Conference* (1971), ed. Peter Foote, Hermann Pálsson and Desmond Slay (London: University College, Viking Society for Northern Research, 1973), p. 91.

Andrew Dennis, Peter Foote, and Richard Perkins, introduction to *Laws of Early Iceland: Grágás I* (Winnipeg: University of Manitoba Press, 1980), p. 3.

Chapter 6.

Eyfirðinga sǫgur, ÍF 9 (Reykjavík, 1956).

Chapter 7.

Yu. M. Lotman and B. A. Uspensky, "On the Semiotic Mechanism of Culture," *New Literary History* 9, 2 (1978): 215.

Björn M. Ólsen, "Um Íslendingasögur," *Safn til Sögu Íslands* 6 (Reykjavík, 1937–1939), p. 44.

Chapter 8.

Íslendingabók, ÍF 1 (Reykjavík, 1968), ch. 3.
Richard Tomasson, *Iceland: The First New Nation* (Minneapolis: University of Minnesota Press, 1980), pp. 6–7.

Chapter 9.

Brennu-Njáls saga, ÍF 12 (Reykjavík, 1954).

Chapter 10.

Tzvetan Todorov, "The Origin of Genres," *New Literary History* 8 (1976):163–164.

1 Introduction

In the Middle Ages Iceland produced literature entirely unique in both quantity and variety. There have been countless attempts to comprehend and interpret the origin and the creative process involved in this branch of the European cultural tradition. It seems most natural to conclude, however, that it was the legitimate offspring of an extraordinary society rather than the bastard of an ordinary society. If the structure of Icelandic society was thus different from that of other European societies in the Middle Ages, then a study of that society must offer a key to an understanding of the literature it produced.

—Björn Þorsteinsson

It is impossible to understand the Old Icelandic sagas without comprehending the function of feud in medieval Iceland. Feud stands at the core of the narrative, and its operation reaches into the heart of Icelandic society. The dominant concern of this society—to channel violence into accepted patterns of feud and to regulate conflict—is reflected in saga narrative.

This study concentrates on feud in the family sagas and in the *Sturlunga saga* compilation. Both are collections of sophisticated, realistic narratives akin to but different from the heroic epics and folktales that flourished on the European continent during the same medieval period. The family sagas, the best-known and the largest group of Icelandic prose writings, have a long-standing reputation for violence. Just what the nature of this violence was is an important question, but little attention has been paid to it.

The violence did not arise from war. Unlike most European societies, Iceland was never embroiled in conflict to establish its boundaries or to expand them. Medieval Icelanders were never called upon to repel a foreign invasion; in fact, military defense was so distant a concern that Iceland's otherwise extensive medieval laws made no provision for it. Internally, Iceland was not divided into tribal regions or quarrelsome petty states. The competition for territorial control by warring clans, as in Ireland, was absent. Instead, medieval Icelanders were concerned with private feud of a particular Icelandic style. In examining Icelandic dispute and its forms of settlement, I suggest that the society engaged in an insular type of feud which channeled most violence into a socially stabilizing process. This vital process, in turn, provided the formal model for saga narratives about Iceland. The relationship between social and literary feud is not the precise reflection of a mirror image but the sharing of common features between the real lives of a people and the narrative form they created in order to tell stories about their island existence.

Feud in the sagas is structured in the context of the island's social, judicial, and governmental forms; it is quite different from the epic conflict found in many other medieval literatures. Saga conflicts, unlike epic struggles, are not contests between men and monsters, demons, or foreign or pagan forces. The outcomes of conflicts in the sagas do not decide the safety or the destruction of a people or a nation. Most epics deal with heroes on whom the society depends in the event of attack, describing the martial deeds of war leaders and their nemesis, treachery. In contrast, the Icelandic prose tales are primarily about disputes between ordinary people over ordinary matters, such as landownership, insult, inheritance, dowries, hay, and beached whales.

Epic heroes take risks on behalf of the greater good, often killing real or imagined agents of chaos to ensure continuity for a society. Roland is a warrior who fights for his homeland and for his emperor against pagan forces and traitors. Beowulf battles destructive creatures on behalf of a foreign society and later of his homeland. The Icelandic hero does not reach the lofty heights of the epic hero because his actions do not determine success or failure for his society. Unlike epic heroes, the Icelandic hero looks primarily to his own self-interest. He exemplifies the attitude of a society that has never confronted a foreign military threat. He is not an Odysseus pitting the values of his mortal society against the immortal world. He is not a Cú Chulainn guarding the border of a tribal region or an Alexander pushing the borders of a civilization to its limits. The hallmark of saga literature is its presentation of characters as rational, though at times exceptional, human beings functioning in the nonfabulous world of the Icelandic Free State. The Icelandic tales are complex expressions of medieval social thought in which character, action, and audience judgment are usually prescribed by rigid cultural norms.

Scholars have argued that, of all family saga characters, Grettir Ásmundarson and Egill Skalla-Grímsson are closest to epic heroes. Such a comparison is based largely on the similarity of a few unmistakably epiclike deeds. Beyond the affinity of specific exploits, however, the sagas of these heroes, when viewed as narrative wholes, suggest only marginal resemblances to continental epics. Almost as an exception among saga heroes, Grettir, while at home in Iceland, actually fights monstrous apparitions whereas most Icelandic revenants are put to rest by legal means or by moving grave sites (see saga selection 2 at end of this chapter). Even though Grettir's deeds have epiclike traits, his actions fail to have the repercussions of those of an epic hero and do little to alter the basic nature of the tale. *Grettis saga* is the story of a misfit who is most memorable for staying alive for many years while being hunted as an outlaw. Egill, too, has epic and heroic attributes, especially his extraordinary skill as a warrior. While abroad, Egill is a viking and a mercenary serving foreign kings. Primarily a fierce, independent Icelander, Egill wanders and fights his way through the Baltic and the North Sea regions, more for monetary gain than for loyalty to a liege, a people, or a cause. When he returns to Iceland, he adapts his behavior to Icelandic norms and fights his antagonists in the law courts in the manner of a native chieftain. These and other attributes of *Egils saga*, the outlaw sagas, and the poets' sagas are discussed more thoroughly in chapter 10.

Icelanders did produce sagas similar in content to narratives that developed on the continent; in fact, four of the seven broad categories of sagas narrate events taking place primarily outside Iceland and strongly reflect the influence of hagiography and continental epic: the *konunga sǫgur* (kings' sagas) relate the history of the kings of Norway; the *fornaldar sǫgur* (sagas of antiquity) tell the fabulous and sometimes mythic tales of epic heroes such as the dragon slayer Sigurðr Fáfnisbani, and Bǫðvarr bjarki, the bear's son; translated texts, such as the *riddara sǫgur* (knights' sagas) and the long *Karlamagnús saga*, which gathers together several chansons de geste about Charlemagne, relate continental tales of chivalric romance and epic; and the *lygi sǫgur* (lying or legendary sagas) form a category based on a mixture of the *fornaldar sǫgur* and the *riddara sǫgur*. These late sagas recount the fantastic adventures of wanderers in mythic lands.

The other three categories of sagas tell of events that take place mostly within Iceland: the *biskupa sǫgur* (bishops' sagas) concentrate on the lives of distinguished churchmen: the *Íslendinga sǫgur* (family sagas) describe characters and events from the earliest centuries of the Icelandic Free State, especially the so-called saga age (ca. 930–1030); and the *Sturlunga saga*, a compilation named after the famous political and literary family, the Sturlungar, recounts events mostly contemporary with the period when the sagas were written, from the late twelfth to the early fourteenth century.

Most literary studies of the sagas do not include the Sturlunga compilation. Yet if we investigate the formal characteristics of feud in the family sagas and the early Sturlunga sagas, we find more similarities than differences. In the family sagas, feuds tend to build into more elaborate narrative segments and resolutions are more a community affair. Conflicts in the Sturlunga sagas occur at a faster pace, one after the other, and the resolutions are more private and also more violent. I propose to demonstrate in this study that medieval Icelanders used a traditional means of saga composition for relating stories of their society, whether in the family or Sturlunga sagas.[1] These two groupings of tales describe disputes set in a rural society whose stable cultural development began in the period of settlement in the late ninth century and continued until the loss of independence to Norway in 1262–1264. It would be incorrect to assume that events narrated in the family sagas really happened, but accepting the sagas as revealing the tensions and dynamics of a rural medieval society is a different matter. We cannot agree that any text gives a factual representation of reality regardless of the author's intention. Even a chronicle is colored by the author's point of view. With this reservation in mind, I examine this corpus of consciously plausible medieval narratives for insight into their compositional technique and for an understanding of the place of feud in the sagas.

Although conflict is everywhere present in the sagas, the most recent comprehensive study of feud is Andreas Heusler's *Zum isländischen Fehdewesen in der Sturlungenzeit* (1912).[2] Focusing on the thirteenth-century Sturlung period, Heusler here builds upon his earlier study of crimi-

---

[1] I am sure examples of similar narrative construction can be found in the later Sturlunga sagas and in the *biskupa sǫgur*, but that is not within the scope of this book.

[2] Andreas Heusler, *Zum isländischen Fehdewesen in der Sturlungenzeit*, Abhandlungen der königlich preussischen Akademie der Wissenschaften, Phil.-hist. Klasse, 1912, no. 4 (Berlin, 1912).

nal law in the family sagas, *Das Strafrecht der Isländersagas* (1911).[3] As a scholar of his time, Heusler collected a mass of descriptive information. He recognized that system prevailed in the operation of Iceland's social order, but he offers little analysis of it. Although Heusler's discussion of saga character roles and of the legal history of the island is detailed, he evinces scant knowledge of how feud worked as an underlying narrative or social process.

Nevertheless, Heusler was aware of what he understood to be an undefinable force inherent in transactions and obligations among saga characters as they gathered forces in assembly cases. He notes that legal success or failure depended upon this *formlose Gewalt* ("formless power"):

> The criminal law was unjust to certain social levels of the country only insofar as the small farmer would never have been able successfully to bring suit against the chieftain without higher protection. The plaintiff's bringing of an action at the thing was, as stated, a move in feud itself, which, as in every other kind of feud, requires its means of power. But when the important farmers and the chieftains quarreled with their own kind, they did not find themselves to be above the legal process. Or, more cautiously expressed, they knew very well how to value the legal weapon, the bringing of actions. That they also called upon this formless power to aid them during the process of their action was of course a prerogative of those in power.[4]

Heusler perceived the essential relationship between chieftain and farmer as one of power; that power, however,

[3]Andreas Heusler, *Das Strafrecht der Isländersagas* (Leipzig: Duncker and Humblot, 1911).

[4]Heusler, *Fehdewesen*, pp. 69–70: Ständisch ungerecht war dieses Strafrecht nur darin, dass der Kleinbauer ohne höheren Schutz nie gegen den Häuptling hätte erfolgreich klagen können. Die Dingklage war, wie gesagt, eine Art Fehdezug, der seine Machtmittel erheischte wie jede andere Fehde. Aber wo die Grossbauern und Goden mit ihresgleichen stritten, da fanden sie sich über Gesetz und Recht nicht erhaben—oder vorsichtiger gesagt: sie wussten auch die gesetzlichen Kampfmittel, die Dingklage, gar wohl zu schätzen. Dass sie auch auf dem Klagewege die formlose Gewalt zu Hilfe riefen, war freilich wieder ein tatsächliches Vorrecht der Mächtigen.

was certainly not formless. Heusler never determined that this relationship of power was a formal element in feud; in this study I point out that it is this recurring element that defines Icelandic feud. With foresight, Heusler consistently approached the sagas in terms of Icelandic society and throughout *Strafrecht* argues that the sagas, more than any other source, give information about the operation of law within the context of the society.

The fact that one has to go as far back as Heusler to find a treatment of saga feud as both a social and a literary phenomenon reflects the lack of attention to textual and extra-textual liaisons. Saga scholarship during the past half century has tried to pry the sagas loose from their traditional social moorings in order to raise the status of these tales from bits and pieces of folklore and history to the realm of great literature. This effort was led by scholars who became known as "bookprosists" because of their belief in the written origin of the sagas.[5] Beginning in the first decades of the twentieth century, they came into conflict with "free-prosists," who advocated a theory of oral origins and stressed the historical roots of the family sagas. Neither the bookprosists' nor the freeprosists' position is tenable by today's standards, although the bookprosists have been highly influential since the 1950s.[6] They implanted the

---

[5]The leading bookprosist Sigurður Nordal argued this point strongly. In *Hrafnkatla*, Studia Islandica (Íslenzk fræði) 7 (Reykjavík: Ísafoldarprentsmiðja H. F., 1940); English translation, *Hrafnkels saga Freysgoða: A Study*, trans. R. George Thomas (Cardiff: University of Wales Press, 1958), he wrote that character portrayals in *Hrafnkels saga* were "far in advance of the disjointed and simple portrayals of character in folk sagas and oral tales" (p. 55).

[6]Different aspects of the bookprose/freeprose controversy have been reviewed by Theodore M. Andersson, *The Problem of Icelandic Saga Origins: A Historical Survey*, Yale Germanic Studies, I (New Haven: Yale University Press, 1964), and Marco Scovazzi, *La Saga di Hrafnkell e il problema delle saghe islandesi* (Arona: Paideia, 1960). Also see Peter Hallberg, *The Icelandic Saga*, trans. Paul Schach (Lincoln: University of Nebraska Press, 1962), pp. 49–69; Jón Helgason, *Norrøn litteraturhistorie* (Copenhagen: Levin and Munksgaard, 1934), pp. 109–120; and Richard F. Allen, *Fire and Iron: Critical Approaches to Njáls saga* (Pittsburgh: University of Pittsburgh Press, 1971), pp. 3–28.

prevailing concept that the sagas, instead of being a traditional narrative form, are the creation of a literary movement whose writers were interested in antiquarian lore.

By today's standards this concept is hard to accept, principally because it is based on three outdated assumptions. The first assumption is that elaborate prose narratives, such as the family sagas, with their intricate feuds and large numbers of characters, were beyond the memorization capacity of an oral storyteller. Memorization, however, is not the issue. These prose texts are built according to a simple compositional technique which enabled the sagaman to narrate in detail a specific instance of feud while preparing future conflicts and the involvement of other characters. The result is a method of narrative construction which at any specific instance is straightforward and simple, whereas, from the perspective of the entire tale, it appears marvelously complex. The method, quite suitable for literary composition, most likely grew out of oral compositional techniques that were not dependent upon memorization. The narrative elements form groups, which in turn link into longer feud chains. These groups, or clusters of narrative elements, are arranged not by some mechanical process but according to the logic of Icelandic feud. Within the clusters, the feud elements combine in a variety of ways and are not sequentially bound. What emerges is a narrative composed of simple basic elements. The clusterings of these elements indicate movement within Icelandic feud and, like any process essential to social operation, have a certain predictability. The technique of prose composition is simple because it is adaptable; in this quality lies its vitality. Within a society constructed around feud, this arrangement of the narrative not only meant something, but it lent an aura of plausibility to the saga.

The second assumption, historically related to the first, is that the thirteenth-century saga authors needed to look outside native traditions for the narrative tools adequate for constructing sophisticated tales about their not-so-distant forefathers. In keeping with this view, some scholars have tried to explain the sagas as either end products of ancient Germanic heroic tradition or innovative Icelandic adaptations of contemporary continental Christian thought and narrative forms, especially hagiography. Certainly both heroic tradition and Christian thought are present in the sagas, but as graftings, not as underpinnings.

The third assumption is that the sagas' realism is determined by whether or not the sagas are factually accurate. The bookprosist Sigurður Nordal used this complex line of reasoning in his monograph, *Hrafnkatla*,[7] to counter the freeprosists' belief in the historicity of the sagas. He argues against the reliability of specific facts in *Hrafnkels saga*, such as the importance of the sons of Þjóstarr and the habitability of certain highland valleys.[8] From his demonstration of the lack of "historical" accuracy in *Hrafnkels saga*, Nordal and subsequent scholars drew the conclusion that the realism of the sagas was little more than a literary artifact.

Each of these three assumptions in its time has been helpful in bringing us to a closer understanding of the sagas, but together they have compounded inherent errors. Notable scholars have initiated change in the critical approach to saga literature. Peter Foote has consistently stressed the need to consider medieval Icelandic society in studies of the sagas.[9] Aron Ya. Gurevich explores the giving of gifts and the place of economic issues in medieval Scandinavia.[10] Preben Meulengracht Sørensen presents a brief but salient

---

[7]See n. 5, above.

[8]Óskar Halldórsson doubts many of Sigurður Nordal's findings. See his *Uppruni og þema Hrafnkels sögu*, Rannsóknastofnun í bókmenntafræði við Háskóla Íslands, Fræðirit 3 (Reykjavík: Hið íslenska bókmenntafélag, 1976).

[9]See, for instance, Peter Foote and David Wilson, *The Viking Achievement* (London: Sidgwick and Jackson, 1970), p. xxiv.

[10]A. Ya. Gurevich [Aron J. Gurevitj], "Wealth and Gift-Bestowal among the Ancient Scandinavians," *Scandinavica* 7 (1968):126–138, and *Feodalismens uppkomst i Västeuropa*, trans. Marie-Anne Sahlin (Stockholm: Tidens förlag, 1979).

argument for reconceiving the association between saga and society.[11] Vésteinn Ólason, in reviewing formal studies of the sagas, questions their correlation with the texts.[12] The historians Björn Þorsteinsson, Gunnar Karlsson, Björn Sigfússon, and Sveinbjörn Rafnsson[13] discuss different aspects of Iceland's social and political history, which, if taken together, illustrate the essential continuity of Icelandic society and its cultural norms from the saga age to the thirteenth century.

Two of my conclusions in this study are that feud stories set in Iceland, though appearing to be quite different from one another in content and in form, may have many formalistic similarities, and that the realism in these sagas is not tied to factual accuracy but to the societal normative code. In order to illustrate these and other conclusions I have included throughout the book numerous examples from the sagas. In the following pages I present a sampling of nine saga selections for two reasons: to give the reader examples to serve as points of reference, and to show that these samples of narrative, although at times quite different, have a great deal in common. The sagas are constructed according to a shared narrative base and, in order to understand that base, we must consider the correlation and modeling between the society and its literature. Although not obvious now, the compositional similarities of the texts and the repetitive use of three basic narrative elements will become clearer as the study progresses.

[11]Preben Meulengracht Sørensen, *Saga og samfund: En indføring i old-islandsk litteratur* (Copenhagen: Berlingske forlag, 1977), esp. "Samfunds-bygningen," pp. 26−58.

[12]Vésteinn Ólason, "Frásagnarlist í fornum sögum," *Skírnir* 152 (1978): 166−202, and "Nokkrar athugasemdir um Eyrbyggja sögu," *Skírnir* 145 (1971): 5−25.

[13]See, for instance, Björn Þorsteinsson, *Ný Íslandssaga* (Reykjavík: Heims-kringla, 1966), and *Íslensk miðaldasaga* (Reykjavík: Sögufélag, 1978); Gunnar Karlsson, "Goðar og bændur," *Saga* 10 (1972):5−27; Björn Sigfússon, "Full goðorð og forn og heimildir frá 12. öld," *Saga* (1960):48−75; Sveinbjörn Rafns-son, *Studier i Landnámabók: Kritiska bidrag till den isländska fristatstidens historia*, Bibliotheca Historica Lundensis 31 (Lund: C. W. K. Gleerup, 1974).

Selections from the Sagas

Selection 1: *Egils saga* (ch. 81)

That day men went to the thing slope and discussed their lawsuits, for in the evening the courts would convene to consider prosecutions. Þorsteinn was there with his following and had the greatest say in the conducting of the thing, because that had been the custom while Egill was still a leader and was in charge of the *goðorð* [chieftaincy]. Both sides were fully armed.

From the thing site men saw a group of horsemen come riding up along the Glúfr River. Their shields shone in the sun and there in the lead, as they came toward the spring assembly, was a man in a blue cape. On his head was a gilded helmet and at his side was a shield worked with gold. He held in his hand a barbed spear, the socket of which was inlaid with gold. A sword was bound to his waist. This man was Egill Skalla-Grímsson, come with eighty men, all well armed, as if they were prepared for battle. It was a carefully picked troop; Egill had with him the best of the farmers' sons from south in the Nesses, those whom he thought most warlike. Egill rode with his following to their booths, which Þorsteinn had had tented but which had stood empty. There they dismounted. And when Þorsteinn learned of his father's arrival, he went to meet him with his entire following and greeted him well. Egill and his men had their gear taken into the booths and their horses driven out to pasture. When that was done Egill and Þorsteinn went with all their followers up to the thing slope and sat down where they were accustomed to sit.

Then Egill stood up and spoke loudly: "Is Ǫnundr sjóni here on the thing slope?" Ǫnundr replied that he was, "And I am glad, Egill, that you have come. It will help to mend those breaches which here divide men." "Is it your doing," asked Egill, "that Steinarr, your son, is bringing charges against Þorsteinn, my son, and has gathered together a large crowd in order to make my son an outlaw?" "It is not my fault," replied Qnundr, "that they are involved in a dispute. I have put in quite a few words and asked Steinarr to come to an agreement with your son, for it seems to me that in each instance Þorsteinn ought to be spared dishonor. In this matter my feeling is based on the old and dear friendship [*ástvinátta*] that has been between us, Egill, since we were raised next door to each other."

"It will soon be clear," said Egill, "whether you are making this statement in earnest or are lying, although I think the latter less likely. I remember the time when it would have seemed unlikely to either of us that we might press charges, or that we might fail to prevent our sons from behaving with such foolishness, as I hear they are doing now. It seems advisable to me that, while we are alive and so close to their affairs, we should take over this case and settle it and not let Tungu-Oddr and Einarr bait our sons to fight like old nags. From now on we should let them [these chieftains] find other means of increasing their wealth than by meddling in such affairs."

Selection 2: *Eyrbyggja saga* (ch. 55)

But when these wonders had reached this stage [of destroying the people on the farm], Kjartan [from Fróðá] journeyed to Helgafell to meet with his uncle Snorri goði from whom he sought advice about the specters who had descended upon them. By that time the priest, whom Gizurr hvíti [the white] had sent to Snorri goði, arrived at Helgafell. Snorri sent the priest to Fróðá with Kjartan along with his son Þórðr kausi [cat] and six other men. Snorri advised them that the bed furnishings of Þórgunna [a deceased Hebridean woman] should be burned and then all the revenants should be summoned to a *duradómr* [a door court, held at the entrance to a farmhouse]. He asked the priest to conduct holy services, to consecrate with water, and to hear confessions. They then set off for Fróðá and along the way they called on men from the nearby farms to ride with them.

They arrived at Fróðá the evening before Candlemas, as the kitchen fires were being laid. By then Þuríðr, the mistress of the house, had taken sick in the same way as the others who had died. Kjartan immediately went inside and saw that Þóroddr and his companions [the previous master of the house who along with his men had drowned] were sitting by the fire, as was their custom. Kjartan took down Þórgunna's precious bed hangings and went into the kitchen. There he took glowing embers from the fire and went outside and burned all Þórgunna's bedclothes. After that Kjartan summoned Þórir viðleggr [wooden leg] while Þórðr kausi summoned farmer Þóroddr. They charged these [dead] men with going about the dwelling without permission and depriving people of life and health. All those who sat by the fire were summoned.

Next a *duradómr* was convened. The charges were announced, and all procedures were followed as if it were a thing court. Witnesses were heard, the cases were summed up, and judgments were made. When sentence was passed on Þórir viðleggr, he stood up and said: "We have sat as long as we could sit it out." After that, he went out a door, other than that before which the court (*dómr*) was held. Then sentence was passed on the shepherd; and when he heard that, he stood up and said: "Now I will leave, though I think that this would have been more fitting earlier." And when Þorgríma galdrakinn heard sentence being passed on her, she stood up and said: "I stayed here while it was safe." Then one after the other, the defendants were called and each in turn stood up as judgment was handed down. All said something as they went out; their remarks indicated that they departed unwillingly. Then sentence was pronounced against farmer Þóroddr; and when he heard it, he stood up and said: "Friendships here are few, I think. Let's flee now, all of us." After so saying, he left.

Then Kjartan and his companions entered. The priest carried consecrated water and holy relics through the entire house. Later in the day the priest sang holy services and held a solemn mass. After that all the ghosts disappeared, and the hauntings at Fróðá ceased. Þuríðr recovered from her sickness and became healthy. In the spring after this wonder, Kjartan took on a new servant couple. He lived for a long time afterward at Fróðá and became a most outstanding man.

Selection 3: *Laxdœla saga* (ch. 47)

Þórarinn the farmer at Tunga [in Sælingsdalr] announced that he wanted to sell his farm Tunguland [the Tongue lands], both because he needed money and also because he felt enmity was growing among people in the district, and he was a close friend of both sides. Bolli felt he needed to buy a residence, for the people of Laugar had much livestock but little land. On Ósvífr's advice, Bolli and Guðrún rode to Tunga; they thought it would be convenient to obtain land so close by, and Ósvífr told them not to let any small details block a deal. Guðrún and Bolli discussed the sale with Þórarinn, and they reached agreement on what the price should be and also on the terms of payment. A deal was struck between them. But the sale was not witnessed, for there were not enough men present that it could be considered legal. After this, Bolli and Guðrún rode back home.

When Kjartan heard about the sale, he rode at once with eleven men to Tunga and arrived there early in the day. Þórarinn greeted him warmly and invited him to stay; Kjartan said that he would be riding back in the evening but would pause there for a while. Þórarinn asked him what his errand was.

Kjartan said, "My errand is to discuss a sale of land which you and Bolli have made, for it is against my wishes that you sell this land to Bolli and Guðrún."

Þórarinn said that anything else would not suit him, "for the price Bolli has promised me for the land is a very fine one and is to be paid quickly."

"You will not suffer if Bolli doesn't buy the land," said Kjartan, "for I will buy it at the same price, and it will not avail you much to go against what I want done, for you will find that I intend to have my way in this district and to oblige others more than the people of Laugar."

Þórarinn replied, "Costly to me are the master's words in this matter. It would be most to my liking that the deal made between Bolli and myself should stand."

"I don't call anything a sale of land that isn't witnessed," said Kjartan. "Now either sell me the land here and now on the same terms as you agreed upon with others, or else live on the land yourself."

Þórarinn chose to sell him the land, and this time there were witnesses to the sale. Kjartan rode home after the purchase.

Word of the sale spread throughout Breiðafjǫrðr, and the people of Laugar heard about it that same evening. Then Guðrún said, "It seems to me, Bolli, that Kjartan has given you two choices, rather harsher than he offered Þórarinn: either you leave this district with little honor, or else you confront him and show that you have a sharper bite than you have evidenced up to now."

Selection 4: *Gísla saga Súrssonar* (ch. 21)

. . . and for another three winters he traveled throughout Iceland, meeting with chieftains and asking them for support. But because of the curse that Þorgrímr nef had laid on him through magic and the power to cast a spell, he did not succeed in convincing any of the chieftains to give him aid. When at times it seemed that some chieftains might take up with him, something always got in the way.

Selection 5: *Guðmundar saga dýra* (ch. 3)

There was a man called Guðmundr, the son of Þorvaldr. He was called Guðmundr inn dýri [the worthy] and lived in Qxnadalr at that farm which is called Bakki. He was the brother of Ásgrímr, who was the father of Þorvarðr inn auðgi [the rich] and of Álfheiðr, whom Gizurr Hallsson had as a wife, and of Vigdís whom Forni Sǫxólfsson married and after whom the family called the Fornungar are named. Guðmundr also shared the same mother with Þórðr Þórarinsson from Laufáss.

Guðmundr had the *goðorð* in his keeping which his brother Ásgrímr and Þorvarðr auðgi had owned. He sided with neither party in the case over the property Helgastaðir. Guðmundr gathered together men, both his thingmen and others, and went with this following to the *várþing* [spring assembly].

But when men came to the *várþing* they found it impossible to arrange a settlement because neither side [in the Helgastaðir dispute] was willing to give up any part of its claim. Each side asserted that it owned everything that was the subject of the dispute. Þorvarðr and Qnundr [the allied chieftains] made it known that they were ready to fight for their claim rather than to make a legal defense. Guðmundr with his band went between the two opposing sides with the result that the matter advanced neither to a fight nor to a legal prosecution. But the plaintiffs now prepared to prosecute their case [against Þorvarðr and Qnundr] at the Althing, because they had not been able to move legally at the *várþing*. And with this the *várþing* ended.

Selection 6: *Víga-Glúms saga* (ch. 11)

The saga now speaks of a man named Arnórr, who was called *rauðkinnr* [red cheek, a type of savage bear]. Arnórr was the son of Steinólfr the son of Ingjaldr, and first cousin to Glúmr. He had been abroad for a long time and was highly esteemed. When he was in Iceland, he was constantly with Glúmr. He requested Glúmr to offer a marriage proposal on his behalf, and when Glúmr asked what woman he wanted to marry, Arnórr answered, "Þórdís, the daughter of Gizurr, the one who was refused to Þorgrímr Þórisson." Glúmr said, "To look in that direction seems unpromising, because I think there is no difference between you two as men. But Þorgrímr has a good home, much wealth, and many kinsmen to rely upon, while you own no dwelling and have little wealth. And further, I do not want to offer any injustice [*ójafnaðr*] to Gizurr and place him in a position where he will not be able to marry off his daughter as he chooses. Gizurr deserves only good from me." Arnórr replied: "Then I'll benefit from good kinship if I get a better match by your pleading my case. Promise your friendship [*vinfengi*] to him. He will give me the woman, for it would have been called a fair match if a man as good as Þorgrímr had not already been turned away." Glúmr gave in to Arnórr's urging. Together they went to Gizurr. Glúmr pressed the case on Arnórr's behalf. Gizurr answered: "It may be, Glúmr, that it will be said I made a mistake if I give my daughter to your kinsman, Arnórr, when I did not choose to give her to Þorgrímr." Glúmr said. "That is correct, and yet there is still something more to be said: if you decide to honor our request, I offer in return my *vinfengi.*" Gizurr answered: "I consider that of much worth, but I suspect that in return I will earn the enmity [*óvinfengi*] of other men. "Well," Glúmr said, "You must see your own way in this matter, but your decision will greatly affect my dealings with you whatever you choose." Gizurr, who replied, "You won't leave this time without succeeding," then extended his hand and Arnórr committed himself to take a wife. Glúmr added that he wanted the marriage to take place at his farm, Þverá, in the fall. Glumr and Arnórr then left.

Arnórr had some malt stored at Gásar [the ship landing], and he and one houseman set out to fetch it. On the day they were expected back with the malt, Þorgrímr Þórisson rode out to the hot springs. Þorgrímr had with him six of his housemen, and they were at the baths at Hrafnagil when Arnórr returned, expecting to cross the river. Then Þorgrímr spoke up: "Wouldn't it be a lucky chance to meet up with Arnórr now? Let's not lose the malt even if we have lost the woman." Þorgrímr and his men went toward Arnórr and his servant with drawn swords, but when Arnórr saw what the odds were, he plunged into the water and made it across the river. His packhorses, however, were left on the other side of the river. Then Þorgrímr said: "Our luck is not all bad; we'll drink the ale but they will decide in the matter of the woman." Þorgrímr then rode to South Espihóll [his father's farm]. Þórir [his father] was blind by that time. Þorgrímr's companions were in high spirits and laughed a lot. Þórir asked what seemed so funny to them. They said that they didn't know which group would be first to hold its feast, and then they told him of their catch and about the chase—"but the bridegroom took a plunge." And when Þórir heard that, he asked: "Do you think you've done well, since you're laughing so much? And what are your plans now? Do you intend to sleep here tonight, as though nothing else is required? In that case, you do not know Glúmr's temper should he approve of his kinsman's journey. I call it prudent counsel to collect our men; most probably, Glúmr has gathered many men together by now."

There was a ford in the river then, which is no longer there. They collected eighty fighting men during the night and waited, prepared, at the bottom of the hill facing the ford in the river. But of Arnórr there is this to be told: he found Glúmr and told him of his trip. Glúmr answered: "It comes as no surprise to me that they did not remain quiet, but the matter is now rather difficult. If we do nothing, we reap dishonor. Yet it is altogether unclear that we will find honor if we seek to right the wrong. Nevertheless, we will now gather men." When it was light the next morning, Glúmr came to the river with sixty men and wanted to cross over. But the Esphœlingar [the men of Espihóll] pelted them with stones, and Glúmr was unable to advance. Instead, he turned back and they carried on the fight across the river with stones and shots. In this way many were wounded, though none are named. When men of the local region became aware of what was happening, they rode up during the day and went between the two groups and arranged a truce. The Esphœlingar were asked what satisfaction they wished to offer Arnórr for the dishonor they had done him. But the answer came back that no compensation would be forthcoming even though Arnórr had run away from his own packhorses. Then something new was proposed. Glúmr should seek Gizurr's other daughter Herþrúðr as a wife for Þorgrímr, and the marriage of Arnórr and Þórdís was to be consummated only if Glúmr was able to procure this other woman for Þorgrímr. And she whom Þorgrímr married was considered better matched.

Now that so many had a hand in the matter, Glúmr promised his aid. He went to Gizurr and brought the matter up. "It may appear to you, Gizurr, by asking for wives for my kinsman and the Esphœlingar, that I am overstepping my bounds. In order to put an end to dissension here in the district, however, I think I must offer you my faith and friendship, if you do my will." Gizurr answered: "It seems to me best that you decide what is to be done, for I think my daughter will gain from this good offer." And so both marriages were agreed upon. Arnórr settled at Uppsalir and Þorgrímr at Mǫðrufell. A short time after these events Gizurr died. His wife Saldís then moved to Uppsalir. Arnórr had a son with Þórdís who was called Steinólfr. Þorgrímr also had a boy who was called Arngrímr, who was promising in all things as he grew up.

Selection 7: *Eyrbyggja saga* (ch. 31)

When his slaves were killed, Þórólfr bægifótr [lame foot] became angry at his son [Arnkell] and asked for compensation. But Arnkell flatly refused to pay even a penny, and Þórólfr became even more infuriated.

One day Þórólfr rode out to Helgafell to find Snorri goði and Snorri invited him in. But Þórólfr replied that he had no need to eat Snorri's food. "My reason for coming here is that I want you to reestablish my rights, because I call you the leader of the district [*héraðshǫfðingi*] and believe you are obligated to set things right for men who have been ill-treated."

"Who is doing you an injustice, farmer?" said Snorri. "Arnkell my son," said Þórólfr. Snorri replied: "That is not an accusation for you to make; you should think in all things as Arnkell does, since he is a better man than you."

"That is not possible," Þórólfr said, "because he is directing such aggression against me. What I want now is to become your full friend, Snorri, and to have you take up the prosecution for the killing of my slaves, the ones whom Arnkell caused to be killed. And I won't reserve for myself all the fines." When Snorri answered, "I have no desire to become involved in a dispute between you and your son," Þórólfr replied: "You are no friend of Arnkell's. It may be, however, that you think that I am close with my money. That will not be the case now. I know," he said, "that you want to own Krákunes and the forest that goes with this property—the greatest treasure here in the region. Now I am prepared formally to transfer [*at handsala*] to you all this property if you take up the case for the killing of my slaves. Press the matter in so manly a way that you will increase your stature and that those who disgraced me will know that they have gone too far. Further, I do not want any man spared from among those who had a part in the killing, whether he is more or less my kinsman."

Snorri felt a strong need to own the forest. It is said that he took charge of the land with a *handsal* agreement and in return received the prosecution for the slaves. Þórólfr then rode home and was well pleased with himself, but the bargain was not much liked by other people.

Selection 8: *Vápnfirðinga saga* (ch. 7)

Þormóðr then left and traveled home no better off than before he had come there. It was told to Brodd-Helgi that Þormóðr had gone to tell Geitir his problems. "And I'd like it," Helgi said, "if Þormóðr didn't have to travel more often on such errands."

A little later Helgi called his tenants together and ordered them to travel with him, along with his servants and guests. They traveled to the wood that Þórðr and Þormóðr owned together, and there they cut down all the trees and brought them all home to Hof. When Þormóðr learned what he had suffered, he went to see Geitir a second time to report what injustice [*ójafnaðr*] had been done to him. Geitir answered: "I can see much more reason that you find this injury worse than the last one, which I thought of little importance. I don't want to yield to Helgi in this case, and moreover I will give you some advice. Find your relatives, the sons of Refr inn rauði, Steinn and Hreiðarr, and ask them to go with you to deliver a summons at Hof. Go also to Guðmundarstaðir and ask Tjǫrvi to travel with you, but you must not be more than eight altogether. And you will summon Þórðr for cutting the wood. You must arrange it so that Brodd-Helgi is not at home. Otherwise, you will not succeed."

Selection 9: *Hœnsa-Þóris saga* (chs. 11–12)

Gunnarr Hlífarson went to see his daughter, who was fostered with Þórðr gellir [yeller], and asked her if she was interested [in the marriage proposal from Hersteinn Blund-Ketilsson]. She answered that there wasn't such longing in her for a husband that she wouldn't just as soon sit at home, "because I am well provided for here with my kinsman Þórðr. But I will do as you wish in this and other matters."

Then Gunnarr pressed the matter with Þórðr, saying that the match seemed to him most honorable. Þórðr answered: "Why don't you yourself give your daughter to Hersteinn if it is to your liking?" Gunnarr responded: "Because I will give her in marriage only if it be as much your will as mine." Þórðr replied that they both should make the decision together. "I want you, Þórðr," said Gunnarr, "to betroth the woman to Hersteinn." "You should betroth your daughter yourself," said Þórðr. "There seems to me to be more honor in it," answered Gunnarr, "if you betroth her, because it would be more fitting."

Þórðr now let himself be led, and the betrothal took place. Then Gunnarr said: "I ask one other thing: that you let the wedding take place here at Hvammr [Þórðr's home]. Then it will be done with the most honor." Þórðr asked him to decide the question, and Gunnarr said: "We will plan that it will take place in a week's time."

Then Gunnarr and his companions mounted and turned to go. Þórðr, going to the path with them, asked again if there was any news. Gunnarr answered: "We know nothing newer than the burning to death of the *bóndi* Blund-Ketill." Þórðr asked how it had happened, and Gunnarr told him all the circumstances of the burning, who had caused it and who had carried it out. Þórðr replied: "This match would not have been made so quickly, had I known about the burning. You may think you have outsmarted me and trapped me with a trick, but I'm not sure that you would have been able to carry this case yourself."

"It is good to count on help from one such as yourself," said Gunnarr. "In any case you are now obligated to help your son-in-law [Hersteinn] just as we are obligated to help you, for many men heard that you betrothed the woman, and it was all done with your agreement. Besides, it would be good for you chieftains to see once and for all which of you is the best, for you have long been snapping at one another like wolves."

They then parted. Þórðr was very angry, thinking that they had made a fool of him. Gunnarr and his companions rode first to Gunnarr's farm, Gunnarsstaðir. They thought they had played their part well in bringing Þórðr into the dispute and were very pleased with themselves.

2 Feud in Saga Narrative: Its Roots in Icelandic Society

> The provocation [disregard for moral criteria of a community] is against a very delicate equilibrium of complicated ideal norms that has not been secured judicially and institutionally but rather left to the free play of the various forces. A man must fight for his rights in the Icelandic Common-wealth. There is no social hierarchy as in the mother country, Norway—from *bóndi* to *hersir, jarl, lendr maðr* and *hirðmaðr*. One's status must be defended constantly, positively and steadfastly.
>
> —Heinrich Beck

> Distanced from the rest of the world, without a sovereign, Iceland had no navy, no army, not even a foreign policy. Thus Iceland never experienced anything analogous to feudalism. There were no towns, not even villages, and nothing was built with stone. Iceland's economic history, like its artistic evolution, separates its people from the rest of the world.
>
> —Lucien Musset

Iɴ the main, saga scholarship has taken little cognizance of the nature of dispute in the sagas, and researchers who have proposed theories of narrative form have not seriously considered the influence of Icelandic feud upon the construction of Icelandic tales. Instead, they either have emphasized the entertainment value of the sagas or have assumed that the sagaman pursued an over-riding goal of moral edification. Neither approach gives much credit to the intelligence of medieval Icelanders, and both are directed largely toward stressing aspects of saga literature which are borrowed from ancient Germanic and Latin medieval cultures. In so doing, formal studies have ignored that the bulk of saga narrative reflects issues inhe-rent in societal decision making, the acquisition of status and wealth, and the formation and maintenance of net-works of obligations. Turning to continental literary mod-els for a key to the structure of saga narrative neglects much of what is traditional in the sagas and often overlooks what we know about the society that produced them. Propo-nents of this search for foreign sources have given us needed insight into influences on the sagas, but in their efforts to define the sagas in terms of European literature, they say very little about the traditional narrative and cog-nitive core of these Icelandic tales.

Two factors made saga literature a suitable vehicle for expressing the interests and anxieties of medieval Ice-landers. First, a model of feud is at the core of saga con-struction. Second, the peculiarly Icelandic way in which feud operated was a vital rather than a destructive force within the medieval community. The relationship between these two factors has been investigated only marginally, even though it enables us to explore, and understand, the traditional narrative art of Iceland's prose literature.

Each extant saga must to a greater or lesser extent be the product of an author, but the sagas as a group are an identifiable art form with roots far deeper than the inven-tiveness of an individual. In this book I concentrate less on the intent of the author than on his method of constructing a text. The goal is not to create a picture of an individual sagaman but to examine the traditional method by which this prose literature is composed. Working within a tradition does not deny the creativity of the individual artist; it merely narrows the scope of permissible innovation.

Although we cannot know with certainty the intentions of individual sagamen, clearly one of the requirements of saga construction was that the tale have a realistic tone. Attainment of this goal was not very difficult, and scholars are in general agreement that the thirteenth-century sagaman was well equipped to give a semblance of actuality to his writings. On the one hand, he had access to traditional oral tales and family genealogies. On the other, sources first written in the twelfth century, such as the historical *Íslendingabók* and *Landnámabók* and the extensive legal compilations, called *Grágás*, were known to him. Equally important, the sagaman was equipped to tell a realistic tale by the very nature of cultural continuity in Iceland's settled rural society.

In writing and telling their sagas, medieval Icelanders were well aware of their historical background. They were attempting to tell the stories of the past and to describe the contemporary aspects of their isolated North Sea society. Region by region, family by family, the Icelanders assembled a social and historical picture of their country. A rarity among European peoples, they recognized that their roots were not in a distant, almost timeless, past, but in relatively recent memorable events.

The *Landnámatíð*, the time of settlement (literally the time of the landtakings), lasted from ca. 870 to 930. This sixty-year period of founding was fundamental to the Icelanders' self-perception. After the uninhabited island was discovered by Norse sailors in the mid-ninth century, reports of the availability of free land quickly circulated. They sparked a boom response throughout the North Sea Scandinavian cultural area, stretching from Norway to Ireland, and between 10,000 and 20,000 persons journeyed across the North Atlantic, with goods and livestock, in small boats. The Icelanders never forgot that they were an immigrant society. They reckoned the generations back to their first settler ancestors, not as myth but as history. Iceland was the first new society formed by transmarine European migration,[1] and its societal forms were as innovative as its literature. Protected by the barrier of northern seas, the island was free to develop with little external interference. The country was never invaded after the Norse settlement; nor did it develop the military infrastructure so important in continental medieval societies. Furthermore, Iceland remained entirely rural during the 350 years of its medieval independence. The movement toward the creation of towns did not take place in Iceland in this period, as it did on the continent and in the rest of Scandinavia.

Iceland had no governmental executive, whether king, prince, or council of nobles. The only centralized decision making was therefore the responsibility of legislative and judicial bodies at the annual national assembly, the Althing (see App. A). This loosely organized government left the maintaining of order and the enforcing of judicial decrees to concerned private parties. The open granting of official power to individuals differentiated Iceland from continental governments whose executive components, to the best of their abilities, guarded princely prerogatives and often tried to expand the governmental power to command. This difference meant that Icelandic and continental political roles and intentions were sharply divergent; unlike the underlying philosophy of government that held sway throughout medieval Europe, Iceland's societal order did not seek to supplant private feud. Instead, Iceland organized its judicial apparatus, indeed its entire society, to assist and expedite the resolution of feud.

The concentration on feud had far-reaching conse-

---

[1]The settlement of Iceland, recorded in many histories, is well known. In *Iceland: The First New Society* (Minneapolis: University of Minnesota Press, 1980), Richard Tomasson has taken an important step in discussing the Icelandic settlement within the broader perspective of later European transmarine migrations.

quences for the development of this insular northern society. Rather than an aberrant and socially destructive force to be controlled by sheriffs, bailiffs, marshals, and royal justiciars, feud in Iceland was a socially stabilizing process. This situation was brought about early on in the period of Iceland's settlement by the type of relationship which developed between the farmers, the *bœndr* (sing. *bóndi*) and the chieftains, the *goðar* (sing. *goði*). The fluidity and originality in the Icelandic system lay in the fact that the *goðar* did not rule territorial areas within which the most important legally defined supporters, the *þingfarar-kaupsbœndr* (thingtax-paying farmers), lived. Instead, the chieftains served as leaders of interest groups and vied for the allegiance of the *bœndr* who lived interspersed among them. The result was a patchwork of alliances that were largely unconstrained by territorial limitations.[2] Loyalty depended on personal interest, and both farmers and chieftains were expected to adhere to a code of conduct whose central value was *hóf*, a term implying moderation in the seeking of personal power. By the thirteenth century, six large families had gained unprecedented wealth and power. The nature of their power, however, was more in keeping with the Icelandic tradition of farmers and chieftains relying upon each other for mutual support than with autocratic control by petty princes or warlords. The concentration of power in fewer hands was a disruptive evolutionary factor, but it would be going too far to say that Iceland in the thirteenth century experienced a radical break with its past. Even in regions where the centuries-old traditions were most weakened—the Southern and Northern Quarters—the traditional rights of farmers were not uprooted.

The origin of the amalgamation of power was not sudden. Rather it was a development that took place over

---

[2]This subject is discussed in greater depth in chap. 5; see esp. map 3. For a more detailed explanation of terms such as *þingfararkaupsbœndr*, see App. A.

centuries and was, as I show in this book, closely connected to the process of feud. In many instances, an individual's or a family's increase in power and status came about when a more aggressive chieftain succeeded in dominating one or more of the other local *goðar*. Even in the last decades of the Free State, the conservative nature of Iceland's centuries-old societal forms is evident in the fact that few of the lesser chieftaincies were abolished. Instead, they still had a role to play as part of an operative decentralized governmental structure. Only in a few exceptional and short-lived instances at the end of the Free State were any of the new regional leaders, in modern studies called *stórhofðingjar* or magnates, successful in setting up an organization with even the semblance of a small dependable regional state. Rather, the *stórhofðingjar* in their few short decades of struggles tried with only middling success to adapt traditional societal forms to the control of larger areas. One of the main reasons for their lack of success was that the *stórhofðingjar* depended to a large extent on their families for their power, and families like the Sturlungar were not cohesive political groups. Thus, whereas one family might control several chieftaincies, these *goðorð* would probably be divided among different relatives who not only were often unsupportive of one another but at times were at each other's throats.

In the confusion of the mid-thirteenth century, the *boendr*, although threatened, retained a large measure of their traditional rights as free landowners. The *boendr* even at the end of the Free State controlled the major portion of the land and the economic and human resources of the island. The Icelandic farmer was adept at holding onto his privileges, for he had had a long history of maintaining himself in the face of individuals who sought to extend their powers at his expense.

The threat posed to the rural decentralized society of Iceland by men unwilling to act with moderation creates one of the severe tensions in the literature. The sagas have a specific term for ruthless and overly ambitious men. They are called *ójafnaðarmenn* (sing. *ójafnaðarmaðr*) meaning "uneven," unjust, or overbearing men. *Ójafnaðarmenn* took advantage of the fact that social defenses against a thoroughly ruthless individual were cumbersome and potentially inadequate, a major weakness of Old Icelandic society from its inception in the early tenth century. These overbearing men ignored the Icelandic code of restraint, which held that, for the common good, the *goðar* and other powerful leaders must not let feud grow into serious and long-term regional warfare. Instead, powerful leaders, in order to protect their own power as well as to ensure a modicum of stability in the community, were expected to allow both their own and others' disputes to be settled by arbitration. Examples of *ójafnaðarmenn* abound in the sagas where, instead of compromising, they push for the ultimate political and often physical destruction of their opponents. For example, in *Vápnfirðinga saga*, Brodd-Helgi twice uses force to prevent the courts from deciding a case. His goal is to destroy his rival Geitir Lýtingsson. In *Hœnsa-Þóris saga*, the chieftain Tungu-Oddr, with several hundred men, bars another *goði*, Þórðr gellir, from reaching the local thing. Oddr's action is one of a series that have given him the reputation of being a dangerous and unjust man to deal with. In the end his power is broken by an alliance of other leaders who recognize his behavior as antisocial.

Christianity, coming peacefully to Iceland in 999 or 1000, did not uproot the established rural culture. The new religion was adopted in a manner that is a tribute to the stability and strength of the Icelandic system of dispute settlement. Whereas in Norway and in other parts of Scandinavia the conversion was accomplished only after long years of upheaval and bloodletting, in Iceland the change in religions was quickly and efficiently resolved at the Althing. The process was similar to the settlement of a serious feud. When it became clear that large-scale violence might occur in a confrontation between believers in the old religion and those who embraced the new, an arbitrator acceptable to both sides was selected and a compromise was proposed that each side could live with. All Icelanders would accept baptism, but the old religious rituals could be observed in private.

The old religion soon died out and was outlawed. The *goðar* used the change in religion to their own advantage by transferring their previous role as keeper of the pagan temple into a Christian context. In many instances *goðar* became Christian priests; along with powerful *bœndr* they assumed the guardianship of church wealth, controlling church property and administering the highly lucrative tithe after it was made law in 1096.

Earlier, sometime in the eleventh century, Icelandic churchmen and farmers had adapted a procedure that was compatible with older traditions of secular landownership whereby land given to the Church for the purpose of maintaining a local church remained under the control of the grantor and later of his heirs. Scholars in recent decades have made much of this important development, showing that secular "owners" of *staðir* (sing. *staðr*), farmsteads with church buildings on them, were able to garnish a large part of the tithe revenue. Buttressed by this new wealth, families in the twelfth century, such as the southern groups, the Oddaverjar (Jón Loftsson's family) and the Haukdœlir (Gizurr Þorvaldsson's family), rose to prominence and began to dominate unusually large regions. The effects of *staðr* wealth should not be overemphasized, however, for this kind of wealth alone does not explain how individuals such as Sturla Þórðarson (Hvamm-Sturla, d. 1183) in the Western Quarter acquired large tracts of land, including *staðir*. Nor does it explain, as Björn Sigfússon has pointed out,[3] how leaders such as Hafliði Másson in the northwest at the beginning of the twelfth century and Guðmundr inn ríki (the powerful) in the northeast at the end of the tenth

---

[3]Björn Sigfússon, "Full goðorð og forn og heimildir frá 12. öld," *Saga* (1960):48–75.

century gained control over large regions before church wealth and *staðir* became factors. *Staðir* were the later twelfth- and thirteenth-century prizes of a traditional system of land acquisition which was based on older patterns of feud.

The custom of secular control of *staðir* hobbled the power and wealth of the Icelandic Church throughout the Christian centuries of the Free State. The situation persisted because the Church at first lacked the ability to manage its property and later, when it had aggressive reform bishops in Þorlákr Þórhallsson the saint (1178–1193) and Guðmundr Arason the good (1203–1237), it lacked the power to repossess the property.

Because of the *staðr* arrangement the Church controlled only a limited amount of its potential wealth. Thus the size and the effectiveness of the followings and the bureaucracy of Iceland's two bishops, one in the north at Hólar and one in the south at Skálaholt, were sharply restricted. The dilemma faced by the Church in the late twelfth century and the strength of secular traditions are illustrated by the refusal of the famous chieftain, Jón Loftsson, to acquiesce when Bishop Þorlákr Þórhallsson demanded that his church administration be given control over Jón's church property in accordance with a dispatch from the archbishop in Norway:

> I will listen to the archbishop's ordinance, but I am resolved to disregard it. I do not think that he knows better than my forefathers, Sæmundr the learned [d. 1133] and his sons. Nor will I condemn the conduct of our bishops here in this country, who honored that custom of the land, that laymen had authority over those churches which their forefathers gave to God, and that they reserved for themselves and their offspring power over them. [*Þorláks biskups saga, hin yngri*, ch. 19][4]

In the end, the bishop had to back down. He consecrated Jón's new church building and dropped his claim to admin-

---

[4]*Biskupa sögur* I, ed. Guðbrandur Vigfússon and Jón Sigurðsson (Copenhagen: Hið íslenzka bókmentafélag, 1858), p. 283.

istrative control over Jón's church property.

The conflict over control of church land was not settled until the end of the thirteenth century, or well after Iceland's loss of independence to Norway. The fact that the conflict between reform churchmen and secular political leaders in Iceland turned on the control of actual property and not, as often on the European continent, on the control of church offices is an indication of the position that landownership held in this island society. In part the Icelandic emphasis on the ownership of productive land was owing to the general lack of opportunity in other economic endeavors.

Besides property ownership, Icelanders possessed several other forms of wealth. Of movable goods, the most valued was silver. Most of the small amount of available silver in circulation had been brought to Iceland by the original settlers, although there were sporadic minor influxes of silver from successful journeys abroad. At first, Icelanders relied heavily on silver to purchase goods from abroad, but by the eleventh century many families had exhausted their reserves. Because silver was in such short supply, most goods and services were bartered. Fines in the sagas, although normally computed in silver, were often paid in goods, especially homespun, foodstuffs, and livestock. Marketing was held to certain standards of payment. Prices of goods were based on a computation of value in relation to measurements of silver. The standardized ounce, *þinglagseyrir*, was set at the local assemblies (see App. A).

Limited agricultural production, coupled with the lack of manufacturing or concerted commercial fishing ventures, of necessity restricted Iceland's trade with the world.[5] From the late tenth century on, trade was in-

---

[5]This situation did not change until the early fourteenth century when the export of stockfish developed. Once started, the trade in stockfish (*skreið*) grew rapidly. By the mid-fourteenth century the export of *skreið* and the industry that grew up around this extensive trade had become firmly entrenched. The intro-

creasingly dependent on Norwegian partners and boats since wood was so limited in Iceland. Imported goods that were not paid for in silver were purchased through a small but consistent export traffic in wool and agricultural products. It was a basic fact, however, that Iceland could barely feed itself; in most years, therefore, there was little in the way of foodstuffs to export. The trade in sulfur and such luxury items as white falcons and walrus ivory was always small. The sources suggest that within the country there was a good deal of cottage industry, especially the production of woolen goods and dairy products. These products served as an internal barter currency and were the means by which most debts were settled and landlords received payment. The immediate and small-scale use of agricultural products was, as was also true of the ownership of livestock, directly tied to the accessibility of productive land. These factors further enhanced the value of real property.

The consistent central importance of landownership indicates the continuity that characterized the experience of Icelanders from the tenth to the mid-thirteenth century. Throughout these centuries land sufficiently productive to satisfy the type of agriculture practiced was scarce. Iceland's northern location, with short, cool, and damp summers, made the growing of cereal crops an unpredictable and minor concern. The vast interior of the country was uninhabitable because of the severity of the long winter, and the population was concentrated in the lowland regions along the coast, warmed by the Gulf Stream, and in a few sheltered inland areas. Ownership of valuable land in these regions was a primary cause of contention because it produced the two major sources of food on which the population depended. The first source was meat and dairy products from sheep and cattle herds. Since the population of approximately 60,000 was not nomadic but lived at settled

---

duction of an enormously important new form of employment brought about radical change in Icelandic life, though after the period under consideration here.

farmsteads, ranching required that each farmer have at his disposal large expanses of grazing land. Owners of land adjacent to the ocean had a proprietary access to the second source of sustenance, natural foodstuffs such as birds' eggs, fish, seal, and occasionally a beached whale. Beginning in the tenth century, Iceland suffered repeatedly from famine; even in good years the country was capable of producing only a small agricultural surplus. The natural limitations on the island's productivity did much to shape Iceland's social and legal forms, which in turn had a profound effect on the sagas.

Scholarly focus in recent years on individual events, like the battles of the thirteenth century, has magnified the differences between chronological periods. The result is that the tenth- and eleventh-century saga age and the thirteenth-century age of writing have acquired reputations of being thoroughly different. This view, always assumed rather than proved, neatly and simplistically divides medieval Iceland into two distinct cultural periods. This "fact" is then used to support the argument that the saga as a literary form must be a late invention because the sagas were written in the thirteenth century, considered so culturally changed from the earlier period. In reality, the concept is circular, based as it is on conclusions that become tenuous when the thread of continuity is traced. The Old Icelandic Free State—lacking religious wars, foreign invasion, or devastating social or economic change—was, at any point in its development, part of a stable cultural continuum.

The roots of Icelandic culture were firmly established in the formative tenth and eleventh centuries. Christian teaching did much to enlarge the world view of Icelanders in the twelfth and thirteenth centuries, but it did not change the fundamental nature of the society. One reason for the failure of Christianity to alter the societal structure was that Icelandic clergymen did not form a powerful priestly caste. Their church organization, unlike that in many other medieval lands, was politically and economically weak. Many priests functioned in their traditional role of secular farmers as well as church officials. Most lived on the land, married, looked after their children's inheritances, and maintained a vested interest in their kin groups. *Sturlunga saga*, a semireliable historical source, offers a graphic picture of the widespread participation of priests and bishops in feud. Rather than trying to stamp out feud, Iceland's clergy early on adapted their church responsibilities to the dominant codes of the society.

Feud was the bedrock of Icelandic medieval culture, and its consistency is an element of continuity throughout Iceland's medieval history and literature. The roots of the society and of its system of feud lay in independent family landholding, whereby free farmers controlled the major portion of the island's productive land. This tradition, established by the first generations after the settlement, continued well after Iceland had lost its independence to Norway in 1262–1264. Just as landownership and the functioning of feud in the society underwent a smooth transition from the preconversion period to Christian times, so, too, did the stories the Icelanders told about this important social behavior change from oral tales of feud to written sagas about feud. In the eleventh century, in a matter of decades, Iceland passed from a preliterate to a literate stage of culture. Icelanders, both clergy and laymen, quickly began writing vernacular prose, often about secular matters, with almost no intermediary stage of learned Latin writing.

In other words, Iceland, unlike other medieval European countries, did not go through a lengthy period in which learning and writing were limited to a cloistered clerical group. Instead, eleventh- and early twelfth-century Icelanders saw the obvious advantages of writing and quickly adopted it. The importation of new ideas and technologies is a normal phenomenon and does not demand the revolutionary reshaping of a culture. It must be remembered that the Icelanders were not forced by an external authority or a conquering power to accept radical innovations, either social or cultural. Instead, beginning in the eleventh century, they selected from continental usages those aspects of Latin-Christian culture which by general consensus could be grafted onto already well-established societal forms. The Icelandic process of decision making, with its traditional dependence on feud to regulate wealth and status, was too strongly established to be shaken.

Over the years scholars have grappled with the problem of defining Iceland's system of self-government. Various terms—republic, democracy, commonwealth, oligarchy— have been used. In an attempt to come closer to understanding Iceland's unique sociopolitical system, Andreas Heusler proposed that Icelandic government was a hybrid of aristocracy and democracy. Einar Olgeirsson argued that the extraordinary nature of Icelandic culture was a late and isolated phase of older Germanic tribal society.[6] Whereas each of these terms reflects aspects of Old Icelandic society and culture, none conveys the fact that Iceland was a nonhierarchical society which had for centuries maintained itself through a highly original system of advocacy. This system, the product of the convergence of social, economic, and geographical factors, made up for the lack of a hierarchical chain of authority. Advocacy tended to cool hotheadedness by giving the right to make decisions about feud to persons who chose not to risk their power recklessly. The intrusion of advocates turned private feuds into community concerns which were so closely watched by dwellers in the district that, if a feud mushroomed, it became a concern at the Althing—that is, a concern of the entire island. The system of advocacy worked to keep a lid on random violence, while at the same time giving ambi-

---

[6]Einar Olgeirsson, *Från ättegemenskap till klasstat*, trans. Cilla Johnson (Stockholm: Pan/Norstedts, 1971), esp. p. 44.

tious men the opportunity to prosper by brokering what power and influence they were able to acquire.

The attempt to create out of the system of advocacy a permanent state form is one of the distinguishing characteristics of Old Icelandic society—an aspect that sets it in sharp contrast to other contemporary European cultures. Instead of being hampered by the lack of a central executive authority, Icelandic society developed, and thrived on, an extraordinary governmental process. The establishment of a complex and well-conceived apparatus of local and national courts with fixed dates and responsibilities provided the Icelanders with forums for negotiating. The development of Icelandic legal standards strengthened and gave legitimacy to those who played the role of advocate. The social and governmental order that the advocacy system reinforced made Icelandic feud possible.

In studying the sagas, scholars have tended to confine their investigations within the limits of a single academic discipline. Literary scholars often lament what they consider to be superfluous material in the sagas; historians regret that the wealth of information in these stories cannot be considered factual because the sagas are a created, and therefore a fictional, literature. Medieval Icelanders, however, had no such difficulties. They told the tales of their people not as history or literature, but as narratives springing from societal relationships. Their stories are about the conflicts and the anxieties inherent in their society; between the medieval audience and the sagaman there was a contract of *vraisemblance*. Only a reconsideration of the functioning of feud can provide a sense of this contract and illumine the compositional technique of saga construction.

Let us turn to an example from the family sagas. By plotting specific occurrences of feud instead of looking to larger sequential schemas we begin to see the construction of saga narrative. The example is a small feud from *Droplaugarsona saga* (ch. 5), which is set in the East Fjords and narrates a series of feuds stemming from insult, seduction,

property dispute, disrupted claim to a *goðorð*, stealing, and
killing. These are all typical reasons for dispute in the sagas.
Reproduced here in its entirety, the feud examined is
divided into segments to demonstrate how saga feud is
constructed of three active narrative elements: conflict,
advocacy, and resolution. These elements are not bound to
a fixed sequential order but are shifted about according to
the decision of the sagaman.

When this small feud takes place, another feud is already
underway. It began when a freedman of Helgi Ásbjarnarson, a local chieftain, insulted a woman named Droplaug.
Her son Helgi kills the freedman, but then is made to pay a
fine to Helgi Ásbjarnarson. The fine angers the young man.
He then learns the law from Þorkell Geitisson, a man
famed for his legal knowledge, and begins to take part in
cases that others have against Helgi Ásbjarnarson and his
followers. The feud here considered describes the second
case Helgi brings against the chieftain. Like most of the
small feuds in *Droplaugarsona saga*, this one concerns the
problems of a local farmer, in this instance Þorgeirr.

Saga text: Information

> Later during the following winter there was a great famine
> with much loss of livestock. Þorgeirr, the farmer at Hrafnkels-
> staðir [Hrafnkelsstead], lost many animals. A man called
> Þórðr lived at Geirólfseyrr [Geirólfs bank] on the west side of
> the Skriðudale River. Þórðr was a wealthy man and was
> bringing up the child of Helgi Ásbjarnarson. Þorgeirr went to
> him and bought fifty ewes, paying for them in homespun. He
> received little use from these ewes because they ran away from
> him.

Small descriptive blocks like this one stud the narrative and
give information about new characters, their families and
lands, and present other background material.

Next, a problem arises when Þorgeirr finds the ewes at
Þórðr's farm. He obtains vital information about his loss of
milk from a farmwoman.

Saga text: Information that provides a source for dispute

> In the fall Þorgeirr himself went to look for his ewes and found eighteen of them in the milking pen at Geirólfseyrr. They had been milked.

Saga text: Information passing

> He asked the women who had ordered the milking, and they said it was Þórðr.

Armed with this evidence, Þorgeirr confronts Þórðr. What occurs next is a fairly typical event in the sagas. The damaged party seeks settlement and proposes terms. Either he himself makes this attempt at resolution, or he gets a more powerful person to serve as his advocate, an action I call brokerage. The damaging party may also suggest terms or seek a broker. If a broker is called upon, the process of attempting a resolution is delayed until the new party acquires the necessary information to fulfill his role.

Saga text: Resolution (rejected)

> Þorgeirr went to see Þórðr and asked him to make up the loss. He set reasonable terms, offering Þórðr the choice either of giving him an equal number of two-year-old wethers or of feeding the ewes for the coming winter. Þórðr said that he would do neither.

Þórðr's rejection engenders a new stage in the dispute. Although Þorgeirr is unsuccessful at resolving the issue, it is likely that many confrontations were quickly and reasonably settled at this point in a feud and were not worth a story. The sagas, however, are about disputes that continued and involved other people.

The reason for Þórðr's refusal is that he has previously entered into an obligation with an important leader in the district. Þórðr's motivation is stated clearly.

Saga text: Information

> Þórðr said that he would find little benefit in his fostering of Helgi Ásbjarnarson's child if he had to pay for the sheep.

Saga text: Advocacy (brokerage)

Next, Þorgeirr went to see Helgi Ásbjarnarson and told him what had happened. Helgi said: "I desire that Þórðr pay you a settlement, for you are in the right. Tell him what I said."

Saga text: Resolution (rejected)

Þorgeirr went back to Þórðr but got nothing for his trouble.

As this attempt to resolve the matter comes to naught, the dispute continues. Þorgeirr tries another local leader who, although not a chieftain, is experienced in the law and is a rival of Helgi Ásbjarnarson's.

Saga text: Advocacy (brokerage)

After this Þorgeirr went to see Helgi Droplaugarson and asked him to take the case, adding: "It is my wish that you keep whatever is to be gotten out of this matter." On these conditions Helgi took over the case.

Seeking the support of others, particularly powerful men, to help solve a problem occurs constantly throughout the sagas. I have termed this type of advocacy brokerage because it has a contractual nature: a person with knowledge, expertise, or power acts on behalf of another as a middleman in times of trouble. Icelanders in need of an advocate usually turned to family members or to important farmers, who were often chieftains. Since none of these sources of support was necessarily reliable, a person needing help at times had to solicit, as Þorgeirr did, several brokers before finding one willing and qualified to do the job. Brokerage depended almost entirely on self-interest. Brokers could increase the level of conflict or resolve the dispute, depending upon their motivation and the current state of district feuds.

The Icelandic social milieu provided a number of ways to induce another party to act as one's broker. One could call upon existing obligations, among them kinship or fictitious kinship bonds such as fosterage, marriage, blood brotherhood. The prudent man created such obligations ahead of time so that he would have a powerful broker to turn to in time of need. Obligations could be kept alive by giving gifts and feasts.

Payment was another means of obtaining support. Usually, wealth was transferred to the broker in the form of land, livestock, silver, or profit from a case, though compensation could also be in terms of power. Men of equal power often allied themselves through contractual pledges of mutual support and friendship, called *vinfengi* or *vinátta*, or they could bond their families in a marriage alliance. Men of lesser status often created bonds of support by fostering a child of a more powerful man. This practice was usually advantageous to the more powerful man, for the foster father often promised to endow the child with an inheritance.

Advocacy, especially brokerage, worked because the society had no public institutions to fulfill an individual's needs. When asked to intervene in disputes between individuals, even the chieftains, the society's only local governmental officials, acted as private parties. Brokerage is not a complex process, and it is found in all societies in one way or another. What was unusual in Iceland was that brokerage was so pervasive and became the normal way in which Icelanders dealt with one another. As a process, brokerage maintained the order of social relationships in a society lacking military and governmental chains of command and possessing only minimal social and political hierarchies. It was the process of brokerage that guided conflict and violence into the social arena of the courts where, through arbitration, resolutions could be proposed. In saga literature brokerage is characterized as a form of worldly societal interchange rather than as the heroic actions of an individual. In the example from *Droplaugarsona saga* given above, the intricacies of this process can be seen.

When Þorgeirr goes to Helgi Ásbjarnarson, there is no talk of payment. Þorgeirr is seemingly hoping that reason will prevail, but Helgi Ásbjarnarson does not lend the full force of his power nor does he accept payment. To do so would be to create an obligation. If Helgi should fail to negotiate a compromise between the two antagonists, he would have to renege on one of the two obligations. When Þorgeirr goes to Helgi Droplaugarson, he is already aware that the matter will not be settled easily, and he offers Helgi Droplaugarson whatever compensation he can get from the case. The two men strike a bargain. Helgi Droplaugarson wants the case because of his ongoing feud with his name-sake, and Þorgeirr sweetens the prize by offering the entire profit to Helgi. For his part, farmer Þorgeirr receives a much needed service.

In turning over this right of prosecution to Helgi Drop-laugarson, Þorgeirr realizes that he will not be compensated materially for his sheep. There are many analogous incidents in the sagas, with an injured party transferring his right to material compensation to a broker. Two of these, one in *Vápnfirðinga saga* (ch. 7) and one in *Eyrbyggja saga* (ch. 31), begin with similar disputes over the use of land or its produce. Like the feud that builds out of Þorgeirr's problem, these incidents initiate tight narrative segments which feed into ongoing feuds.

Why would a person such as Þorgeirr give up his right to compensation? There could be many reasons. One might be the knowledge that his opponent Þórðr, in return for his determination to cheat a neighbor, will now have to defend his person and property against Helgi Droplaugarson, a dangerous and motivated antagonist. Another could be Þorgeirr's awareness that if he leaves the case open, his honor is at stake. Faced with a humiliating situation, he might be goaded by others into challenging and attempting to kill Þórðr—a risky venture. Instead, Þorgeirr turns to a broker and proves himself a difficult man to humiliate. Nor can Þorgeirr, once he has contracted with a broker, be intimidated into dropping the case. The right of prosecution has been assumed by Helgi Droplaugarson, and Þorgeirr is relieved of all responsibility. Within the context of the saga, Þorgeirr plays a secondary but important role. He introduces a dispute that forms a link in the feud chain of the saga, and now he is out of the tale. Why does a broker like Helgi get the entire reward? Again, the answer is tied to risk and honor: Helgi, a farmer, puts his reputation and perhaps his life on the line when he goes against a chieftain. If he loses the case, he may be forced to pay fines. By merely taking the case, Helgi assumes the expensive burden of bringing a large following to the local springtime assembly or to the summer Althing. A group of followers was often necessary if one feuding party was to show enough force to equal his opponent's. To be successful, Helgi Droplaugarson will have to depend on others for support. He will need either to generate new obligations or to call in previous commitments. By whatever means Helgi, as a broker, obtains the required support, it will always have to appear at least to match or, better, to overshadow his opponent's strength in men or influence.

Saga text: Conflict

> In the spring Helgi Droplaugarson went to Geirólfseyrr and summoned Þórðr to the Althing. He charged that Þórðr had concealed the ewes and stolen their milk.

Helgi's prosecution of Þórðr is in accordance with *Grágás* (Ib, 162) for both the stealing of the sheep and the use of the milk.[7] As brokers preparing for the Althing, the two

---

[7]The standard edition of *Grágás*, the books of Old Icelandic law, was edited by Vilhjálmur Finsen and published in three volumes. Ia and Ib: *Grágás: Islændernes Lovbog i Fristatens Tid, udgivet efter det kongelige Bibliotheks Haandskrift* (Copenhagen: Brødrene Berlings Bogtrykkeri, 1852); II: *Grágás efter det Arnamagnæanske Haandskrift Nr. 334 fol., Staðarhólsbók* (Copenhagen: Gyldendalske Boghandel, 1879); and III: *Grágás: Stykker, som findes i det Arnamagnæanske Haandskrift Nr. 351 fol. Skálholtsbók og en Række andre Haandskrifter* (Copenhagen: Gyldendalske Boghandel, 1883). An English translation of Volume I appeared in 1980: *Laws of Early Iceland: Grágás I*, trans. Andrew Dennis, Peter Foote, and Richard Perkins (Winnipeg: University of Manitoba Press). Translations of Volumes II and III are expected. For a short discussion of *Grágás* see Appendix A.

Helgis call upon those obligated to them so as to be well represented at the court. At times the process of collecting followers forms an entire narrative segment, as when Flosi and Kári in *Njáls saga* go around the countryside gathering support for the case resulting from the burning of Njáll (see chap. 9). At other times a saga simply states that a man has gathered followers, and it may name the important ones. As in this example of feud between Þorgeirr and Þórðr, the initial conflict over disputed wealth often recedes into the background. The confrontation engenders new acts of feud and becomes one more step in the development of the saga, which, as the sum of small repetitive narrative parts, focuses the audience's attention on questions of honor, of the strength and influence of brokers, and of their ability to gain supporters.

Saga text: Information

When the case was later heard at the Althing, both Helgi Droplaugarson and Þorkell Geitisson came with extremely large followings. With them was Ketill from Njarðvík. Helgi Ásbjarnarson did not have a following sufficient to void their suit.

The dispute has advanced to the Althing, and the feudists are at loggerheads. The stalemate persists until third parties intervene.

Saga text: Advocacy (arbitration)

Then men asked that they arrange a settlement.

Advocacy in the form of arbitration or brokerage is often the "breathing space" between conflicts, cooling potentially violent responses by channeling them into community issues and sometimes legal avenues. It may also be the calm before the storm, for bringing in an advocate is the way in which the sagaman feeds the smaller unit of feud into the conflicts of more powerful men. Members of the community or arbitrators, advocating the community good, often intervene to bring about a settlement when two groups or individuals fail to find a solution themselves. In some instances this narrative slot is developed into a full description of advocacy, or repetitions of advocacies, which can go on for pages. In others, advocacy simply leads into the coming action. In this example from *Droplaugarsona saga* the sagaman chose to pass quickly through the mechanism of arbitration, noting the presence of intervention, and to turn at once to its result.

Saga text: Resolution (direct)

> Helgi Droplaugarson wanted nothing less than self-judgment [*sjálfdoemi*], and this he got. Helgi awarded himself as many payments of a cow's worth as there were ewes that Þórðr had ordered milked. They separated now with this decision, and Helgi Droplaugarson thought that the case had gone according to his wishes.

This example is typical of saga feud. A mundane dispute over livestock starts off the quarrel. A failed resolution occurs before the injured party turns to a broker; when the second broker responds aggressively, the feud grows. The eventual resolution of the specific matter of sheep stealing clearly does not end the longer feud of the saga, but it does complete a chain of events that forms a small feud. Often such resolutions did not hold, and the process would begin again.

In the above example, even if we did not know that the saga continues with several more feud chains, we could guess it. Not only has Helgi Droplaugarson won a case from the other Helgi, but in forcing his opponent to pay the value of cows for the loss of sheep, he has broadcast his scorn for Helgi Ásbjarnarson's authority. A response by Helgi Ásbjarnarson is called for. Although the story of the feud was certainly well known to the medieval audience, the form and elaboration of the responses of one Helgi to the other and the decision of whether or not to have an intervening small story was in the hands of the sagaman. This is the stuff of Icelandic saga feud.

3 The Syntax of Narrative Elements

The saga-writer is, to a certain extent, bound to unwritten tradition, sometimes to its contents, at any rate to its narrative style. In spite of the enormous rift which, certainly, has often separated a written from its corresponding oral saga, the written saga as a whole must be regarded as an ennobled continuation of the oral one, and not a complete departure from it, not an absolutely new *Formwille*.

—Einar Ól. Sveinsson

MANY established terms could be borrowed to describe narrative units in the sagas, but few would reflect the way in which the sagas were constructed or what these tales are about. At issue is the basic perception of why the sagas took so strong a hold on the medieval Icelanders. The question is: Are these prose narratives an introspective creation of an island people or are they a thinly veiled adaptation of continental literary forms, easily categorized by sequential patterns?

Vladímir Propp proposed the word "function" to describe units of narrative action in Afanás'ev's collection of Russian folktales and fairy tales. Propp's seminal work, *Morphology of the Folktale*, first published in Russia in

1928, became widely available in translation in 1958 and since then has influenced studies of traditional narrative.[1] Propp distinguished thirty-one functions whose order in individual tales he describes as strictly uniform; he also determined that all the folktales in this particular group are structurally of one type.[2] Propp argues that the action in each tale is part of a movement directed toward liquidating either a lack or a villainy. The functions, he says, follow in a fixed sequence the events of an individual tale, and in most instances the motivating lack or villainy was a specifically determinable element, such as absence of food, wife, or wealth, or the oppression of a villain, whether a robber, a wicked stepmother, or a witch.

After laying out the order of the thirty-one functions, Propp shows that some of them can be dropped and others repeated while the tale advances toward the liquidation of the lack or the villainy. His innovative analysis suggests that a group of folktales progresses according to episodic "moves" of groups of these functions. One of Propp's contributions to analysis of narrative was his demonstration that the tales could be understood in terms other than those centered on motif analysis. The weakness of his approach is that it concentrates on form while ignoring content.

Alan Dundes recognized the shortcomings of motif analysis as well as the limitations of Propp's concentration on form. In his *The Morphology of North American Indian Folktales*, he used Kenneth Pike's structural term "motifeme" to correspond to Propp's "function," but he corrected the deficiency of referring only to form by retaining the use of motif.[3] Using Propp's terms, Dundes proposed

---

[1] Vladímir Propp, *Morphology of the Folktale*, trans. Laurence Scott, intro. by Svatava Pirkova-Jakobson; 2d ed. rev., ed. Louis A. Wagner, intro. by Alan Dundes (Austin: University of Texas Press, 1968).

[2] Ibid., pp. 22–23.

[3] Alan Dundes, *The Morphology of North American Indian Folktales*, Folklore Fellows Communications, Vol. LXXXI, no. 195 (Helsinki: Academia Scientiarum Fennica, 1964).

that the movement from "lack" to "lack liquidated" forms a nuclear two-motifeme sequence in the North American Indian tales. He also describes four- and six-motifeme sequences, as well as some that are more complex. The combination of the terms "motifeme" and "motif" has taken on a specific meaning in descriptions of syntagmatically set progressions in a certain type of traditional narrative.

Theodore Andersson, in *The Icelandic Family Saga*, also relied on Propp's principles in developing a set of terms for his schema of saga structure.[4] Because his approach has been influential in structural studies of the sagas, I consider it here at some length. Andersson joined to the concept of sequential progression the presumption that the sagas arose from a heroic legacy of Germanic epic. Following the lead of W. P. Ker in the nineteenth century and of Andreas Heusler in the early twentieth century, Andersson argues that in thought and structure the sagas are an adaptation of Germanic epic poetry:

> In view of the evidence it seems more fruitful to regard the literary form of the saga as an adaptation of heroic models rather than as history, as an older generation held, or as a novelistic innovation, as a newer generation believes. The narrative material may be historical, or at least traditional, and some of the techniques are unprecedented, but the author's mode of thought and many of his stylistic habits are certainly heroic. His interpretation of the action as conflict and climax and his polarization of the conflict are a clear legacy from the heroic pattern. A recognition of this literary line clarifies some of the saga's uniqueness and some of the mystery surrounding the sudden appearance of such a fully contrived form. The saga authors did not need to create an entirely new literary type, but were able to elaborate on a traditional literary mold, the heroic mold.[5]

---

[4]Theodore M. Andersson, *The Icelandic Family Saga: An Analytic Reading* (Cambridge: Harvard University Press, 1967).

[5]Ibid., p. 93.

Whereas Propp grounded his sequential progression in a movement set off by determinable small units of story with motivational effects on the tale, such as acts of villainy or the lack of an object or a person, Andersson bases his progression on the mounting of epic tales to a dramatic climax. His schema divides plot into gross thematic categories: introduction, conflict, climax, revenge, reconciliation, and aftermath. These bind each saga to a pyramidal structure with only one occurrence of each category. In Andersson's words, the "dramatic line of the saga is thus a simple pyramid, the peak of which is the climax. The incline before the peak describes the events that produce the climax and the decline describes the subsequent events that set it to rest. In simplest terms a saga is the story of a dramatic climax, which everything else is calculated to put in relief."[6]

Andersson later reversed his view of the heroic model. In a 1978 article he writes: "Despite many gestures borrowed from the heroic tradition, the underlying outlook is not heroic, as has been often argued, but social."[7] As more scholars come to this position, it is likely that the tendency to isolate characters and events from their social context will reverse itself. The change in overview has not, however, been accompanied by adjustments in the concepts of structure and origins of the texts. Even in his 1978 article Andersson maintains the importance of climax as the focal point of his six-part sequential order. This proposed structure, which is ill-fitting in many cases, serves only to summarize the action rather than to tell us anything about the particular nature of Icelandic narrative.[8]

Andersson's central placement of climax produces an

    [6]Ibid., p. 34.
    [7]"The Icelandic Sagas," in *Heroic Epic and Saga*, ed. Felix J. Oinas (Bloomington: Indiana University Press, 1978), p. 157.
    [8]Vésteinn Ólason considers the shortcomings of such structures in, "Frásagnarlist í fornum sögum," *Skírnir* 152 (1978):166–202, and "Nokkrar athugasemdir um Eyrbyggja sögu," *Skírnir* 145 (1971):5–25.

artificial schema and forces the tale into an unyielding mold. Rather than depending on a fixed sequence as Andersson has suggested, saga narrative is formed by numerous feuds, each containing repetitions of conflicts, acts of revenge, and resolutions, often with introductions and aftermaths of their own. In support of his theory Andersson cites the short story (*þáttr*, pl. *þættir*) of Þorsteinn staffstruck, *Þorsteins þáttr stangarhǫggs*, to illustrate the schema he then uses for the family sagas. According to this schema, climax must follow the conflict of the saga and must precede revenge. Andersson places climax at the point when an important character in the saga, farmer Þorsteinn, kills an unimportant stableman at the farm Hof because of an uncompensated blow at an earlier horsefight. Every other indication from the *þáttr* shows that the killing is not the dramatic peak of the tale, but only that it is the event that brings into the tale one of the story's two major characters, the well-known chieftain Bjarni Brodd-Helgason of Hof.

Employing Andersson's terms, one could just as easily determine that Þorsteinn's killing of the stableman was an act of revenge for the stableman's blow, the initial cause of conflict. Then revenge would precede climax and so would disrupt the syntagmatic order. Another problem with Andersson's fixed schema is that the *þáttr* includes another confrontation and resolution which, coming after Bjarni and Þorsteinn's reconciliation, do not fit into the six-part schema. Bjarni initiates a playful conflict with Þorsteinn's father in which he deceives the old man into thinking that Þorsteinn has been killed. The new conflict, an attempted revenge on the part of the father, and the reconciliation between Bjarni and the old man are simply dropped by Andersson, presumably because they do not fit into his strict sequence of six nonrepetitive parts.

Andersson sets up his schema according to an entirely literary decision. He fails to consider the medieval audience, which we may safely assume was far less interested in the killing of a hired hand than in the actions of the famous chieftain Bjarni. Nor from the nature of this tale does it seem that the sagaman was much interested in the stableman. If one is looking for climax, this unusually short and uncomplicated saga contains an encounter far more dramatic, elongated, and memorable than the brief exchange between Þorsteinn and the stableman. After building tension through a series of repetitious goadings of Þorsteinn and Bjarni, the sagaman finally brings the two major characters together in single combat, *einvígi*, to settle the issue of honor. The *einvígi*, presented with humor, results in a peaceful settlement through which Þorsteinn becomes Bjarni's faithful follower. After the final mock conflict between Bjarni and Þorsteinn's father, in which the feeble old man tries to stab the *goði*, the saga ends with a short eulogy of Bjarni, a description of his death, and a recounting of the chieftain's numerous descendants. The final concentration on Bjarni and not on Þorsteinn is a further indication that Bjarni's presence is of central importance to this *þáttr*.

Even in the longest of sagas, Andersson insists on the fixed placement of a climax. For instance, he outlines the lengthy *Njáls saga* as a sequence of two pyramidal structures, saying that "each of the two climaxes is cradled in the standard six-part structure," and that each of these structures, one centered on Gunnarr of Hlíðarendi and the other on Njáll Þorgeirsson, forms its own saga.[9]

Although *Njáls saga* at some point may well have been two or more small sagas, the saga at hand is but one saga, as Andersson agrees, but it is not two separate structures, as Andersson contends. Instead, *Njáls saga* as we have it is a skillfully interwoven narrative whole in which the sagaman first concentrates on Gunnarr's feuds and then moves on to the feuds of the sons of Njáll, including his foster son and his son-in-law. A common thread in the feud chains is how

---

[9]*Icelandic Family Saga*, p. 304. See also pp. 291–307.

initially Gunnarr and later the Njálssons are embroiled in violence while Njáll, with varying success, maneuvers first Gunnarr and then his sons out of trouble by providing legal resolutions. Throughout the feuds of Gunnarr and the Njálssons the sagaman presents a series of double resolutions, one violent and one legal. This pattern is evident in the short feud in which the wives of Gunnarr and Njáll respond to each other's actions with violence, while the husbands settle matters legally (see chap. 9). The final set of resolutions in the saga follows the same pattern: Kári Sǫlmundarson, Njáll's son-in-law, kills several of the burners to avenge the death of Njáll and his family. Finally he and Flosi reconcile and seal the resolution with a marriage tie.

Even if we pare down Andersson's schema to fit single feuds instead of entire sagas, we are still burdened with the fact that sagas do not follow a single syntagmatic pattern. Traditional narratives such as folktales and heroic epics may be built upon the expectation of a climax, but the sagas are not. They certainly have many memorable high points, but these do not fill the same formal role as those in either epic or folktale. Partly for this reason, the sagas have defied the analysis successfully applied to these two other forms of traditional narrative.

Other saga scholars have followed Andersson's lead in imposing syntagmatic structures on the sagas. For example, Lars Lönnroth, theorizing about the general composition of the sagas, proposes two sequential "action patterns."[10] The first, which he terms the "feud pattern," consists of "introduction, cause for conflict (balance disturbed), first punitive act plus x number of revenge acts leading up to climax, more revenge acts, and final settlement (balance restored)." This linear sequence is a modified version of Andersson's six-part structure which, although still cen-

---

[10]Lars Lönnroth, *Njáls saga: A Critical Introduction* (Berkeley, Los Angeles, London: University of California Press, 1976), pp. 68 ff.

tered on climax, is cut down to a more reasonable episodic level. Lönnroth's second action pattern is proposed for stories of Icelanders abroad. This "travel pattern," composed of "departure, a series of tests, including court visits and viking adventures, and homecoming,"[11] does in a general way reflect the progression of events when Icelanders travel abroad. Its success lies not only in its simplicity but in the nature of the tales described, for the tales of Icelanders' journeys abroad are in many ways different from feud stories at home. Iceland's island location required that tales of journeys abroad by Icelanders be bracketed by travel out and travel in. Accounts of such journeys include many *þættir* and, far more so than the indigenous sagas of feud, they take on aspects of folktale and epic journeys. The exotic settings of foreign travels, replete with kings, queens, jarls, royal maidens, berserkers, and monsters, stand in contrast to the tales of feud set in the well-understood social, political, and legal world of Iceland. It is not surprising, then, that Lönnroth's travel pattern, while reflecting aspects of journeys out from Iceland, does not fit normal saga journeys within Iceland.

Richard Allen, in *Fire and Iron*,[12] proposes an eight-level hierarchy of saga narrative which employs many terms. Using *Njáls saga* as the prime example, he suggests that the sagas have a mythopoeic underpinning which he schematizes,[13] using as models the Bible and mythic and heroic poetry: "It is tempting to suggest a parallel evolution of Judeo-Christian creation and hero myth with Germanic creation and Germanic heroic myths in order to explain why many of Auerbach's remarks on Christian literature seem applicable to the sagas."[14] Allen's levels of saga narrative are as follows:[15] Level I.A is "minimal fact," which

---

[11]Ibid., p. 71.
[12]Richard Allen, *Fire and Iron: Critical Approaches to Njáls Saga* (Pittsburgh: University of Pittsburgh Press, 1971).
[13]Ibid., p. 46. See also p. 56 for schema.
[14]Ibid., p. 46.
[15]Ibid., pp. 71–74.

he substitutes for the poetic formula, and Level I.B is "figurative and gnomic statements"; Level II is "motif (small units of typical acts)"; Level III is "scene (level of sustained personal or social action)"; Level IV is "the level of the chapter unit . . . the patterned sequences of events which are components of a large theme." Levels V and VI are "episode" and "episode cluster," which he compares with the oral term "theme" and which are marked off by "interludes." On Levels V and VI, Allen writes, "the theme has broad cultural and psychological implications and may be sensed as referring back to mythic origins. . . . But the origin of these stylized episodes, scenes, and motifs can be assigned not only to the myth, but to the ritual upon which myth took shape."[16] Level VII is "plot" and Level VIII is the "archetypal level," which Allen concludes curves back to Level I.B.

The overtones and undertones of religion and ritual in Allen's hierarchy preclude the possibility that his terms can effectively describe a literature long recognized for its realistic tone. To propose that the sagas are generated from mythic roots is to build bridges that fall from the very weight of the argument.

The sagas have long been understood in a general way to be scenic or episodic, and Allen defines "scene" as "the level of sustained individual or social action, as a compact unit of significant action which has a beginning, middle, and end."[17] Building on Allen's definition, Carol Clover argues in her article about saga composition, that scenes have "a remarkably fixed tripartite schema" and theorizes that, within the context of what she calls "structural traditionalism," scene has a key generative function in saga narrative.[18] To this end she proposes that the beginning, middle, and end of dramatic scenes in the sagas can best be

---

[16]Ibid., p. 73.

[17]Ibid., p. 65.

[18]Carol Clover, "Scene in Saga Composition," *Arkiv för nordisk filologi* 89 (1974):57–83.

termed "preface," "dramatic encounter," and "conclusion." Clover's supposition that a three-part formulation of scene, similar to more extensive sequential schemas, was the primary compositional tool or modus operandi of the sagaman ignores the depth and sophistication of the literature. The progression whereby a dramatic encounter is first introduced and then followed by a brief conclusion is not exclusively a characteristic of saga narrative; it is seen in many medieval literatures, as well as in the modern novel. In any story, after all, characters appear, encounter one another, and part. Recognition that scenes in the sagas have three general parts tells us very little about the constituent elements of saga narrative and less about the techniques employed by the medieval storyteller in clustering the active and nonactive elements of his tale. That one can, in examining the sagas, repeatedly find occurrences of the basic form of the paragraph is not surprising in a prose literature.

In a ground-breaking study of oral storytelling, Albert Lord set forth the Parry-Lord thesis that oral poetry is not memorized but is constructed mnemonically.[19] The singer composes during a performance by means of a traditional technique. Lord has shown that the singer of oral poetry relies on a substitution system employing metrically set formulas to construct units which he terms "themes" and defines as "groups of ideas regularly used in telling a tale in the formulaic style of traditional song."[20] Examples of themes are the repeated arming of the hero, the sending of letters, and the preparations for a journey. Lord's approach to traditional narrative is quite different from those of the studies previously mentioned in that neither formula nor theme is sequentially set. His terms "formula" and "theme" are useful for studies of Old Norse verse, but they

---

[19]Albert Lord, *The Singer of Tales*, Harvard Studies in Comparative Literature 24 (Cambridge: Harvard University Press, 1960).

[20]Ibid., p. 68.

were not designed to take into consideration prose feud tales constructed without concern for metrics. These terms would probably be extremely useful in studying *rímur*, a late medieval to modern form of Icelandic rhymed narrative verse, some of which are about saga characters.

Theories of fixed sequential order do little more than bring attention to gross patterns in the sagas, and the determination to find such an order has remained for years a stumbling block in the study of the sagas' narrative form. The results of the search have been chiefly a system of summarizing the sagas which touches only the dramatic high points and separates us even further from the sagaman, the saga texts, and the means by which the texts were composed. The major problem with theories of sequential order is that the sagas were not constructed according to uniform sequences. They were built, rather, by combining three active elements—conflict, advocacy, resolution—which define the Icelandic process of dispute and its settlement. In this study, these terms designate only single incidents, however small, and have no sense of encompassing whole segments of the story. Conflict and resolution are, of course, familiar, but eminently suitable and direct, terms to describe compositional elements within a narrative devoted to stories of feud. Resolutions are not separated into categories such as lasting or temporary and successful or unsuccessful. If the resolution is temporary or unsuccessful, the feud chain continues until an acceptable settlement is reached. The third element, advocacy, is a key concept in the world of the sagas which has not yet been defined as an important structural element. Advocacy is tied inextricably to the kind of society that produced the sagas, a society that thrived on building and realigning bonds of support to make up for the lack of governmental institutions.

Conflict, advocacy, and resolution, as small units of action, substitute one for the other in no fixed order. That is, these active narrative elements, which I call feudemes, are not bound to a linear progression; rather, they cluster together in a variety of ways, and the results often form what critics have described as scenes or episodes. A cluster, because it may begin with any feudeme, is free of a rigid schema. The clusters form chains of feud, which are the backbone of Icelandic prose narrative; one or several chains make up an entire saga. Since the variety of the feudemes and the formation of clusters and chains are taken up in later chapters, the discussion here is limited to introducing the feudeme as the sagaman's basic narrative tool.

Feudemes represent only action that takes place, not action that can be inferred, even logically, from the narrative. For instance, in *Víga-Glúms saga* (ch. 10), Þorgrímr Þórisson is refused the hand of Gizurr Kaðalsson's daughter, Þórdís. This occurs as an action. However, when this event is later referred to in the saga (Ch. 11, saga selection 6) action does not occur, it is only implied; therefore, the category is information. In a second example, if a person is killed and a character in the saga learns of the action or gets involved in a dispute only because someone informed him about the killing, such giving of information would be advocacy (information passing). Only if a killing takes place "on the scene," that is, as an action, is it conflict or resolution, depending upon the circumstances. Another example is the difference between a vision of a killing or a prophecy of a death (information) and the actual event.

Feudemes, then, differ from units of information in that they are active, whereas the latter are nonactive; both are essential to the construction of saga prose. Awareness of feudemes provides a means for understanding the sagaman's choice of active and nonactive narrative elements. And that choice is the heart of the method by which the sagas were constructed.

The analogy of "feudeme" with linguistic terminology suggests that the role of a feudeme in feud is similar to the role of a morpheme in language. The feudeme forms a relatively stable indivisible unit of feud within the context of the Icelandic saga. Another similarity to linguistic construction is that each feudeme can be expanded by attaching a unit of travel as a prefix or a suffix. In the sagas set in Iceland, most journeys were undertaken for these reasons: to attend feasts or assemblies, to gather supporters, to seek aid from a broker, to create obligations, to bring together parties for a resolution, or to visit another farmer for the purpose of acquiring foodstuffs, laying claim to land, or initiating conflict.

In using feudemes to construct his narrative, the sagaman did not have to be aware of how he composed. He fashioned stories about disputes among Icelanders by means of action units which reflected the different stages of feud. The point should be stressed that if the feudemes arise from the society on which the sagas are modeled, they are not precise representations of everyday procedure. As a literature, the sagas have a way of heightening daily life and introspectively concentrating on issues of social and personal tension. These tales, however, give strong indications of social modes of action. In many instances the distinction between acceptability and unacceptability of action is defined by the result rather than by the specific action itself. For example, in an instance from *Hoensa-Þóris saga*, Hœnsa-Þórir burns his opponent Blund-Ketill to death in his farmhouse. As the tale progresses we can see, from the character of the burner and the result of the burning, that the action was unacceptable. A burning is treated differently in *Njáls saga*. Flosi burns Njáll and his family in their house, but from the outcome of the tale it is clear that this action was not a wholly unacceptable move on Flosi's part. Similarly, saga society did not condemn all aggressive behavior that was irrational or exaggerated. It reacted only against conduct that was destabilizing to either its ethical, economic, or political order.

Of primary consideration to the sagaman was the social configuration of traditionally known material. The sagaman had to make his tale conform to a corpus of existing sources. Characters, events, and feuds, from the settlement period to the period when the sagas were written, were components of a traditional store of information. Place-names and famous events, such as memorable Althings, were part of the Icelanders' collective memory. There was little freedom to alter the substance of known events, although they could be embroidered in narrative. Many characters appear in more than one saga, and the Icelandic audience was often aware of an individual's genealogy, the location of his farm, the district in whose political and judicial arena he participated, and what kind of personality he was supposed to have had.

Rather than being antiquarian flourishes, as some have assumed, the genealogies of characters and the historical backgrounds of relationships contribute to the social configuration of specific acts of advocacy and obligation. The reason a man went to one person instead of to another often stemmed, not from chance, but from the history of family, political ties, and landownership. The audience, despite its familiarity with the background of the tales, did not know how the saga would take form in each telling and which parts of the feud would be expanded. Medieval Icelanders were decidedly interested in stories about their ancestors, their districts, famous court cases, political maneuverings, and the passing of land from one family to another.

At times the sagaman developed his story according to phases of dispute, recognizable to and expected by his audience, in which the alignment of events was limited by the possibilities of Icelandic feud. The sagaman's tale often fell into a common formulation of what should be included to make a saga plausible, though the specific way the storyteller arranged his narrative was left to his own discretion. He could digress and elaborate or he could stick to the bare bones of a traditional story. Incidents relating to or acts of certain characters are told in separate sagas and integrated into the tales in different ways. Thus the sagaman was free to draw upon a pool of common material and characters which he adapted to the exigencies of his tale.

Well-known brokers and arbitrators, such as Snorri goði, Guðmundr inn ríki, Jón Loftsson, and Þórðr gellir, appear in a number of sagas. Occurrences like Snorri goði's alliance with Víga-Styrr appear in *Eyrbyggja saga* and *Heiðarvíga saga*. The failed attempt by Gísli Súrsson's sister Þórdís, the mother of Snorri goði, to avenge her brother's death appears in *Gísla saga* and *Eyrbyggja saga*. An incident of feud building out of a divorce is presented illogically in *Víga-Glúms saga* (ch. 16); the same incident is found in *Reykdœla saga ok Víga-Skútu* (ch. 26), where it is described in much more detail and with a logical development (chs. 23–25). Entire sagas, such as *Ljósvetninga saga*, exist in two similar but different recountings; similarly, *Qlkofra þáttr* and *Bandamanna saga* are at heart the same tale, but they are set in different locations with entirely different characters. The story of the divorce and dowry recovery of Unnr, daughter of Mqrðr gígja (the fiddle), appears in *Laxdœla saga* (ch. 19): "Hrútr married and the woman he took was called Unnr, the daughter of Mqrðr gígja. Unnr left him and thus began the feud between the Laxdœlir [the people of Lax River valley] and the Fljótshlíðingar [the people of Fljótshlíð]." The story of the same marriage and divorce opens *Njáls saga* and initiates a feud that, with its background, is strung over twenty-four chapters.

In some instances a story begins in one saga and runs over into another. For example, the feud that erupts in *Sturlu saga* over Birningr Steinarsson's property later appears at the opening of *Íslendinga saga*, where it is continued.

Many of the *pættir* are about characters who play roles in the family sagas. For instance, Bjarni Brodd-Helgason, the chieftain who appears in *Þorsteins þáttr stangarhǫggs*, plays a major but different role in *Vápnfirðinga saga*. Bjarni's cousin and opponent in this saga, Þorkell Geitisson, shows up in several sagas as a supporter and a legal expert. In *Droplaugarsona saga*, for example, he teaches Helgi Droplaugarson the law that Helgi uses to great advantage in his feud with Helgi Ásbjarnarson.

Similarly, characters of one generation are tied to both ancestors and descendants. The comprehensiveness of generational ties and their effect on the tales are apparent when a *bóndi* or a *goði* is introduced into the saga with information about his genealogy and land. Such background information can even lend an air of irony or sarcasm, as when Mǫrðr Valgarðsson, a scoundrel in *Njáls saga*, is introduced with a splendid genealogy.

Besides the similarity of character and situation, there is also similarity in the way feud progresses from one feudeme to another. The challenge is to recognize these recurring elements, although they are clothed in different details and embroidered in a variety of ways. There is nothing mathematical or mechanical about the way in which the sagaman combined feudemes. He simply concentrated on a type of action and fleshed it out with specific names and details. The keys to understanding this method are that most feuds in the sagas progress consistently and logically and that the feudemes, like feud itself, are integrating principles. Although the number of narrative tools was limited by the tradition of feud, the literature gives the impression of a wide array of narrative forms. Feudemic substitution offered the sagaman a variety of possibilities to work with.

4 Units of Travel and Information and the Feudeme of Conflict

"Greatly to find quarrel in a straw" is the rule of their [the Old Icelanders']
conduct. The tempers of the men are easily stirred; they have a general name
(*skapraun*) for the trial of a man's patience, applied to anything that puts a
strain on him or encroaches on his honour. The trial may come from anything—horses, sheep, hay, women, merchandise. From these follow any
number of secondary or retaliatory insults, trespasses, and manslaughters.
Anything almost is enough to set the play going.

—W. P. Ker

Units of travel and information are the nonactive elements of saga prose. Along with the active feudemes, these nonactive units occur many times during a
saga feud and are essential elements in saga narrative. In
this chapter I look first at travel and information, then turn
to the feudeme of conflict. In the following two chapters I

consider advocacy and resolution, respectively. Throughout the discussion, I include examples of the different categories in order to illustrate the variety of ways in which each narrative element is manifested in the medieval texts. So as not to crowd the discussion with a plethora of examples, I have assembled as companions to the chapters on the feudemes three appendixes: B, conflict; C, advocacy; and D, resolution. In these appendixes further examples are grouped according to categories as they appear in the chapters.

Units of Travel

Travel (T), though not a feudeme itself, accompanies feudemes. Like a prefix or a suffix, a single occurrence or a block of travel descriptions may be joined to any feudeme. Units of travel may also stand alone. A walk from booth to booth in search of support at the Althing is an example of travel accompanying advocacy. Another type of advocacy occurs when a group of beggar women travel from one farm to another and pass information (travel/advocacy). Sometimes journeys to seek the support of powerful men end in failure, as happens to Gísli Súrsson (see saga selection 4). Travel/resolution occurs when a group rides out with the intention of carrying out an ambush in the name of blood vengeance, or when a chieftain travels to the farm of an outlaw with the intention of holding a court of confiscation. The juncture of simple travel and a unit of action (travel/feudeme) may also be a dramatic means of repetition, as in Flosi's and Kári's journeys for support in *Njáls saga* (see chap. 9).

Short descriptions of travel often transport characters over long distances with little discussion of nature, except for brief mentions of geographical points of reference. Sagas usually progress from action to action, presenting brief observations, descriptions of how places got their names, and information that bears directly on the ensuing action. When small blocks of travel are introduced, they prepare the audience for change, and, as in the dimmed light of a stage between scenes, the audience observes the preparations as the travel block places the characters. Such blocks often group together the journeys of different persons with the goal of maneuvering them into place for a conflict or a resolution. In saga narrative these concentrated descriptions of movement help to produce the economy of style for which the sagas are famous. For instance, in the following passage from *Njáls saga* (chs. 41–42) the sagaman maneuvers, with utter economy, five characters into place as a prelude to the killing of Þórðr leysingjason (freedman's son):

> "Now I will give you the plan," Hallgerðr said. "You should ride east to Hornafjǫrðr, take care of your goods, and return home just at the opening of the Althing; for if you are at home, Gunnarr will want you to ride to the Althing with him. Njáll and his sons as well as Gunnarr will be at the Althing. It is then you should kill Þórðr." They agreed to carry out this plan. After that they set out for the East Fjords. Gunnarr suspected nothing and rode to the Althing.
>
> Njáll sent Þórðr leysingjason east to the Eyjafell area, telling him to be away for one day. Þórðr went east, but then he was unable to get back from the east because the river was so high that horses could not cross it for a long stretch. Njáll waited one day for him, because he had intended that Þórðr would ride with him to the Althing. Njáll told Bergþóra that she should send Þórðr to the assembly when he returned. Two days later Þórðr returned from the east. Bergþóra told him that he should ride to the Althing—"But first ride up to Þórólfsfell and attend to the farm there, but don't stay more than one or two days."
>
> When Sigmundr and Skjǫldr returned from the east, Hallgerðr told them that Þórðr was at home, but that he would ride to the Althing in a few days. "Now is your chance to get him," she said, "but if you fail this time, you'll never get another chance."

Men came to Hlíðarendi from Þórólfsfell and told Hallgerðr that Þórðr was there. Hallgerðr went to Þráinn Sigfússon and his companions and said: "Þórðr is now at Þórólfsfell and your best chance is to kill him as he rides home."

"This then is what we will now do," said Sigmundr. Then they went and took their weapons and horses and rode out to intercept him.

Units of Information

Just as travel is interspersed throughout the feudemes, so are units of information (I). As one might expect, informational units are often lengthiest at the beginning of a saga. They also repeatedly occur at the beginning of feuds, at the introduction of characters, and at the first mention of valuable property. Units of information may be devoted to one subject or to a mixture of background subjects, such as genealogies, past travels, distinguishing character traits, history of family lands, settings for conflicts, portents, kinship bonds, political alliances, place-names, and proprietary rights.[1] Descriptions of travel often are combined with units of information (T/I). These combinations can be as short as two clauses or sentences, but several travel and information units are routinely alternated, one after the other, to form blocks. Frequently bits of information are interspersed in a section of narrative dominated by a particular feudeme. For instance the description of a killing (an act of conflict) may be imbedded with information about kinship bonds as well as information about how the name of the victim determined a place-name. In these instances, the

---

[1] A different view is expressed by Theodore Andersson in *The Icelandic Family Saga: An Analytic Reading* (Cambridge: Harvard University Press, 1967), p. 9: "These introductions apparently gave information for information's sake and are not integral in the sense that they contribute something vital to the later story. They could be dropped without depriving the reader of any hints about things to come. But a few saga authors seem to have been sensitive to this structural laxity and made an effort to connect their introductions with the plot."

category of information is noted only once to indicate that information occurs in the section of narrative, not how many times it occurs.

The more important a person is the more detailed the introductory information usually is. Characters who do little more than escalate a feud between more important persons usually receive little background attention. The introduction of a major character often includes genealogical ties that determine inheritance, blood vengeance, and kinship responsibilities. Such information is also often a clue to issues and alliances in the coming feud. Descriptions of characters rarely reach the magnitude of Egill's riding into the Althing (see saga selection 1), but they often concentrate on distinguishing attributes, such as a person's *ójafnaðr*, or the telling of a portent that intimates the outcome of the feud, someone's death, or both.

Certain types of information give the audience advance notice of what a conflict will be about. The audience learns, for example, that two farmers jointly own a field, or that a farmer whose wife dies in a boating mishap is reported to have convinced a survivor to change his report of the order of the deaths. In these ways informational units provide signposts so that the audience is able to keep an eye to the thread of action and be prepared for new characters or feuds. Such blocks make understandable the complexities of feud and the interrelationships of feud characters.

The Feudeme of Conflict

Repetitive and often mundane acts such as a scuffle between two small farmers or the withdrawal of support by an angry friend satisfy formal roles in the narrative, just as the more noteworthy act of killing a leader does. All are conflicts, and any such act could initiate or escalate a feud. Like any feudeme, the conflict at hand may be considered most successfully if first it is looked at separately and then viewed in its relationship to other feudemes in the feud chain. The trick is not to identify a conflict simply with the characters involved. Doing so concentrates the analysis on a few acts of great violence, thus building the impression that conflict in the sagas is chiefly the meeting of heroes at drawn swords. This older view of the sagas as epic contests limits our understanding of the suppleness of Icelandic prose, which was constructed by substituting small acts one for the other. This process allowed the sagaman to narrate a specific action, such as a confrontation between two farmers, in one sentence or to extend it into a long passage. Acts of conflict may occur within an ongoing feud or may initiate a new dispute. Series of disputes that stem from repetitive confrontations and acts of violence fill large sections of some sagas.

As a feud continues, the characters concerned in it often change. For instance, the seduction of Valgerðr Óttarsdóttir by Ingólfr Þorsteinsson in *Vatnsdœla saga* (ch. 37) is followed by a series of events that involve more people in killings, the harboring of an outlaw, sorcery, and another seduction. The trouble over Vigdís Ingjaldsdóttir's dowry in *Laxdœla saga* (chs. 15–16) is preceded by conflicts over a fishing catch, a killing, and the harboring of an outlaw. In most instances, conflict (C) initiates the action or the posturing of one individual or group against another. An act of violence can have different repercussions and hence play a dual role. For instance a killing may resolve one feud and thus fulfill the criteria of a resolution. The same act however may engender new acts of feud and thus also be a conflict. Because the action is first a resolution, I have categorized it as such, although the sagaman and the audience were aware that many resolutions formed the seeds of new feuds. For convenience, I divide conflict into two categories: those over material goods, such as wealth, and those over nonmaterial issues, such as honor and status (see introduction to App. B).

The saga selections in chapter 1 narrate numerous examples of conflicts in both categories. In the first saga selection, from *Egils saga*, Steinarr Ǫnundarson is pressing a case against Egill's son Þorsteinn; Steinarr has grabbed some of Þorsteinn's land, a material source of conflict that engenders the events described in the selection. The martial aura of Egill's entrance into the thing has all the trappings of an impending heroic clash; nevertheless, Egill's dispute with Ǫnundr and Steinarr is handled in the traditional Icelandic way of a legal arrangement. The cutting of trees in *Vápnfirðinga saga* (saga selection 8) is an act of conflict in a series of disputes which causes Geitir to kill Brodd-Helgi. Selection 3 from *Laxdœla saga* tells the story of a forced sale of land. A fight between suitors and the stealing of malt are narrated in *Víga-Glúms saga* (selection 6). Haunting is the nonmaterial source of the disturbance for which the revenants are summoned in saga selection 2 from *Eyrbyggja saga*; also in the category of acts of conflict over nonmaterial issues is the insulting of Bolli by his wife in *Laxdœla saga* (selection 3).

Material Sources of Conflict

The primary reason for conflict over material goods was the need for land and its produce. Woods, meadows, and grazing lands were often shared because of their scarcity, and an owner was likely to covet more than his allotment. Similarly, land adjacent to the ocean was at a premium because its owners enjoyed the rights to natural foodstuffs, such as birds' eggs and beached whales. Driftwood was also a valuable commodity in a land with few timber resources. Conflicts arose repeatedly in the sagas over opposing claims to property ownership, dowry, and inheritance rights, as well as over movables such as hay, wood, and livestock. An accusation of theft or the stealing of chattels or foodstuffs and cheating in the division of property frequently initiated feuds between farmers who then turned to more powerful men for help. In this way, important men involved themselves in seemingly unimportant matters, such as which farmer was harvesting more hay from a shared field.

Shared land, like the field "Sure-giver" in *Víga-Glúms saga*, was frequently a source of conflict. In the feud between Hallgerðr and Bergþóra in *Njáls saga*, the initial dispute concerns an insult, but Hallgerðr finds another means of continuing her quarrel: in a piece of land shared by the two families. In an example from *Vápnfirðinga saga* (ch. 7) a dispute between two farmers over a shared meadow escalates into a feud between two chieftains over power in the district.

Arguments over the produce of land set off disputes in a number of sagas. One example from *Eyrbyggja saga* is the stealing of a freedman's hay by Arnkell goði's father (chs. 29–31); another example is Blund-Ketill's attempt to buy hay for smaller farmers in *Hœnsa-Þóris saga* (ch. 5). In *Reykdœla saga* (ch. 9) Vémundr Þórisson knowingly buys wood already purchased by his rival Steingrímr Qrnólfsson. In the same vein, in *Laxdœla saga*, Kjartan Óláfsson buys land in order to insult his foster brother and rival Bolli Þorleiksson (see saga selection 3).

The shoreline was divided into common land and privately owned parcels. In *Hávarðar saga Ísfirðings* (ch. 3) a whale is washed ashore on land where Hávarðr inn halti and Þorbjǫrn Þjóðreksson divide the jetsam. In the opinion of most men, the whale belongs to Hávarðr. Many men gather, and the lawman Þorkell is to settle the question. He decides that both claimants own the whale. Þorbjǫrn rushes at Þorkell with a drawn sword and again asks him to whom the whale belongs. Þorkell drops his head and changes his decision. Thus, Þorbjǫrn gets the whale and Hávarðr goes home. Later Þorbjǫrn kills Hávarðr's son Óláfr.

Stealing and cheating often have to do with livestock. In *Reykdœla saga*, Hánefr at Óþveginstunga is accused by Hrafn at Lundarbrekka of stealing sheep. Hrafn demands an equal number of sheep in return for those stolen, but

Hánefr refuses. Hánefr goes to Vémundr Fjǫrleifarson (Þórisson), who is bound to him because Hánefr is fostering Vémundr's daughter; Hrafn seeks the support of his relative, Steingrímr Qrnólfsson. When Hánefr admits to Vémundr that he did steal the sheep, Vémundr gets Hánefr to transfer all his goods to him by *handsal* and brings his daughter home. Steingrímr then has Hánefr outlawed at the Althing (chs. 4–5). This incident marks the beginning of the dispute between Vémundr and Steingrímr which takes up most of the saga.

Dowries, too, are often at the root of a dispute. In *Vápnfirðinga saga* Brodd-Helgi refuses to give up the dowry of his former wife Halla (ch. 6). Halla's brother Geitir attempts to get the dowry back. *Njáls saga* (ch. 8) takes up the issue of the dowry of Unnr, daughter of Mǫrðr gígja. The divorced husband Hrútr Herjólfsson intends to keep the property.

Rival claims to inheritances stirred animosities especially among kinsmen. In *Laxdœla saga* Hǫskuldr Dala-Kollsson becomes embroiled in a conflict with his half brother, Hrútr Herjólfsson. Hǫskuldr refuses to give Hrútr his rightful share of their mother's inheritance when Hrútr immigrates to Iceland. For three years Hrútr tries to claim his property by lawful means, but he is unsuccessful. Then, when Hǫskuldr is away at a feast, Hrútr takes half of Hǫskuldr's cattle. Hǫskuldr's servants pursue Hrútr and his men. In the encounter that follows, four of Hǫskuldr's servants are killed and the rest are wounded; because of Hrútr's skill as a fighter, his men suffer only minor wounds. When Hǫskuldr hears of the incident, he gathers men. His wife tells him, however, that he would do better to settle with his kinsman, for many people feel that Hrútr's claim to the inheritance is just. Also, she believes that Hrútr has the support of some powerful men, particularly Þórðr gellir. Hǫskuldr takes her advice, and men friendly to both bring about a final settlement between the kinsmen (ch. 19).

Nonmaterial Sources of Conflict

Nonmaterial sources of conflict were primarily issues of power and honor. In some instances, a rejected suitor began or escalated a feud over the loss of a good match or love. This frequently occurred in the poets' sagas, but many other characters, such as Kjartan Ólafsson in *Laxdœla saga* and Þorgrímr Þórisson in *Víga-Glúms saga* (see saga selections 3 and 6), also acted this way. The issue of who was to control a *goðorð* was often a source of conflict within a family or a district. In *Droplaugarsona saga* Hrafnkell Þórisson feuds with his uncle Helgi Ásbjarnarson over the *goðorð* they share. Oddr Ófeigsson in *Bandamanna saga* has to fight twice for the lands and the *goðorð* he purchased with his profits from trade. Once he confronts his overseer Óspakr, who was entrusted with the management of the *goðorð* during his absence from Iceland, and later Oddr is forced to contend with eight *goðar* who banded together to oppose him. Initial acts of conflict are often followed by summoning which in itself is an act of conflict. When one man went through the procedure of publicly summoning another, it established a posture of legal opposition and presented a challenge that had to be answered.

Other familiar sources of conflict in the sagas are of a supernatural kind, such as witching and haunting. These not only were disturbing to the community but they often led to death. The witch Katla tries to protect her son Oddr in *Eyrbyggja saga* (ch. 29), but they are both killed. In the same saga the young farmer Kjartan and Snorri goði's son free the farm Fróðá from ghosts (see saga selection 2).

Conflicts that Could Fall Into Either Category

Although women had certain rights in divorce and marriage, wives and daughters were often treated as possessions, especially in cases of seduction when the honor of the family demanded compensation for the abasement of a kinswoman. In *Vatnsdœla saga* (ch. 37), a long feud ensues over Ingólfr Þorsteinsson's seduction of and love songs to the daughter of Óttarr of Grímstungur. In *Ljósvetninga saga* (A, ch. 21; C, ch. 22),[2] the *bóndi* Ísólfr asks his chieftain Eyjólfr Guðmundarson to take the case against Brandr Gunnsteinsson for seducing Ísólfr's pregnant daughter. Eyjólfr agrees, and the seduction case starts a series of disputes between Eyjólfr and Þorvarðr Hǫskuldsson, who eventually takes Brandr's side.

Conflicts that started over material goods often turned into feuds involving issues of power and honor, while ongoing feuds between powerful men were often fueled by smaller conflicts over material goods between less important persons. Insult, killing, horsefighting, and harboring an outlaw were frequent causes for violent clashes. Honor, in all such cases, demanded that a man preserve his reputation and guard his family name.

---

[2]*Ljósvetninga saga* is preserved in two major manuscripts, A and C. See Björn Sigfússon's discussion of the manuscripts in his introduction to *Ljósvetninga saga*, *ÍF* 10 (1940), esp. pp. xxi–xxvi.

5 The Feudeme of Advocacy

It is hard to think of another literature where so much time is spent persuading, bargaining, advising, whetting, cajoling, bullying, being obstinate, and so forth; where the range of human activity is so severely restricted to the elements of competition and the expressions of willfulness or its opposites.

— Robert Cook

In little more than seventy years a combination of social compromise, political ingenuity, and legal inventiveness had produced a constitutional and judicial system that was extraordinarily comprehensive. . . . In theory every individual was attached to a household; every householder was attached to a chieftain. Through householder and chieftain everyone was attached to an assembly.

— Dennis, Foote, and Perkins

Acts of advocacy could lead to or result from conflicts, resolutions, or other acts of advocacy. Like the other feudemes, all types of advocacy were rooted in the traditional forms of Icelandic feud. The major and most varied form of advocacy was brokerage.

Brokerage (A^b).—Acts of brokerage are evident in many of the saga selections given in chapter 1. In selection 7, from *Eyrbyggja saga*, Snorri goði acts as a broker for the farmer Þórólfr bægifótr, and, in selection 2 from the same saga, a farmer Kjartan from Fróðá on Snæfellsnes appeals to his uncle Snorri goði for aid in ridding his farm of revenants. In the sixth saga selection, Víga-Glúmr twice acts as broker, each time carrying, on behalf of another man, a marriage proposal for one of Gizurr Kaðalsson's daughters. In selection 9 from *Hœnsa-Þóris saga*, Hersteinn Blund-Ketilsson is represented by the *bóndi* Gunnarr Hlífarson and later by the *goði* Þórðr gellir. Gísli Súrsson, in selection 4, tries but is unable to enlist the help of a broker; in the first selection Egill Skalla-Grímsson, acting as a broker for his son Þorsteinn, requests that his opponent Qnundr sjóni and his son Steinarr dismiss their supporters, the *goðar* Einarr Teitsson and Tungu-Oddr. Saga selection 5 gives background and an incident of arbitration by Guðmundr dýri; the eighth selection from *Vápnfirðinga saga* recounts Geitir's plan for Þormóðr to recover his losses.

Through brokerage a contender attempted to acquire the support he needed to maintain or claim his rights. Powerful brokers were at times valued simply for the kinds of advice and the plans of action they could offer. Such counsel was normally based on a wide-ranging knowledge of the current state of obligations. Brokers were identifiable, not by office or by training, but by prestige, power, and wealth. A broker who took on a case often served in the capacity of a lawyer. He decided whether to settle the case in or out of court and what the compensation should be. Brokers ranged from middlemen who simply transacted business, representing a disputant and effecting a resolution without becoming more deeply involved, to active advocates who risked life and wealth to bring about a desired resolution.

The need to gather support and to create obligations was the motivation for brokerage, and brokerage relationships formalized ties of mutual dependence between members of the society. Bonds could be sealed with a formal *handsal*, an agreement of *vinfengi*, the creation of a fictitious kinship alliance of marriage or fosterage, or the exchange of gifts.

Whenever one party supported another, an obligation, sometimes strong, sometimes weak, was generated. The pervasive concept of obligation was founded in the relationship between *goði* and *bóndi*, although it operated in almost all relationships in Icelandic society. The broker who provided the necessary support usually expected something in return from the person he helped. Sometimes the quid pro quo was merely the maintenance of existing kin or political ties, but often the broker sought to gain either in wealth or in future support. A fact that has not been thoroughly understood is that feud in Iceland was often economically profitable. Because brokers, especially chieftains, were in an advantageous position to lend support to others, they were able, through the process of feud, to acquire wealth. Saga literature portrays wealth changing hands most rapidly during the bartering in brokerage and arbitration.

At this point two basic questions arise: Why was feud in Iceland so systematic? What were the roots of this social behavior, which formed so central an element in Icelandic literature? To answer these questions I propose to examine the development of Icelandic brokerage, for in Iceland's first century of statehood, a normally peripheral and private aspect of social behavior was elevated to the position of a central and often public process. Using the possibilities of brokerage, Icelanders in the tenth century expanded the ancient Norse concept of the local freemen's assembly into a complex political and judicial system that for several hundred years answered the needs of a whole country. This societal evolution, beginning around 900 or within the life span of the first few pioneering generations, resulted in a society that did not develop anything more than the basic outlines of a hierarchical governmental order. This turn of events was to have far-reaching consequences for Icelandic culture in a later period.

The most important of the many reasons for Iceland's unusual societal development was the island's geographical location, at the very edge of the known world. Iceland was too distant, too difficult, and perhaps too poor a target even for Norway's vikings. The Icelanders were not bothered by foreign raiders, and although in a few instances invasion was threatened by Norwegian and Danish kings in the tenth and eleventh centuries, it was never a serious possibility. So little did the Icelanders fear foreign attack that nowhere do the Free State laws deal with questions of military defense.

Free from the threat of invasion, Iceland was left alone to develop a societal structure corresponding to its internal needs. In this respect it was completely different from the rest of the Norse cultural area (or from all of Europe, for that matter), where attack could be frequent and swift. For instance, in Norway, whose long coastline and numerous fjords approximate Iceland's coast, the fear of surprise attacks bound regional communities into cohesive military, and hence political, units which could successfully defend their borders. In these small states, led by petty kings or local military commanders (*hersir*), each stratum of society knew its place and its rank. Specific rural areas were responsible for providing elements of military power—a ship and its crew or a band of soldiers. Later, toward the end of the ninth century, after Haraldr inn hárfagri (fine-hair) (ca. 870–930) had united all Norway, these basic structures of local society were reconstituted into a system of national defense, with farmers forming regional units in the Old Norwegian levy (*leiðangr*).

Regional and national order in Iceland evolved differently. Upon arrival, the leaders of the first colonists claimed huge tracts of empty land, at times asserting their authority over entire fjords. In keeping with the traditions of the societies from which they came, many of the first *landnámsmenn* (settlers, sing. *landnámsmaðr*) tried to establish command over entire regions. Soon, however, these leaders or their immediate descendants proved unable to retain ownership or control over their extensive landtakes. Within a few generations the original tracts were divided up into relatively equal farmsteads, and soon there was little to distinguish one prosperous landowner from another. By the mid-ninth century most of Iceland's productive land and the majority of its labor force were controlled by free farmers.

The rapid leveling was possible because the claims to regional authority asserted by the pioneering families quickly proved untenable. For one thing, the resources of the island were not sufficient to support a princely lifestyle. Icelanders in later centuries were well aware of the limitations of their country. In the twelfth century they wrote stories about original settlers like Geirmundr heljarskinn (helskin),[1] which, whether true or not, convey the understanding that the first generations of *landnámsmenn* had to readjust their aspirations to the reality of conditions in their new country. Both *Landnámabók* and *Geirmundar þáttr heljarskinns* tell how Geirmundr, a king's son from one of the many Norwegian royal houses and a successful viking captain, tried to live in a princely style. According to the probably exaggerated story, Geirmundr maintained four large estates and traveled with a bodyguard of eighty men. The expense of living in such a grand manner could not, however, be supported by the land; only the great wealth that Geirmundr brought with him to Iceland, presumably taken in viking raids, enabled him to maintain it. At his death, Geirmundr's holdings were broken up.

In order to retain control over their followers the original settlers had at first shared their lands with them, but this apportionment did not establish a political or governmental hierarchy. Without a military threat sufficient to encourage a sense of loyalty to a local military leader and his family, individual landowners apparently asserted their independence and refused to take orders. The farmers' sense of independence was buttressed by another factor: new settlers streaming in had little reason to recognize the already

---

[1] Skin that was dark or pale as death.

dwindling authority of the first families. It seems that these later colonists were integrated in a relatively peaceful manner into the landowning population. Probably the earlier settlers saw the wisdom of not denying land-hungry immigrants what they had come so far to get. The sources are vague on the process but the results are clear. For about six decades new arrivals either purchased, were granted, or took farmsteads by force (probably dueling) from a constantly diminishing supply of unused but nominally claimed land. In many instances the original settlers presumably granted the new arrivals land in return for promises of future support. Like the obligations incurred when the first *landnámsmenn* granted land to their followers, the ties of dependence, military or financial, agreed to when the new arrivals accepted their lands soon disappeared.

Scholars have often explained the independence of the Icelandic farmer as a product of his viking heritage.[2] There may indeed be some truth in this old romantic notion; more to the point, Iceland's nonhierarchical development may be explained by the fact that Icelandic farmers lacked a good reason to give up their recently acquired wealth and rights of the frontier. Besides the lack of an external military menace and the physical characteristics of the land, other forces that traditionally bind a region into a political entity were absent. Iceland had no regional economies differentiated by specialties in agricultural production, manufacturing, or mining; also, unlike the rest of the Norse world and the continent, Iceland developed no trading centers to focus and support political control. Because of all these disparate factors, Iceland nourished a society that for centuries catered as much to the demands of farmers as to the desires of chieftains.

Of the farmers, the largest and most important group comprised the *þingfararkaupsbœndr*, (farmers paying the

---

[2]See, for example, Hans Kuhn's informative article, "Landbesitz in der Besiedlungszeit Islands," *Zeitschrift für deutsches Altertum und deutsche Literatur*, 97(1968):107–117.

thing tax, see App. A), usually referred to simply as *bœndr*. At the very end of the eleventh century, there were 4,000 to 5,000 such heads of households. These *þingfararkaups-bœndr*, who qualified by possessing a certain amount of wealth, enjoyed, with their families, the full rights and responsibilities of freemen. Among the *bœndr*, on whose properties almost all the entirely rural population lived, there was little differentiation in legal status. The wealthier landholders clearly had more influence over local affairs, but at no time were there legal distinctions establishing grade and rank; in many parts of Norway, in contrast, different types of freemen (for example, *hauldr, árborinn maðr*, and *reksþegn*) made up a complex hierarchical order. Into the thirteenth century, poorer landholders in Iceland retained full legal rights. Even Icelandic tenant farmers in the thirteenth century enjoyed a measure of personal independence unheard of in Europe. It has even been asserted that thirteenth-century landowners had little personal or judicial power over their tenants.[3]

Among the mass of farmers lived the fifty or so men who at any time could call themselves *goðar*, either because they owned outright, or shared in ownership of, a *goðorð*. At times it is difficult to distinguish from the sources whether a man was a *goði* or a *bóndi*, because chieftains lived like farmers and married into farmers' families, and successful farmers bought or otherwise acquired chieftaincies. Possession of a *goðorð* was a mark of power, lending the owner an aura of authority. In some instances the claim to social eminence was augmented by tracing descent back to a prominent *landnámsmaðr*, although by the eleventh century, after generations of intermarriage, most landowners in Iceland could easily find such an ancestor in their family trees.

Whatever claims to authority a chieftain might assert, no

leader, even in the thirteenth century, had more than brief success in coercing or convincing the *bœndr* that they should unite behind him and unify a region into a competitive small state. Instead, for centuries *goðar* vied for the personal allegiances of the surrounding farmers, who often, without regard to territorial proximity, allied themselves to different chieftains in the quarter. The three, at times rival, chieftains of each local district shared the responsibility for holding the *várþing*. A few weeks later, for two weeks at midsummer, the chieftains from all over the country assembled at the Althing. A feud between Tungu-Oddr and Þórðr gellir, about 965, resulted in a series of judicial reforms that made the three-decade-old system of regularly convened courts more accessible and less partial and set the form of Icelandic government for the next few hundred years. The island was divided into administrative quarters, and thirteen thing districts were recognized (three in each of the Southern, Western, and Eastern Quarters and four in the Northern Quarter). Thereafter, each *várþing* met with the understanding that it was soon to be followed by the Althing where difficult issues could be taken to the *fjórðungsdómar* (the four quarter courts) and the *fimtardómr* (the fifth court of appeals) after it was established about 1005. At the national assembly also sat the *lǫgrétta* (the national legislature or law council) with its power to make new laws and to provide decisive interpretations of old ones. The result was a governmental structure that maintained internal order yet bypassed central executive authority.

While each *goði* shared the responsibility of holding one of the district assemblies, farmers living anywhere in the quarter could attach themselves to any chieftain in the quarter, whether or not chieftain and farmer lived in the same district. Out of this complex arrangement a *goði* assembled a following that closely approximated a modern-day interest group, a practice reflecting the fact that few chieftains could claim authority over a geographical area. The interest groups were formed through an awareness of reciprocity between leader and follower. Thingmen gathered around a *goði* for reasons different from those that guided the composition of a territorial state. They, with their leader, remained a cohesive constituency because of consciously expressed self-interest. Because the supporters of individual chieftains were often dispersed over a wide area and interspersed with thingmen of other chieftains, they were able to switch loyalties. The freedom of farmers to choose the stronger chieftain is one of the realities of Icelandic feud.

Because their position in this governmental order did not carry with it the right to obedience, the *goðar* could only solicit the support of the *bœndr* and through them manipulate societal forces. Ostensibly power flowed into the hands of chieftains, but actually much of it remained in the hands of obstinate farmers. The *bœndr*, aided by their sons and farmhands, guarded their own rights and interests. The situation was from the start a compromise that displeased many people. Iceland's medieval history and its saga literature are dominated by the continuous struggle to restrain ambitious men, sometimes farmers and sometimes chieftains, from destroying the balance of power on which the rights of both *goðar* and *bœndr* depended.

The relationship between a *goði* and his followers was a personal bond. It was a contract for mutual support between two parties who rarely worked through functionaries. Although the farmer was limited to choosing from among the available chieftains of the quarter, he did have the right to transfer his allegiance once a year to a new chieftain from the already established district *goðar*. In practice, the free exercise of the right to change leaders was tempered by traditions of personal and family loyalty, as well as by practical considerations, such as proximity to a certain chieftain. *Ójafnaðarmenn*, in seeking to restrict the exercise of this right, threatened both chieftains and farmers. The goal of these overbearing men was often to take control of a whole district, and to the medieval audience the consequences of such action were clearly undesirable.

The creation of regional rule would destroy the traditional Icelandic distribution of power. Tales of dispute in the sagas are often based on the understanding that the feud posed questions as serious as the maintenance of the traditional Icelandic social fabric.

The complicated and nonterritorial relationship between leader and follower was so firmly implanted in the tenth century that toward the end of the life of the Free State the traditional Icelandic *goði/bœndr* system, still intact, was functioning in many parts of the country. This was especially so in the north and the west. An example is the situation described in *Guðmundar saga dýra*, which concentrates on local disputes over land and power in the region of Eyjafjǫrðr in the Northern Quarter at the end of the twelfth century. In this fjord region, more than five chieftains claimed the allegiance of large numbers of farmers interspersed among the rival leaders. Map 3 shows the location, in the years 1184–1200, of thingmen and chieftains mentioned in the saga. It places only those farmers who were referred to in the saga as thingmen of the local chieftains. Clearly many more farmers were living in this rich and important region; some of them are mentioned in other contemporary sagas. The map shows that, even at the end of the twelfth century, the two powerful and bitter rivals, Guðmundr dýri and Ǫnundr Þorkelsson, lived quite close to each other, and that they did not control small states or geographical areas. Nor was the power of these two chieftains understood in such terms. Their strength depended upon the thingmen who were interspersed with one another in the nearby valleys.

The following list of chieftains and their thingmen mentioned in *Guðmundar saga dýra* includes only chieftains and thingmen whose areas of residence and affiliation can be verified from the saga. (The numbers and letters refer to designations on map 3).

A. Guðmundr dýri at Bakki
    2A.   Sǫxólfr Fornason at Myrkárdalr

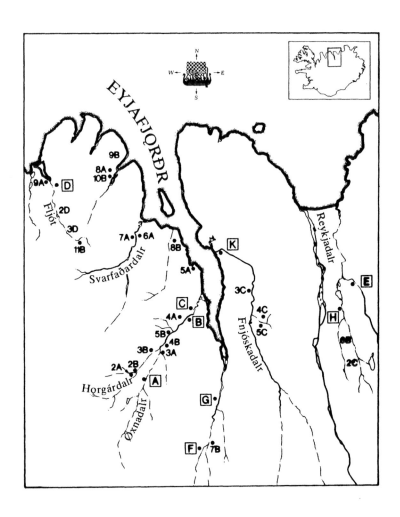

3A. Þorvaldr at Bægisá
4A. Kálfr Guttormsson at Auðbrekka
5A. Hákon Þórðarson at Arnarnes
6A. Sons of Arnþrúðr at Sakka (later sent to Qgmundr Þorvarðsson)
7A. Sumarliði Ásmundarson at Tjǫrn
8A. Þorsteinn Halldórsson at Brekka
9A. Nikulás Bjarnarson at Grindill

B. *Qnundr Þorkelsson at Laugaland* (he later moves to
Langahlíð, and Þorfinnr, his son and follower, moves
to Laugaland).
2B. Erlendr Þorgeirsson at Myrká
3B. Bjǫrn Steinmóðarson at Øxnahóll
4B. Tjǫrvi at Rauðalækr
5B. Langahlíð (see parenthetical note, above)
6B. Halldórr or Bjǫrn Eyjólfsson (farm not specified)
7B. Einarr Hallsson at Mǫðruvellir (shares *goðorð*
with Qnundr)
8B. Helgi Halldórsson at Áskógr
9B. Bjǫrn Gestsson at Sandr (location approximated)
10B. Eyvindr and Sighvatr Bjarnarson at Brekka
11B. Rúnólfr Nikulássson at Mjóvafell (residence of
father)

C. *Þorvarðr Þorgeirsson at Mǫðruvellir*
2C. Halldórr or Bjǫrn Eyjólfsson (farm not specified)

Map 3. Eyjafjǫrðr (ca. 1184–1200), showing locations of
chieftains and their thingmen as mentioned in *Guðmundar saga
dýra*. A chieftain and his thingmen are designated by a letter and
numbers: A stands for a chieftain, and 2A, 3A, and so on, for
that chieftain's thingmen.

3C.   Brandr Knakansson at Draflastaðir
4C.   Hallr Ásbjarnarson at Fornastaðir
5C.   Qgmundr Þorvarðsson sneis at Háls (later be-
      comes *goði*)

D.   *Jón Ketilsson at Holt* (*goðorð* later given to Guðmundr
     dýri)
2D.   Þorvarðr Sunnólfsson (farm not specified)
3D.   Már Rúnólfsson (farm not specified)

E.   *Eyjólfr Hallsson at Grenjaðarstaðir* (a priest, later
     abbot of Saurbær; acts as though he were a *goði*. Son-
     in-law of Óláfr Þorsteinsson at Saurbær).

F.   *Óláfr Þorsteinsson at Saurbær* (probably a *goði*; may
     have shared a *goðorð* with Kleppjárn Klængsson)

G.   *Kleppjárn Klængsson at Hrafnagil* (may have shared a
     goðorð)

Farmsteads that change ownership:
H.   *Helgastaðir*
     First owner is Guðmundr Eyjólfsson, who gives the
       property to his son Teitr.
     Upon Teitr's death, the property is disputed, in the end
       going to Kleppjárn Klængsson and his son Klængr.
     A marriage is arranged between Klængr and the daugh-
       ter of Þorvarðr Þorgeirsson.
     Kleppjárn and Klængr sell to Ásbjorn Hallsson, the
       brother of Eyjólfr Hallsson.

Farmsteads whose owners change allegiance between
chieftains:
K.   *Laufáss*
     Þórðr Þórarinsson is a follower of Þorvarðr Þorgeirsson;
       his sons are followers of Guðmundr dýri.

Kinship bonds complemented political ties but in times of feud were not dependable sources of aid. The family and Sturlunga sagas suggest that even if payment and receipt of compensation for a killing extended by law to individuals who shared a great-great-grandfather with the killer or a great-great-great-grandfather with the dead person, the issue was understood more as an option than as a requirement to enter a feud. Although Icelanders knew their genealogies, the individual could normally count on only a few close blood relatives such as parents, siblings, and uncles and near cousins on both maternal and paternal sides. The determination of kinship was, however, especially important in establishing claims to property through inheritance, and the sagas tell how distant claims fueled many feuds over valuable property.

The limited family group on which the individual depended could be extended by marriage or fosterage. Most of these bonds of fictitious kinship were highly valued. The peer group created by one's foster brothers and brothers-in-law often proved a valuable asset in times of political maneuvering and blood vengeance. But even within so small a group, the gathering of support for a dangerous feud could not be regarded as routine; on the contrary, it required ingenuity and/or gifts. The sagas are sprinkled with examples like the following from *Eyrbyggja saga* (chs. 26–27), where a husband was killed and his widow had to work hard to convince her kinsmen to seek atonement for the loss of a family member.

> After that Snorri goði traveled to Drápuhlíð with six men. They saw the fire as they came up the slope; Vigfúss Bjarnarson and his farmhands were burning charcoal. Snorri and his men came upon Vigfúss's group, surprising them. They killed Vigfúss but spared his farmhands. Then Snorri went home, and Vigfúss's farmhands carried the news home to Drápuhlíð. The following day Vigfúss was buried in a mound.
>
> That same day, Þorgerðr, the wife of Vigfúss, journeyed to

Bólstaðr to tell the news to her kinsman Arnkell goði. She asked him to take up the prosecution for the killing of Vigfúss. Arnkell backed off from her request, saying that the obligation lay with Vigfúss's relatives, the Kjalleklingar family. Arnkell especially directed Þorgerðr to Víga-Styrr and said that it was Styrr's responsibility to bring a case for the killing of his kinsman Vigfúss. In addition, he noted that Styrr liked to get involved in many affairs. . . .

Next Þorgerðr went out to Styrr's farm below Hraun and asked him to take up the prosecution for his kinsman Vigfúss. Styrr answered: "Last spring I promised Snorri goði when he stayed out of my suit against the Þorgestlingar family that I would not go against him as an antagonist in those cases where many were as equally involved as I. Now what you might do in this case is seek out Vermundr, my brother, or others of our kinsmen."

Then Þorgerðr journeyed out to Bjarnarhǫfn and asked Vermundr for his support. She admitted he was faced with a difficult obligation, "since Vigfúss trusted you the most of all his kinsmen." Vermundr answered: "I am indeed obligated to do something here, but I am not inclined to go in advance of our other kinsmen in this matter; I will, however, help out as I can with participation and advice. First, I want you to travel out to Eyrr and meet with Steinþórr, Vigfúss's kinsman. Fighting comes easy to him, and it is time for him to prove himself in some kind of litigation." Þorgerðr answered: "You are putting a lot on me in this case, but I will not spare myself any difficulty, if it will lead to success."

Then she traveled out to Eyrr and met with Steinþórr and asked him to become leader of the prosecution. "Why do you ask this of me?" Steinþórr replied. "I am a young man and have not been involved in lawsuits. Besides, other kinsmen of Vigfúss's, in particular those who are more closely related to him than I, are more contentious types than I am. There is no hope here that I will take this case off their hands. Nevertheless, I will not part ways with those of my kinsmen who might take up your case." Þorgerðr got no other answer there.

After this she journeyed back across the fjords to meet with Vermundr, telling him what had happened. She said that all would be lost unless he became the leader in the case. "The expectation still remains," Vermundr answered, "that the prosecution will bring a judgment in this case which will be of consolation to you. I will even offer one more bit of advice to you, if you want to follow it." She answered: "I will do almost anything in order to bring this about." "Now you should go home," said Vermundr, "and have Vigfúss your husband dug up; then take his head and bring it to Arnkell and say to him that this head would not have left it to others to prosecute after him, if the necessity had arisen." Þorgerðr said that she did not know how this would turn out, but she said she could see that her kinsmen would spare her neither trouble nor grief. "Nevertheless, I will do it," she said, "if it will add to the problems of my enemies."

Then she traveled home and did everything just as she had been instructed. And when she came to Bólstaðr she told Arnkell that Vigfúss's kinsmen wanted him to become the leader in the prosecution for the killing, and they all promised their assistance. Arnkell stated that he had earlier declared how he was disposed in this matter. Then Þorgerðr drew the head out from under her cloak and said: "Here is that head which would not have backed away from prosecuting for your sake, had it been necessary." Arnkell, greatly shaken by seeing the head, pushed her away from him, saying: "Go away and say to the kinsmen of Vigfúss that their support against Snorri goði should not be less than the vigor of my leadership in the case. My thoughts tell me, however, that whatever way the case turns, they will be heading for a safe haven before I do. And I can see that it is Vermundr's plan that you are now following. But he would have no need to egg me on, wherever we kinsmen are placed." Then Þorgerðr went home.

The winter passed. In the spring Arnkell brought suit for the killing of Vigfúss against all those men who had ridden out to the killing, except for Snorri goði. Snorri for his part prepared countersuits: a case for a conspiracy against his life [*fjǫrráðamál*] as well as a case for the blow received by his follower Már [*áverkamál*]. Snorri's intention was to have Vigfúss adjudged *óhelgi*, because, by acting as an outlaw, he forfeited his rights.

Both sides came with a large following to the Þórsnes thing. All the Kjalleklingar supported Arnkell and with them he had the larger following. Arnkell pushed the case with great vigor. When the case came before the court, men intervened and the matter was submitted to arbitration with the proposal of terms and under the care of some *góðgjarnir menn*. The result was that Snorri goði formally agreed by handclasp [*handlag*] to accept the arbitrators' decision and many men received large fines. But Már was exiled from the country for three years. Snorri paid up, and the thing ended with the settlement of all cases.

Although kinship remained important, families never developed into territorially defined large clàns as in Ireland; instead, they lived widely dispersed among other families. Often different members of one family were attached to different *goðar*, clouding loyalties during feuds. Many of the *goðar* and *bœndr* whose farmsteads are shown on map 3 were related by kin bonds. No network of obligation was clearly built on kin or political lines; it is a mistake to say that Icelandic society was dominated by kinship bonds or political alliances. Rather, it was characterized by a combination of the two. Even close relatives could diverge sharply when a kinsman or a foster relative killed another member of the same family, or when heirs squabbled over property after the death of a kinsman or a kinswoman. Such situations, which were common in Iceland, underscored the individual's need for a form of political protection in the absence of any central administration.

The need for protection was filled by brokerage relationships. Given the nonhierarchical social and governmental order of Iceland, the two main political groups—*goðar* and *bœndr*—found in brokerage the opportunity to exchange things of value, ranging from wealth to alliances and friendship. The brokerage system focused not on aristocrats with the power to command but on middlemen with the ability to bargain. Such persons are accurately described as social heroes with "clear insight into the existing social rules" and with "the reputation, wealth, and authority to guarantee a balance, like Óláfr pái," or as bargainers aware of "all the shrewd ways of handling social affairs, like Snorri goði."[4] Christian priests also participated in the system of advocacy. The story of a priest acting as a broker in the year 1173 is told in *Prestssaga Guðmundar góða* (ch. 8). A well-born priest, Guðmundr Arason (later bishop of Hólar, 1203–1237, and called "the good"), takes on the prosecution of a killer, Koll-Oddr. Guðmundr has been asked to handle the case because of his good connections. At first all goes well. Guðmundr succeeds in having the killer convicted and given the full penalty of outlawry, and then he goes through all the aftercourt motions, though we are not told whether the priest manages to confiscate any of the outlaw's possessions. The killer, however, is a dangerous opponent who has no intention of quietly accepting his sentence. Instead, he is taken in and protected by an important man (a relative of the great chieftain Hafliði Másson). But Guðmundr is prepared for this step. He turns to his powerful kinsman, the *goði* Sturla Þórðarson of Hvammr. When Guðmundr arrives at Hvammr, however, Sturla is on his deathbed and dies two days later. The death of Sturla is a disaster for Guðmundr, who is powerless without the backing of his kinsman:

> That aid on which Guðmundr had counted was gone, but his determination remained. Then he racked his brains about how he could proceed in this case. It had to be done in such a way that his having outlawed a man would not work to his dishonor and also that he would not accrue such liability that it would cost him his place in his order and his priesthood.

Guðmundr's quandary points to an important aspect of Icelandic feud: although freemen may have enjoyed rights equal to those of a chieftain, they often had to call on the resources of others. A person needed a chieftain or a

[4]Heinrich Beck, "*Laxdœla saga*: A Structural Approach," *Saga-Book of the Viking Society* 19, 4(1977):383–402.

powerful man if he was to employ the law aggressively and to maintain a claim or a legal action. Individually or in a band, farmers may have had the physical ability to defend their rights or even to kill their opponents (including a chieftain), but when such action was undertaken without the protection of a powerful leader, especially a *goði*, they were exposed to potentially devastating legal consequences.

As a way of establishing and maintaining reciprocal ties, the systemization of advocacy, especially in the form of brokerage, brought the entire island together into a cohesive political body. Disputants in one district relied on neighboring chieftains and farmers. At the Althing a district leader turned to his peers from other districts who might themselves have power or have access to alliances with powerful men. A network of bonds crisscrossed on both local and national levels. The pull of alliances formed new affiliations and broke others that had outlived their usefulness. In this way the society was stabilized; power and wealth fluctuated and some men prospered. It was impossible in medieval Iceland for anyone to be both isolated and powerful. The harsh competition for foodstuffs and land gave a man of stature little opportunity to play the role of judge without also playing the riskier roles of defendant and prosecutor.

Other Forms of Advocacy

Advocacy, especially brokerage, answered two fundamental needs of the medieval Icelander. On the one hand, it supplied a means of enforcing one's rights; on the other, it offered ambitious men extraordinary latitude to improve their own situations. As a pervasive feature of medieval Icelandic society, advocacy naturally became an important compositional feature of the sagas. Besides brokerage, I have identified four other categories of advocacy: self-advocacy, arbitration, goading, and information passing.

Self-advocacy, arbitration, and brokerage most often had a formal, even a contractual, nature, whereas goading and information passing were more personal, usually taking place within a family or a household. Often beggars and vagrants are given temporary shelter in a household and pass information. Arbitration (A^a) had a dual role. Formally, it is an act of advocacy; functionally it is an attempt at resolution. Since arbitration is primarily associated with resolutions, I have considered it in chapter 6.

Self-advocacy (A^s).—As implied by its name, self-advocacy is direct action by a character on his own behalf. Usually he introduced himself into another's affairs in order to further his own interests. Obviously, such conduct could initiate feud. For instance, a man may buy an inheritance right to property to which he has no legal claim. Armed with his acquired right, he challenges the heirs for possession of the property. In *Sturlu saga* (ch. 28), the *goði* Einarr Þorgilsson buys from an ignored daughter by a first marriage an expectation of inheritance to Birningr Steinarsson's valuable land. Einarr then asserts that Birningr's second marriage is unlawful and notifies Birningr that he has to give up his farm. A long feud ensues. In *Laxdœla saga* (saga selection 3), Kjartan Óláfsson forces a land sale to offend his rival Bolli. In other instances of self-advocacy, a person buys cases against a rival, as Guðmundr inn ríki does in *Ljósvetninga saga* in order to avenge slanderous remarks or as Vémundr Þórisson (Fjǫrleifarson) tries to do in *Reykdœla saga*.

Information passing (A^i).—This form of advocacy is usually initiated by someone not directly involved in a feud or not important enough to be a disputant. In a rugged, sparsely populated country such as Iceland, passing of information from one locale to another required a substantial effort. Farms were spread out over a wide area and people were weather-bound for much of the year. Since there were no towns or courtly gatherings—centers in most societies for intrigue and the dissemination of information—information passing took on an exaggerated importance. Sometimes information carriers were paid for their services with money or food; sometimes they acted out of loyalty or good will.

As a narrative device, information passing sparks conflict and even resolution. The sagas are replete with examples of third parties, often minor characters, who warn of the approach of opponents or tell of insults or killings, travels, or witchings. Information passing, like goading, frequently leads to immediate action. An information carrier may have a vested interest in a particular household because he or she works there as a shepherd, a housewoman, or a hired hand, or because he or she visits there as a traveling workman or a beggar looking for food. The information passer may also be a concerned party, perhaps a thingman or a local farmer who wishes to see two rivals start, maintain, or resolve a feud. At other times the information passer may be a man who informs allies of a plan of action or of new developments, including the movement of opponents. This type of information passing is used to galvanize men into action and is employed repetitively in the travels of Kári Sǫlmundarson in *Njáls saga* (ch. 135). Kári's use of information passing is distinctly different from his opponent Flosi Þórðarson's use of brokerage in his corresponding journey to gain support in the East Fjords (ch. 134). Both of these passages are considered later on (see chap. 9).

Goading (A^g).—This type of advocacy is similar to brokerage in that it is often a way of inducing another person to act on behalf of oneself or one's family. It is a way to repair damage done to one's honor, and it usually results in killing, especially blood vengeance. Goading is less socially controlled than brokerage because it usually does not involve payment or consideration of reciprocal obligations and takes place between individuals without the aid of an arbitrator or a court. After an act of goading and the resultant violence, however, an arbitrated resolution usually follows. All too often the goader has been stereotyped as the woman inciter. There are, of course, many fine examples of women who incited their men: Bergþóra and Hallgerðr in *Njáls saga*, Guðrún in *Laxdœla saga*, and Þorgerðr silfra in *Vápnfirðinga saga*, to name a few. Yet fathers such as Þorsteinn's father in *Þorsteins þáttr stangarhǫggs*, or thingmen such as the Þorbrandssons in *Eyrbyggja saga*, just as easily fit into this feudemic slot. Often persons who acted as goaders were those who lacked the power to attain their own objectives and could offer no reciprocal political arrangements such as *vinfengi*. Consequently they found it difficult to induce brokers, even when kinsmen, to lead cases. There are memorable scenes in the sagas in which the severed head of a family member, bloody clothes, or food singed to represent a kinsman burned to death in his home provided the impetus for vengeance.

At times information passing was combined with goading. In *Hrafnkels saga Freysgoða* (ch. 8), for example, the actions of a washerwoman fill the narrative slot of advocacy. Sámr, a man of modest circumstances, has unseated the chieftain Hrafnkell by taking his land and *goðorð*. After Hrafnkell moves to a new farm, all is quiet until Sámr's brother Eyvindr returns from abroad and rides within sight of Hrafnkell's new farmstead. As Eyvindr rides by in the distance, the idea of vengeance takes root at Hrafnkell's farm:

A woman washing clothes down by the lake saw men journeying by. The servant woman bundled the linen together and ran home. She threw the wash down beside the woodpile outside the house and ran in. Hrafnkell had not yet got out of bed, and some of his best men were lying about the hall. The workmen, however, had already left for their jobs, for it was the haymaking season. The woman began speaking as soon as she came in: "It is mostly true, as the old saying goes, 'Age brings out the coward in a man.' Reputation that arises early is of little worth if a man later conducts himself with dishonor and does not have the firmness to uphold his rights when the need arises; and such conduct is a great wonder in that man who had earlier been spirited. Now there is a second path in the lives of some. They grow up with their fathers and you think them in no way your equal. But then just when they are reaching manhood they travel from land to land and are thought most remarkable wherever they go. With that they come home to Iceland and think themselves greater than established leaders. Eyvindr Bjarnason rode by here and forded the river at Skálavað, carrying a shield so beautiful that the sun flashed from it. He is so worthy a man that revenge could be found in him." The servant went on speaking in this way. Hrafnkell got up and answered her: "It may well be that there is too much truth in your chatter, but not because you intend any good in this. It is fitting that you now add to your troubles. Go quickly south to Víðivellir and find the Hallsteinssons, Sighvatr and Snorri. Ask them to come quickly to me with those men who are skilled with weapons."

Within this well-turned passage we see the opportunities afforded a sagaman by feudemic construction and its principle of substitution. When the woman interjects her information, the feud in the saga has been dormant for six years. Ostensibly it has been resolved, for Hrafnkell and Sámr have even met at gatherings, although they never discuss their previous dealings. A new status quo has been established, and a number of sagas end at this point in the story. To present Hrafnkell as a loser, however, clearly was not the sagaman's intention. He uses the tool of information passing to steer the narrative back to the feud. After killing Eyvindr, Hrafnkell catches Sámr in his bed and forces him to relinquish the property and *goðorð*. In this instance, the sagaman used information passing (A^i) and goading (A^g) to rekindle the feud, but he could have achieved the same objective merely by substituting another feudeme. For instance, Hrafnkell might have responded to a breach in the terms of the resolution (R), or a person with a prosecution against Sámr might have appealed to Hrafnkell to be his broker against Sámr (A^b), or the sagaman might have arranged a confrontation between Sámr and Hrafnkell, perhaps at an assembly (C).

Before turning to the chapter on the feudeme of resolution, I emphasize the distinction between the closure of an on-going feudeme and the occurrence of a feudeme of resolution. The first is the completion of an action and is logically embedded in feudemes. For instance, the closure of an act of advocacy conveys either directly or indirectly the result of a meeting between parties where an offer of some sort is proposed. Chapter 7 presents an example from *Víga-Glúms saga*, where Glúmr asks for the hand of a woman for himself (A^s) and later makes two marriage proposals for others (A^b). The acceptance or rejection of such a proposal is part of the advocacy feudeme, as either one closes a proposal rather than initiating a feudeme of resolution.

6 The Feudeme of Resolution

It is your evil habit to settle first and then kill afterward.
—Prándr from Grímsey to Hrólfr Sigurðarson (*Valla-Ljóts saga*)

THE feudeme of resolution (R) falls into three major categories, all of which can occur outside of or at the courts. The first, arbitrated resolution, is a settlement reached by third-party negotiation. Direct resolution between the concerned parties, the second category, was a frequent means of settling disputes in the sagas. It could occur without force as *sjálfdœmi* or as direct compromise, or with force in instances of duelings or killings. Examples of the latter are killings committed in the name of blood vengeance, or those that removed an *ójafnaðarmaðr*. The third major type of the feudeme is rejected resolution, as when one party refused to agree to a settlement or refused even to consider negotiations when a resolution was attempted. This third category is not the same as a failed resolution, for resolution in any of the categories might end in failure.

The issue, as far as the formal characteristics of the tale are concerned, is whether an attempt at resolution was made, not how the resultant settlement came about or whether it was initially successful or long-lived. Very few resolutions in the sagas were final; most engendered more violence. Often a feud was finally arbitrated or resolved when the quarrel was placed in the hands of more powerful men who were able to deal with each other directly. We assume that in many, perhaps most, instances, issues of potential dispute among Icelanders themselves and not just saga characters were settled directly and even amicably. At other times, an aggressive Icelander was interested not in settling a dispute but in carrying out vengeance or acquiring property. Real or imagined resolutions involving such characters sowed the seeds of further saga feud. Within saga narrative instances of resolution usually signal a change in the feud, since they frequently led to new conflicts. The more tangential parties were often compensated or mollified in some way and dropped from the feud at hand. Generally, when resolutions were final, all parties remaining in the feud agreed to some form of compromise.

Þorgils saga ok Hafliða contains a parable about how Iceland functioned through adherence to a goal of compromise settlement. The background for telling the parable, a rare story form in the sagas, is that two powerful *goðar*, Þorgils Oddason and Hafliði Másson, were involved for several years in a growing feud. Men frequently tried to come between them and arbitrate. According to this saga from the Sturlunga compilation, each leader came to the Althing of 1121 prepared for a showdown, Hafliði with 1,200 men and Þorgils with 700. Earlier, when the two men met at the Althing to discuss a settlement directly, Þorgils betrayed the attempts at settlement and viciously maimed Hafliði. Consequently, at the Althing, Hafliði seeks vengeance and steadfastly refuses to adopt a reasonable negotiating stance. This series of types of resolutions—arbitrated, direct, arbitrated, and rejected—does not bring the feud to an end. The matter, already very serious, becomes unusually dangerous as the two weeks of the Althing slip by and a major clash begins to seem likely. At this juncture Ketill Þorsteinsson, a man outside the feud, comes to Hafliði and tells the *goði* about a similar earlier experience of his own.

> It seems a great pity to your friends if a settlement is not reached and this case is not brought to a good end. Yet many think it is hopeless now, or nearly so. I know of no advice to give you, but I have a parable to tell you.
>
> We grew up in Eyjafjǫrðr, and it was said that we were promising. I made what was thought to be the best possible match—with Gróa, the daughter of Bishop Gizurr. But it was said that she was unfaithful to me.
>
> I thought it hard that there was such talk. Trials were held and they went well. But nevertheless the persistent tales were offensive to me, and for this reason I grew very hostile toward the other man [his wife's seducer]. One time when we met each other in passing, I attacked him. But he ducked under the blow and I found myself underneath him. Then he drew his knife and stabbed me in the eye so that I lost the sight of that eye. Then he, Guðmundr Grímsson, let me get up, and it seemed to me there was something wrong about this. I had twice his strength, and so I thought we would compare similarly in other things.
>
> I fiercely wanted to avenge his wounding me with the strength of my kinsmen and to have him outlawed. We prepared our case. But some powerful men offered to support him, and therefore my suit came to nothing. It may now also happen that men come forward to support Þorgils, even though your case is more just.
>
> When my case had reached this point, they [Guðmundr's party] offered to pay a fine in settlement. I thought about what I had had to endure and how heavily it all had weighed on me, and refused the offer. . . . And I found, when thinking about my honor, that no offers could have been paid which would have sated my honor. [chs. 28–29]

Ketill, helped by his religious nature (he later, with Hafliði's backing, became a bishop), comes to realize that his demand for absolute justice is not reasonable and settles the dispute. The point of Ketill's tale is well made, for shortly thereafter Hafliði submits his case to reasonable arbitration and a settlement is arranged which both men then honor. This adherence to rules, which addressed order more than justice, was inherited from Scandinavian legal tradition; it underlies Njáll's famous statement when feuding parties would no longer play by the rules: "Our land must be built with law or laid waste with lawlessness" (*Njáls saga*, ch. 70).

The sagas, with their many descriptions of resolutions, are literary evidence of a national process of limiting violence. The first 300 years of Iceland's medieval independence, beginning in the early ninth century, were characterized by the almost total absence of the murderous pitched battles that routinely took place in Scandinavia and elsewhere in the medieval world. Only in the mid-thirteenth century, in the very last decades of the Free State, is there evidence of the incidence of casualties that might be expected when two groups of committed men battled. As in the confrontation between Þorgils and Hafliði, the sagas often tell of large forces assembled by feudists, though no leader could depend on continued support in a protracted struggle. For one thing, farmers had no tradition of following orders or of being away from home for long periods; and chieftains, for their part, lacked the financial resources necessary to feed, house, and pay large followings for an extended period of time. Instead, the assembling of large forces was usually a temporary defensive measure. The existence of such an assemblage warned an opponent that if he acted too aggressively, men were willing to stand and fight.

Faced with a show of force, a combative leader would have to determine whether his own forces might melt away if he acted aggressively for too long a period. The uncertainty engendered by relying upon farmers to act as soldiers was a factor in limiting violence. Over and over, after an initial show of strength, feudists wisely turned to the extensive court system or to other means of settling disputes. In the absence of a police apparatus, the settlement had to reflect a decision that could be enforced in the face of political realities; otherwise the feud would continue.

In Iceland legal decisions were not primarily governed by moral concepts. The goal of legal resolution was to return the community to a workable arrangement and not to determine who committed a crime, or how it was done. The purpose of court verdicts was to find a compromise that could be lived with even if men grumbled; harmony within the community was more important than justice to the individual. For instance, if one man killed another viciously and without reason, such a killing could be balanced off against another seemingly more reasonable killing or injury when a decision was arbitrated. Similarly, in many arbitrated settlements, a chieftain who was obviously culpable of some deed paid a fine, while one or more of his followers received the brunt of the punishment by being outlawed.

Arbitration.—The usual means by which the society limited violence was arbitration. Sometimes arbitration is referred to in the sagas by the legal term *jafnaðardómr*, a case before an umpire. *Jafnaðardómr* was in many instances understood to be the opposite of *sjálfdœmi*, a common form of direct resolution. Arbitrators might be appointed by the disputants or by the court at the assemblies, if the case was being heard there. Arbitration might also be demanded by men who intervened in a dispute on their own initiative, clear evidence that the community did not want to tolerate the instability of an ongoing feud. Like brokers, arbitrators lacked military or governmental authority, but they were respected and often powerful personages who stepped into socially necessary and defined roles, acting on behalf of the community, the court, or one of the feudists. They were often called *góðviljamenn* or *góðgjarnir menn*, men of goodwill, benevolence, or good deeds. They were, of course, often motivated by self-interest, since an imbalance of power in the district or an unresolved dispute at the assembly could lead to widespread disorder.

Compensation for arbitration, like brokerage, varied from case to case. Sometimes arbitrators were not paid at all; sometimes they received payment in material goods, including a part of the proceeds from a case heard by the *féránsdómr*, the court of confiscation. Often an increase in reputation and honor and the creation of new alliances were the rewards for successful arbitration. Guðmundr dýri accrues all these rewards as a result of his intervention in the feud over the valuable property Helgastaðir (saga selection 5). After Guðmundr demonstrated his abilities in keeping the feudists apart, men began to seek his services as broker or arbitrator. One such instance proved especially advantageous; the year after his intervention in the Helgastaðir feud, two brothers became involved in a dangerous dispute with a powerful *goði*. The brothers were young men and, although they too owned a chieftaincy (the *Fljótamannagoðorð*) which had a large following, they needed the support of powerful backers. "They called on Bishop Brandr and sought his advice. The bishop noted that in each of the most important cases last summer, Guðmundr dýri had provided the best counsel. The bishop advised them to go to Guðmundr and ask him to take on their case" (*Guðmundar saga dýra*, ch. 4). The brothers, following the churchman's advice, went to Guðmundr who finally agreed to act for them, but only after the brothers gave him their *goðorð*.

In many ways arbitration was a face-saving procedure. It relied upon the understanding that the honor of all parties was to be considered, and it allowed the parties to withdraw from a critically dangerous situation. The mechanism of legal arbitration could also be abused by wearing an opponent down rather than solving a dispute. This possibility is often explored in the sagas. A large part of the action in *Droplaugarsona saga* and *Ljósvetninga saga* builds from a consistent attempt by a rival to undercut the power and wealth of an established *goði* by continually bringing legal cases against him and his followers.

At the courts, the forms of arbitration were well defined. The laws addressed the issues of who sat on the court, who could appoint a judge, what procedure to follow in bringing a case, and how to evaluate a fine or balance injuries. At times the court itself appointed a group of men to arbitrate a disagreement, and their decision became binding. When arbitrators wished to ensure the closure of a feud, the resolution might include an offer of alliance, marriage, or fosterage. The creation of fictitious kin bonds often led to the quieting of old animosities.

Because so much of Icelandic feuding was eventually settled through negotiation at the courts, and because judgments there were made by peers, brokerage and arbitration were essential and repetitive aspects of feud. Often a saga-man concentrated on these aspects rather than on conflict in order to explain the course of social interplay or to prepare the audience for the complexity of obligations in a serious case at the Althing. Again and again, litigants gathered support for both aggressive and defensive moves while arbitrators worked to terminate conflicts.

The following passage from *Eyrbyggja saga* (ch. 10) illustrates the milieu of compromise which determined the decisions of Þórðr gellir, a well-known broker and arbitrator. (It is the same Þórðr gellir who in *Hœnsa-Þóris saga* is tricked into holding the marriage feast and acts as Hersteinn Blund-Ketilsson's broker; see saga selection 9). The passage also gives insight into the way in which feud contributed to the regulation of power in a local district. The conflict it describes began when the Kjalleklingar, a rising family under the leadership of Þorgrímr Kjallaksson, challenged the local prominence of the Þórsnesingar (the people of Þórsnes), who followed the *goði* Þorsteinn from Helgafell. Þorsteinn's father, Þórólfr Mostrarskegg Ǫrnólfsson, had been one of the first settlers in the Álpta-fjǫrðr (Swans' Fjord) region on the Snæfells Peninsula, and during his lifetime this *landnámsmaðr* exerted great influence on events in the area. He set up the first local assembly at Þórsnes, a small headland which he had named after his patron god. Because of his devotion to Þórr, Þórólfr declared the ground of the thing sacred to the god and forced men to go to a distant skerry to relieve themselves. The challenge to Þorsteinn Þórólfsson's authority was centered on this burdensome interdiction, although the underlying issue was the refusal of the new generation to bow to Þorsteinn's claim that he had inherited the authority wielded by his father. By the time Þórðr gellir is sent for, blood has been spilled in a confrontation at the Þórsnes thing and strong enmity has developed between the parties:

> Friends of both sides adopted the plan to send for Þórðr gellir, who at that time was the greatest leader [*hǫfðingi*] in the area around Breiðafjǫrðr. Þórðr was a kinsman of the Kjalleklingar and a close relation to Þorsteinn Þórólfsson by marriage. Men thought that he was the most likely to bring about a settlement between them. When the message came to Þórðr, he set out with many men and sought to make peace. He soon found that the differences between the two sides were very great. Nevertheless, he succeeded in establishing a truce and arranged a meeting. There it was concluded that Þórðr should arbitrate, but with the following conditions: the Kjalleklingar demanded that they should never again be required to go to Dirtskerry for their needs, and Þorsteinn stipulated that the Kjalleklingar should not foul the field now any more than they had done previously. The Kjalleklingar declared all the dead on Þorsteinn's side had fallen outside the law [*óheilagr*, hence they had forfeited their rights to personal security and indemnification] for the reason that they had come intending to fight. For their part, the Þórsnesingar said that each of the Kjalleklingar was *óheilagr* because he had breached the law at a hallowed assembly place.
>
> Although Þórðr could see that it would be difficult to effect a resolution, he agreed to try it, for he wanted to reach an agreement rather than allow the two parties to separate unreconciled. Þórðr began his arbitration by declaring that each side should retain the benefit that it had won. He determined that no death or blows suffered in the fight at the Þórsnes thing

would be compensated, and he said the field was defiled by the blood spilled there. He declared that ground to be now no more sacred than any other, and he said that those who struck first were the cause of the fight and that this action was itself a breach of the peace. He also said that no assembly should be held again at that place.

In order that the two sides should be satisfied with the settlement and live peacefully from then on, he set the following conditions: Þorgrímr Kjallaksson would be responsible for the upkeep of half of the pagan temple. In return, he would receive half of the temple dues as well as the allegiance of half of the thingmen. He would also from then on support Þorsteinn in all his legal cases and back him in enforcing whatever degree of holiness he wished to establish for the future thing site.

In addition, Þórðr gellir arranged a marriage between his kinswoman Þórhildr and Þorgrímr Kjallaksson. She was the daughter of Þorkell meinakr, Þórðr's neighbor. Because of this agreement, he was then called Þorgrímr goði. They then moved the thing farther in on the ness, where it is now.

Direct resolution.—This method of settlement usually meant compromises, killings, or humiliations. In Iceland a threatening challenge did not, as in heroic societies, demand a violent response. Instead, successful Icelanders like Snorri goði tried to avoid risking their lives foolishly. Even if a peaceful solution should bring humiliation, they attempted to find a compromise before risking violence.

In narrating a compromise resolution, humor is possible. In *Ljósvetninga saga* the powerful and ambitious chieftain, Guðmundr inn ríki, is brought up short when he visits a farm and sits in the high seat normally reserved for another local personality, Ófeigr Járngerðarson. Ófeigr, who at first contents himself with a lesser seat, waits until the tables are set up. Then

> Ófeigr set his fist on the table and said, "Do you think this fist is large, Guðmundr?" He answered, "It is certainly large." Ófeigr said, "Would you imagine that there was strength in it?" "That is certain," Guðmundr replied. Ófeigr said,

"Would you expect it could deliver a great blow?" "A huge one," Guðmundr said. Ófeigr: "What would you expect would be the result of it?" Guðmundr: "Broken bones or death." Ófeigr: "And how would you find such a death?" Guðmundr: "Terrible, and I would not want to die that way." Ófeigr: "Then don't sit in my place." Guðmundr: "As you wish." And he sat himself on the other side. [ch. 11]

Besides compromise, specific forms of direct resolution were *einvígi* or *hólmganga* (a duel), *sjálfdœmi*, killing of an *ójafnaðarmaðr*, and blood vengeance. Another form of violent, direct settlement was the burning of an opponent in his house. As to be expected, this form of resolution usually did not end a saga but initiated new violence, often blood vengeance, which in turn led to direct or arbitrated settlement. *Hólmganga* and *einvígi*, likewise, often failed to settle matters permanently.

Hólmganga (literally 'to go to a small island') was formal, following precise rules; *einvígi* was less formal.[1] Duels are infrequent in the sagas, probably because they were outlawed at the very beginning of the eleventh century. Sometimes duels were fought when legal decisions were unacceptable to one of the parties. After Gunnarr of Hlíðarendi in *Njáls saga* loses the case for the reclamation of the dowry of his kinswoman Unnr, he challenges the other litigant to a duel. His opponent, Hrútr Herjólfsson, declines to fight and releases the dowry, but the enmity springing from the case embroils Gunnarr in a series of disputes. In *Eyrbyggja saga*, Þórólfr bægifótr arrives in Iceland late in the settlement period and is successful in a duel. He first moves in with his mother but then decides there is not enough land on her claim. He then challenges a man with no near relatives who could pursue a charge of manslaughter should he be killed. By this means Þórólfr gains his landtake.

[1] Olav Bø, "*Hólmganga* and *einvígi*: Scandinavian Forms of the Duel," *Mediæval Scandinavia* 2 (1969):132–148.

Þórólfr thought there was too little good land there, and he challenged Úlfarr kappi [the champion] to a *hólmganga* for his lands because Úlfarr was old and childless. But Úlfarr chose to die rather than be bullied by Þórólfr. They fought on an island in Álptafjǫrðr and there Úlfarr fell. Þórólfr was wounded in the foot and afterward walked with a limp. For this reason he was called *bægifótr* (lamefoot). Þórólfr settled at Hvammr in Þórsárdalr and took possession of Úlfarr's land. He was the most unjust and overbearing man [*inn mesti ójafnaðarmaðr*]. He sold land to two freedmen of Þorbrandr from Álptafjǫrðr. To the freedman Úlfarr he sold Úlfarsfell, and to Ørlygr [Úlfarr's brother] he sold Ørlygsstaðir. These men lived there for a long time afterward. [ch. 8]

The farms of Úlfarsfell and Ørlygsstaðir later become major points of contention between Þórólfr bægifótr's son, Arnkell goði, and the sons of Þorbrandr from Álptafjǫrðr.

Often the sagaman filled large segments of the narrative with a series of attempted settlements, drawing on different types of resolution. In *Vápnfirðinga saga*, for example, after Geitir kills his former brother-in-law Brodd-Helgi, the saga details a number of attempted resolutions, first between Geitir and his nephew Bjarni Brodd-Helgason, and then, after Bjarni kills Geitir, between Bjarni and his cousin Þorkell Geitisson. The resolutions include attempts at *sjálfdœmi*, blood vengeance, arbitration, and direct compromise.

Sjálfdœmi occurs when one party is given the right to designate the terms of the settlement. There are two primary possibilities in such a circumstance. First, when one party wants to maintain friendly relations it shows good faith by granting self-judgment to the opposing side; such a grant assumes a response of moderation. More often than not, *sjálfdœmi* takes this form, but at times, even when offered in good faith, it backfires. For example, Sturla Þórðarson in *Sturlu saga* awards himself a huge sum of money after being given the right to set his own award by the priest Páll Sǫlvason. Similarly, after the events depicted in saga selection 1 from *Egils saga*, Egill, granted *sjálfdœmi* by his old friend Qnundr sjóni, takes advantage of the opportunity to lay a crushing decision upon Qnundr and his son Steinarr.

Second, *sjálfdœmi* is invoked when one of the parties to a dispute has the upper hand and is determined to set the terms of the decision. In *Víga-Glúms saga*, Víga-Glúmr's mother is forced to give *sjálfdœmi* to her aggressive neighbors Sigmundr and his father. The woman has no supporters: one son, who has already taken his inheritance, does not come to his mother's defense; another son has died; the third boy, Glúmr, is considered slow-witted. The neighbors nibble away at the woman's property and, as settlement to a lawsuit, award themselves through *sjálfdœmi* a valuable field previously shared by the two families. The land is not returned even after the reason for the *sjálfdœmi*, an allegation of a theft of livestock by workmen from the woman's farm, is made moot when the livestock are found. Víga-Glúmr eventually retaliates by killing Sigmundr and reclaiming the field.

Killing of an *ójafnaðarmaðr* is an example of a violent settlement resorted to only after other attempts at resolution have failed. Such a settlement often follows feuds caused by the naked ambition, intolerable conduct, or plain injustice of an *ójafnaðarmaðr*. A passive character, who has given way for a period of time, may be forced to risk his life in attacking an opponent whose *ójafnaðr* is no longer tolerable. In *Vápnfirðinga saga* (see saga selection 8), Geitir kills Brodd-Helgi because Brodd-Helgi, an extremely ambitious man, threatens to destroy him. Other powerful men, particularly *goðar*, sense a threat to themselves in Brodd-Helgi's actions and tacitly support Geitir. By doing so they permit Geitir to break the rules of the game and kill a fellow *goði* with few or no legal reprisals. For similar reasons and with similar support, Snorri goði kills Arnkell goði in *Eyrbyggja saga* and Hávarðr kills the goði Þorbjǫrn Þjóðreksson in *Hávarðar saga Ísfirðings*. In each of these instances, the violent death of the *ójafn-aðarmaðr* stems from his unwillingness to settle matters through compromise or from his refusal to abide by an arbitrated agreement.

Blood vengeance was not limited to an unruly few. Although the Church had an international standard of conduct by which its members were to live, for Icelandic clergy the indigenous process of feud often took precedence. Even toward the end of the Free State, clergy participated in blood vengeance and the ethos of feud, although, when involved in a dispute, they often showed a certain reluctance to bloody their own hands. Like other Icelanders, priests in the *Sturlunga saga* were subject to goading. For example, *Guðmundar saga dýra* tells us that in 1198, two years after the chieftain Ǫnundr Þorkelsson had been burned to death in his home, his three sons, two of whom were priests, sat down to a breakfast prepared by Ǫnundr's daughter. The woman served only the singed feet and heads (*svið*) of sheep. When asked by her husband what kind of food this was, she replied that for her "nothing went so far as *svið*." Her brother Vigfúss, a priest, then commented: "There is no denying that you are reminding us of what is our concern where burnt flesh is" (ch. 17). That same day the men rode out to seek vengeance. These two types of direct settlement, burning and blood vengeance, produced some of the more spectacular killings in the sagas.

Rejected resolution.—Even though the terms in the following example are favorable to Guðmundr dýri, the questions of former rivalries and honor prevent his accepting them. In *Guðmundar saga dýra* (ch. 12) a series of conflicts develops when an unimportant farmer's son, Rúnólfr Nikulássson, wounds a thingman of Guðmundr dýri's in an encounter at a horsefight. Guðmundr's reputation is at stake, and the incident stirs older animosities. Guðmundr finally burns Rúnólfr's chieftain, Ǫnundr Þorkelsson, in his home (ch. 14). With Ǫnundr during the attack was Gálmr

Grímsson, a respected farmer in the district, who tries to negotiate a compromise:

> Inside was a man called Gálmr, the son of Grímr. He was a good farmer and lived at the place called Dynhagi. He was a friend of all the burners, but of none more than Kolbeinn Tumason [an ally of Guðmundr dýri's and a leader of the burners]. Gálmr went to the door and spoke with the attackers; as yet the fire had not gone so far that all might not be saved. He asked Guðmundr and Kolbeinn to leave, offering them all his wealth in return. He was a very wealthy man and had the best of farms. Kolbeinn answered that he would give Gálmr as much money as he wanted if he would come out of the house. Gálmr answered: "For a long time now you have laughed at me because I liked to take baths and often drank a lot. Now there's a bath in the offing but it seems to me now unclear what the outlook is for a drink of mead." And he did not go out.

In some sagas series of resolutions fill whole sections of the narrative. The recurrence of temporary resolutions gave the sagaman a framework for competently handling a seemingly huge number of characters and their conflicts. At times a sagaman would play on the ways a settlement was perceived by different characters, thus interjecting new life into his tale at the very point when a feud chain was ending and familiar characters were leaving the saga. The conflict then narrowed to a few participants and the terms of the resolution led to a new dispute, initiating a new feud chain.

When two or more resolutions occur, for example, the first logically paves the way for the second, the second, for the third, and so forth. The sagaman who composed *Njáls saga* used this stylistic device with exceptional skill, often playing on the ways different people perceived the same resolution. For example, during the court case brought after the Njálssons killed their foster brother, Hǫskuldr Hvítanessgoði, the sagaman catalogs a series of resolutions, each of which comes to the brink of success only to fall back in failure. The first attempt at a court resolution fails because of a legal technicality. But Njáll, who wants the case resolved, rescues the proposed settlement by calling upon arbitrators. When they cannot agree, the resolution again seems to be in jeopardy. The arbitrators then cast lots to decide who will propose the terms of the settlement. Snorri goði, winning the draw, suggests that the unusually large award of treble compensation be paid for Hoskuldr's death and that payment be made there at the Althing. Knowing that settlement is close and that Njáll and his sons cannot meet the full payment with the funds they have brought to the Althing, the arbitrators themselves provide half of the award; their generosity again saves the settlement from collapse. Njáll's family pays a third of the award, and others at the assembly make up the difference. When Njáll finally throws a silk cloak and a pair of boots onto the pile of silver, the feud truly seems to be on the verge of closure. Flosi Þórðarson, Hoskuldr's relation by marriage, however, senses an insult in the giving of the cloak and asks who gave it. When he asks a second time and again receives no answer, he guesses that Njáll is the donor, and he calls Njáll's manliness into question. Skarpheðinn Njálsson, always ready with a comeback, retorts that Flosi is used as a woman every ninth night. Flosi is so angry that he kicks the pile of money and swears he will accept no other compensation for Hoskuldr than blood vengeance. The sagaman, having recounted a whole series of failed resolutions, has set the stage for new acts of violence.

In another series of multiple resolutions in *Njáls saga*, Gunnarr of Hlíðarendi kills twice in the same family. In a legal settlement he is banished from Iceland for three years with the proviso that if he does not go abroad, he may be killed by the kinsmen of the dead men. At the last moment Gunnarr decides not to go abroad, and for this breach of conduct his opponents attack and kill him. To some parties the killing was a legally sanctioned resolution. The day Gunnarr was to leave had passed, and he was not only unprotected by the law, but he was also guilty of violating his oath. To other parties, however, the killing of Gunnarr was not acceptable. The sons of Njáll now avenge Gunnarr by killing some of his killers. In each of these instances, the act designed to bring closure to a specific dispute engenders a new act of feud. *Njáls saga*, which before this series of resolutions had been so deeply concerned with Gunnarr and his feuds, now shifts attention to the sons of Njáll and their quarrels. They, like Gunnarr, turn primarily to violent acts to resolve their feuds, even though Njáll urges compromise.[2]

[2]Gunnarr's decision to remain home in Iceland resulted in partial loss of his legal status and personal immunity. In narrating this part of the tale and the subsequent repercussions, the sagaman assumed that his audience had knowledge of immunity and the different types of outlawry. Dennis, Foote, and Perkins, in the introduction to their translation of *Grágás* I, describe the general aspects of immunity and the different types of outlawry:
"All free people enjoyed the same legal status but their immunity or right to legal redress might be diminished or lost by their own act. Their forfeit of immunity might be conditional (in relation to one or more specified persons or for a specified time and place) or absolute (i.e., anyone, anywhere and at any time, could do them hurt with legal immunity). In a sense this forfeit existed from the moment the act causing it was committed, but it received retrospective legal recognition when it was accepted as grounds for a clearing verdict in a lawsuit. Otherwise, forfeit of immunity was made an essential part of the public penalties of outlawry that were imposed for many offenses. Lesser outlawry meant confiscation of property, dealt with by a confiscation court held at the outlaw's home, and exile for three years but with temporary rights of residence and passage—reasonable arrangements in a remote island with unreliable sea traffic. Full outlawry meant loss of all goods through a confiscation court, loss of all status, and denial of all assistance—virtually a death penalty. An intermediate form allowed an outlaw passage abroad for life-long exile, but this mitigation of full outlawry was not decided by the judges of a court but depended on permission from the Law Council, as did other forms of mulct and banishment (often within Iceland itself) that might be imposed in cases privately settled by mutual agreement and arbitration. The standard penalty for minor offenses was a fine of three marks, and the Lawspeaker and chieftains faced loss of office as an additional penalty. In general, however, outlawry is the predominant feature of the penal system. We cannot tell what effect it had—it may have deterred both wrongdoing and litigation. It has often been pointed out that private settlement, though ultimately subject to public sanction by the Law Council, probably played a much larger part in ending disputes than the law texts reveal." *Laws of Early Iceland: Grágás I*, trans. Andrew Dennis, Peter Foote, and Richard Perkins (Winnipeg: University of Manitoba Press, 1980), pp. 7–8.

7 Feud Clusters and Feud Chains

Every culture creates its own model of the length of its existence, of the continuity of its memory. This model corresponds to the concept a given culture has of the maximum span of time practically comprising its "eternity." Insofar as culture acknowledges itself as existing, only identifying itself with the constant norms of its memory, the continuity of memory and the continuity of existence are usually identified.

—Y. Lotman and B. A. Uspensky

If we take a collective look at our sagas, it is quite evident that the art displayed in their composition is uneven. Some are composed with more skill than others. Nevertheless they all follow, in various respects, set rules in their art, rules that are common throughout. But it is doubtful whether the sagamen were conscious of these rules, which are nowhere in the sagas set out in plain words. Nonetheless they display themselves probably as an unconscious reflex in the writers' handling of saga material.

—B. M. Ólsen

FEUDEMES combine to form clusters which are usually separated from one another by shifts in location, character, season, and time. Normally there is only one, if any, feudeme of conflict in a feud cluster. This conflict can be resolved quickly or it can engender further disputes which, along with acts of advocacy and resolution, motivate succeeding clusters.

Because saga narratives progress by clusters, the focus at any one time is on the conflict or the resolution in the cluster at hand rather than on the first major conflict or the final resolution in the saga. This narrative strategy freed the sagaman to develop the tale as he composed without having to memorize a fixed saga-long structure, and it was suitable whether the sagaman was writing or telling his story.

The nuclear, most typical cluster formation comprises conflict, advocacy, and resolution (abbreviated C, A, R); the sagaman, however, also used a variety of other feudemic formations and was not bound to one type. The way in which feudemes form clusters, as words form clauses, distinguishes one saga narrative from another in construction, emphasis, and style. Each cluster is a unit of story. Two premises govern the employment of feud clusters: (1) a saga feud is not one or several fixed sequences; (2) there is no set order of feudemes within a feud cluster.

A feud chain is a series of feud clusters. For instance, an insult may engender a killing or a breach of the terms of a settlement, and this act may start a new cluster centered on the killing or the failed resolution. Or a series of feud clusters may start with the desire of one man for another's land. The resulting confrontation may engender insult. Insult may lead to killing; killing may cause the victim's family or followers to seek support or blood vengeance; either of these may lead to an arbitrated settlement. The settlement may end the saga or it may be joined with a new feud chain filled with still more acts of advocacy, more conflicts, and more resolutions.

Feudemic construction—building from feudemes to clusters to chains—is tied to the development of feud in traditional social terms rather than to the artistic originality of the individual saga author. By linking feud clusters into feud chains, the sagaman relied on a narrative vehicle that fitted his purpose in telling about feuds. Grouping feudemes into clusters was a way of putting meaning into simple, repetitive actions. Arranging clusters in small chains and then linking the chains together was a way of constructing long prose stories. Occurrences of feudemes and the beginnings and endings of feud chains are easily recognizable. The formation of clusters within a feud chain is at times less clear, though distinct patterns appear in certain chains and sagas. The whole was a narrative strategy by which the sagaman could direct his tale to issues that touched the anxieties of the medieval people from whom the narratives sprang.

The feudemes in a passage from *Droplaugarsona saga* which begins with a farmer named Þorgeirr and his need for milkable ewes have been discussed earlier (see chap. 2). They fall into the following clusters: (1) information (the source of the dispute—milking livestock), advocacy (information passing), resolution (rejected); (2) information, advocacy (brokerage), resolution (rejected); (3) advocacy (brokerage), conflict (summoning for stealing); (4) information, advocacy (arbitration), resolution (direct). This series of clusters is a small feud chain. In *Droplaugarsona saga* several such feud chains are linked together to form the feud between Helgi Ásbjarnarson and Helgi Droplaugarson. Thus this saga, like most sagas, is a series of interconnected small feud stories.

A series of feuds between two well-known men or families may develop into a contest that carries through a complete saga, as in *Droplaugarsona saga* or *Vápnfirðinga saga*, where a feud spans two generations of opposing fathers and sons. In *Heiðarvíga saga*, Víga-Styrr, the central *ójafnaðarmaðr*, feuds with a series of opponents. The feuds of three generations of one family with different opponents, including kin, are the main subjects of *Laxdœla saga*. In *Eyrbyggja saga*, the feud chains concerning Arnkell goði and Snorri goði do not run consecutively but are interspersed with other feuds.

The nuclear cluster is highly adaptable. For instance, if

the sagaman wanted two disputants to resolve a matter successfully and without violence, he could have continued the action from conflict through advocacy (whether the characters acted as their own advocates or sought brokers) to a peaceful settlement. On the other hand, the sagaman could have just as easily narrated a violent resolution (failed or successful) by the same progression. The standard form of this progression occurred, for example, when two farmers engaged in a conflict. Each goes to his chieftain for support, and a legal resolution between the *goðar* is arranged. If, however, one of the parties was dissatisfied with this settlement, he might have initiated new acts of conflict. Arbitrators might have to intervene to bring about peace in the district before a mutually agreeable resolution was reached.

A particular meaning animates some clusters. When one party aggressively confronts another for reasons of wealth, power, or blood vengeance, the result is often a series of alternating conflicts and resolutions (C, R, C, R, C, . . .). This pattern emerges in the actions of an *ójafnaðarmaðr*, who seldom seeks brokerage and often prevents resolution. To strengthen his own hand, the opposing more passive party is then forced to solicit the help of others, and often he ends up killing the aggressor. When one party refuses to allow a case to be settled, either because the terms are not satisfactory or because he desires blood vengeance, the cluster becomes a series of unsuccessful resolutions with intermittent advocacies, primarily unsuccessful brokerages. This situation arises at the very end of *Vápnfirðinga saga*, when Þorkell Geitisson repeatedly tries to avenge the killing of his father by his kinsman Bjarni Brodd-Helgason.

In *Njáls saga*, a type of cluster dominates the narrative during preparation for major court cases. It is characterized by the repetition of a single feudeme in conjunction with units of travel and information. For example, the spring journeys of Kári, Njáll's son-in-law, and Flosi, leader of the burners of Njáll and his family, are described (see chap. 9).

Both leaders traverse the countryside in search of support (travel/advocacy). Each leader visits chieftain after chieftain before the approaching Althing. Then, at the Althing, each man engages in still another repetition of support seeking. A counterexample, exhibiting the same travel/ brokerage coupling, comes from *Hœnsa-Þóris saga*. The petulant farmer Hœnsa-Þórir refuses to sell hay to Blund-Ketill, a wealthy and respected farmer. A conflict ensues and the frustrated Blund-Ketill, whose generous offers have been turned down, takes some but not all of the hay. In order to get backing against Blund-Ketill, Þórir seeks support from various important men. Each time he describes the robbery to a potential broker, Þórir accuses Blund-Ketill of stealing all his hay. The broker then asks Þórir's foster son (son of the powerful chieftain Arngrímr Helgason) if what Þórir says is true. Each time the boy says no, and Þórir leaves without gaining support.

Clusters are not necessarily initiated by conflict. For instance, Einarr Þorgilsson's act of self-advocacy from *Sturlu saga* (see chap. 4) illustrates a cluster beginning with advocacy. Einarr Þorgilsson purchases an expectation of inheritance to a parcel of land (self-advocacy) and then challenges the rights of the still living landowner and his son (conflict). In some instances, a legal resolution is unacceptable to one party, and, instead of ending the feud, it initiates more feud. This situation arises, for example, when a court case ends in a decree of outlawry. Normally such a decree is enforced at the *féránsdómr* (court of confiscation) held on a specified date at the defendant's farm. A new cluster begins if the defendant gathers a force of armed supporters (advocacy) and by threat of force refuses to allow the holding of the *féránsdómr* (conflict). In this way a potential resolution quickly yields to further developments in the feud. In order to avoid violence an arbitrator often steps in and proposes a new resolution.

In the following example of a foiled *féránsdómr* from

Guðmundar saga dýra, two powerful chieftains in the Eyjafjǫrðr region, Ǫnundr Þorkelsson of Laugaland and Þorvarðr Þorgeirsson of Mǫðruvellir, have joined together and are vying with others for the ownership of Helgastaðir, a valuable property (see map 3). Both sides are determined to win the land and neither will compromise. When Ǫnundr and Þorvarðr threaten violence at a local assembly, Guðmundr dýri, a man new to the feud, steps in with his followers and keeps the two groups apart (saga selection 5). Although Ǫnundr and Þorvarðr themselves stay at home, their enemy Eyjólfr Hallsson takes the case to the Althing, where the two allied chieftains are outlawed. Ǫnundr and Þorvarðr, having no intention of accepting the court decision, gather men to block the holding of the *féránsdómr.* Guðmundr, however, sees that the coming confrontation will serve his own interests. He collects 150 men and sets out to intervene. First he stops Eyjólfr's band and then Ǫnundr and Þorvarðr's. The progression of the active elements in this cluster is Aᵃ, C, Aᵃ, R.

A^a/I: Then he [Guðmundr] went between them because Eyjólfr called it the law that the *féránsdómr* should be held there within his following, because they were unable to come any further.

C: But Ǫnundr and Þorvarðr swore that if this was done, they would immediately start a battle.

A^a: Then Guðmundr went between them and said that he would turn against the side that would not follow his counsel.

R: The result was that no *féránsdómr* was held and no battle ensued.

T/I: Toward the afternoon men started to leave because it was stated in the laws that the presentation of the formal proof at the *féránsdómr* should be done while the sun was in the south.[1]

---

[1]Formal proof of the action could not be presented until the court had been convened, before noon, with all parties in attendance.

T: Men on each side now rode away to their local meeting places, and those men who had come a longer distance returned to their regions. [ch. 3]

The feud continues throughout the summer with the usual small skirmishes and large threats. But by then other men in the community, and apparently the feudists themselves, have begun to tire of the feud. The saga tells us that some of the farmers participating in the feud had difficulty that winter in supplying their farms with food. Arbitrators, one of whom is Guðmundr dýri, come forward and tell both sides that the disturbances cannot continue. The dispute is then negotiated and a settlement is reached. The decree of outlawry is dropped.

In many feuds, if a broker refuses to lend his help the conflict does not escalate but remains limited to the original participants. This frustrating and suspense-building situation may prevail when thingmen of a chieftain are wronged by another powerful chieftain and are unable to get their own *goði* to act. In a segment of feud from *Eyrbyggja saga* (considered more thoroughly in chap. 8), a major character Arnkell goði is taking lands that clearly are part of the inheritance of the sons of Þorbrandr, who fail repeatedly to persuade their chieftain, Snorri goði, to take action against Arnkell. In such a situation the feudemes alternate between the request for brokerage and the return to the initial conflict.

Although it might seem, at first glance, that there is not much of a story in such a progression (A, C, A, C, . . .), many sagamen employ this or similar retarding devices in order to concentrate on the emotional aspects of feud. Almost as a rule, the sagas that center on dispute in Iceland do not stop to examine or comment on the psychology of the characters. Yet the development of anger and the frustration that leads to violence are admirably conveyed to the reader by the repetitious presentation of small actions, especially failed advocacies and resolutions. At the same time the sagaman, by repeating a feudeme, such as unsuccessful brokerage, has at his disposal a technique for enlarging an often simple story line into a longer tale. The repetition of the cluster of failed brokerage and the return to the unresolved initial conflict are evident in situations where women fail in successive attempts to goad their men to action. In *Eyrbyggja saga*, for example, in the long passage quoted in chap. 5 Þorgerðr Þorbeinisdóttir goes from kinsman to kinsman trying to persuade one of them to lead the case against the killers of her husband Vigfúss from Drápuhlíð. The repetition of unsuccessful attempts to find an advocate forms scenes and, in the hands of a skillful sagaman, creates moments of dramatic tension.

Clusters may be tightly constructed or may span a large section of narrative punctuated with descriptive or informational passages. The format, sequence, and events of feuds between major characters were well known to the medieval audience; plausibility in terms of the shared memory of Icelanders was essential. Within this tradition a sagaman had latitude to expand or to contract a tale in a manner commensurate with his own artistry. For instance, the authors of *Laxdœla saga* and *Njáls saga* were more skillful in creating complex narratives than were the authors of *Fóstbrœðra saga* and *Heiðarvíga saga*. Yet the compositional technique is the same in all the family sagas mentioned above, as it is in a passage from *Landnámabók*.

The consensus among scholars is that a thirteenth-century sagaman fashioned his tale from a mixture of written historical sources, preexisting oral tales, and his own imagination. Among the written sources for saga stories, *Landnámabók* has long been regarded as the most important. This text, first written in the early twelfth century, builds on older oral traditions. Its series of entries tell, in both skeletal and embroidered prose, stories of the original landtakes and events of the settlement.[2] *Landnámabók* concentrates on approximately 430 of the most important *landnámsmenn* and supplies often detailed information about the size and boundaries of property claims. A major source book for medieval Icelanders, the text was altered and expanded in the thirteenth and fourteenth centuries, and several versions of the later revisions

---

[2]In recent years doubts about the veracity of the factual information in the sagas have spread to more historical works, such as *Landnámabók* and *Íslendingabók*. Olaf Olsen, *Hørg, hov, og kirke: historiske og arkœologiske vikingetidsstudier* (Copenhagen: Gad, 1966), has argued that the information concerning heathen practices and sanctuaries is unreliable. Other aspects of the story of Iceland's settlement and development into a state have been questioned by Sigurður Líndal in "Sendiför Úlfljóts: Ásamt nokkrum athugasemdum um landnám Ingólfs Arnarsonar," *Skírnir* 143 (1969):5−26, and by Preben Meulengracht Sørensen in "Sagan um Ingólf og Hjörleif: Athugasemdir um söguskoðun íslendinga á seinni hluta þjóðveldisaldar," *Skírnir* 148 (1974):20−40. In *Saga og samfund* (Copenhagen: Berlingske forlag, 1977), Sørensen notes that the authors of *Landnámabók* probably exaggerated the importance of Norwegian colonists and tended at times to reflect conditions at about the year 1100, but he never doubts that underlying *Landnámabók*'s entries there is much old and authentic material (p. 28). Hans Bekker-Nielsen, in his chapter "Frode mænd og tradition," in *Norrøn fortællekunst: kapitler af den norsk-islandske middelalderlitteraturs historie*, ed. Hans Bekker-Nielsen, Thorkil Damsgaard Olsen, and Ole Widding (Copenhagen: Akademisk forlag, 1965), pp. 35–41, emphasizes the continental influences on those twelfth- and thirteenth-century sources that tell of Iceland's earlier periods. Bekker-Nielsen stresses that families and individuals equipped to record information about the history of Iceland were probably educated by clerics and therefore were markedly influenced by Christian thought.

Sveinbjörn Rafnssön, *Studier i Landnámabók: Kritiska bidrag till den isländska fristatstidens historia*, Bibliotheca Historica Lundensis 31 (Lund: C.W.K. Gleerup, 1974), has reconsidered the very purpose of *Landnámabók*. He argues that the information was altered to verify twelfth- and thirteenth-century claims to landownership. For a discussion of Rafnsson's views see Jakob Benediktsson, "Markmið Landnámabókar: Nýjar rannsóknir," *Skírnir* 148 (1974):207–215. Also see Jakob Benediktsson's introductions to *Íslendingabók* and *Landnámabók* in *Íslenzk fornrit* 1, and his article, "Landnámabók: Some Remarks on Its Value as a Historical Source," in *Saga-Book* 17, 4(1969):275–292.

are extant.[3] *Landnámabók* is an extraordinary testament to the ability of medieval Icelanders to recount their origins in a historical manner, an option not open to contemporary European narrative chroniclers, such as Geoffrey of Monmouth, who wrote about older continental peoples whose origins were in a mythic past. For the original compilers of *Landnámabók* the saga age was only two or three generations earlier, a distance easily bridged by memory. Three or four more generations took the compilers back to the settlement period.

The recounting of events and names found in the terse entries in *Landnámabók* has been assumed to lack the kind of narrative art evident in the family sagas. Yet in both, action is presented by feudemes and grouped into clusters while informational sections, such as genealogy, kin relationships, land status, and dating, provide the social background. The fact that cluster construction is evident in the family sagas, in *Sturlunga saga*, and also in *Landnámabók* shows the extent and the stability of the Icelandic technique of prose narrative. The common existence of feudemes and clusters in all these texts is also noteworthy when the scope of these writings is considered. The family sagas and the sagas of the Sturlunga compilation concentrate on disputes in the later centuries, when all the valuable land was owned, whereas *Landnámabók* tells how the new land was taken and catalogs the creation of kinship relations which determined property ownership and family bonds in the later years. The following passage from *Landnámabók* (number 376 in the thirteenth-century version, *Sturlubók*, and number 331 in the fourteenth-century

---

[3]Differing views as to the age and importance of the different versions have been advanced. See Jón Jóhannesson, *Gerðir Landnámabókar* (Reykjavík, 1941); Jakob Benediktsson, introduction in *Íslenzk fornrit* 1, esp. pp. i–cxx; and Sveinbjörn Rafnsson, *Studier i Landnámabók*.

Hauksbók version) tells the story of the *landnámsmaðr* Qzurr hvíti (the white), a settler in the Southern Quarter. After giving Qzurr's reasons for emigrating from Norway to Iceland, the account follows the status of part of his landtake through the tribulations caused by a dissenting claim.

Information		Feudemic progression
genealogical setting	There was a man named Qzurr, the son of Þorleifr of Sogn [in Norway]. Qzurr killed a man in a sanctuary in the Upplands, when he was on a bridal journey with Sigurðr hrísa [the bastard?]; on that account he was exiled to Iceland.	*Cluster 1.* (past: how Qzurr came to Iceland) C: killing T: bridal journey R: exile
how the settler came to Iceland location of land dating information fictitious kin bonds heir to Qzurr genealogy location of landowner and freedman shared land status of inheritance	He was the first to claim Holtaland between Þjórs River and Hrauns Brook. He was seventeen years old when he committed the slaying. He married Hallveig, daughter of Þorviðr. Their son was Þorgrímr kampi, the father of Qzurr, the father of Þorbjǫrn, the father of Þórarinn, the father of Grímr Tófuson. Qzurr lived at Kampa Hill. His freedman was Bǫðvarr, who lived at Bǫðvarr's Knoll near Viðiwood. To him Qzurr gave a share in the wood, but he stipulated that he himself was to get it back after Bǫðvarr's death if Bǫðvarr should be childless. Qrn of Vælugerði, who has been mentioned previously [in *Landnámabók*], cited Bǫðvarr for sheep stealing. For that reason Bǫðvarr gave over his possessions by *handsal* to Atli,	*Cluster 2.* (present: Icelandic feud) C: stealing A[b]: *handsal*

Information   Feudemic
                                                              progression

	the son of Hásteinn, who quashed Qrn's case. Qzurr died while Þorgrímr was young. Hrafn, son of Þorviðr, was trustee for Þorgrímr's property. After the death of Bǫðvarr, Hrafn claimed Víðiwood and banned Atli from it, though Atli thought himself to be the owner. Four men, led by Atli, went to get wood. Leiðólfr was with him. A shepherd told this to Hrafn, and he rode after Atli with eight men; they met in Orrostudalr [Battledale] and fought there. Two of Hrafn's housecarls fell and he himself was wounded. One of Atli's men was killed and he himself rode home with his death wound. Qnundr bíldr [the axe] separated them and invited Atli to stay with him.

dating
information

control of
prosecution for
land claim

size of groups

location

condition of
wounds for legal
purposes

R: case
   overturned
(time break)
Cluster 3.

C: counterclaim
   to land

T: to land in
   question
A^{i}: information
   passing induces
   fighting
T: to woods

R: violent resolu-
   tion

T: home

R: action of
   góðviljamaðr

dating
information

dating
information

omen of death

location

place-names

Þórðr dofni [the drowsy], Atli's son, was then nine years old. When Þórðr was fifteen, Hrafn rode to Einarr's Harbor to meet a ship. He was wearing a dark-blue hooded cloak and he rode home again at night. Þórðr waited alone for Hrafn at Haugaford, a short distance from Traðar Hill, and killed him there with a spear. Hrafn's mound is to the east of the road, and to the west is Hásteinn's mound and Atli's mound and Qlvir's. The killings were balanced off against each other.

(time break)
Cluster 4.

T: commerce

T: home

R: killing,
   blood vengeance

R: arbitrated
   resolution

Information		Feudemic Progression
status of heir	Þórðr gained in reputation from this exploit. He married	(future: potential for new feud)
marriage bonds	Þórunn, the daughter of Ásgeirr, "the terror of the Easterners," who killed a Norwegian ship's crew at the	
location	mouth of Grímr's River because he had been robbed in Norway. When Þórðr was	
dating information	twenty-two years old, he bought a ship in Knarrar Sound and set out to claim his	T: to claim
inheritance considerations	inheritance. He hid a great deal of money and for that reason Þórunn did not want to	inheritance
dating information about rightful heir	move; she stayed on the land. Þórðr's son Þorgils was two years old at the time. Þórðr's	
death of landowner	ship was lost. A year later Þorgrímr ørrabeinn [scar-leg], the son of Þormóðr and Þuríðr, the daughter of Ketilbjǫrn,	
marriage bonds new inheritance considerations (potential problem with half brother)	came to manage the property for Þórunn. He married Þórunn, and their son was Iæringr.	

Much information is given in the above passage. It describes how Qzurr's original land claim was established, and then how part of it was taken from his family, forcibly regained, and then taken again. At the conclusion of the passage the issues of feud are resolved, at least to a certain degree, although we are left with the portentous information that Þórðr dofni's son and rightful heir Þorgils is three years old when his mother remarries and has a second child. The passage names several generations of two families that were involved in the contest. The entry closes with the land in the possession of a man and a widow, neither of whom is a blood relation of the original families.

The passage from *Landnámabók* is a feud chain. There is nothing fixed about a feud chain in terms of length, breadth, or syntagmatic pattern. The determinant is what an Icelandic storyteller chose to do with certain basic information. If a sagaman wanted to he could expand a compact narrative such as the above *Landnámabók* entry—with a feud stretching over generations—into a saga composed of numerous feud chains. By its very nature such a saga would focus on the events of a region as different families competed for a limited amount of land and for power. On the other hand, a sagaman could just as easily have chosen to emphasize the feuds of a single generation. The saga would then tend to concentrate on the antagonism among a few individuals or families. What is constant is that feud stories, whether elaborated into a saga or truncated as in the *Landnámabók* example, are composed of the three active narrative elements. The passage has the following clusters of feudemes: C/T, R; C, A, R; C, T/A, T/R, T/R; T/T/R, R; T. Cluster 2 is a nuclear cluster and cluster 3 is a variation on the nuclear cluster. The other clusters each have two feudemes, some with the element of travel attached. The final unit of travel is imbedded in a block of information.

The primary concern of this passage from *Landnámabók* is to outline the history of Qzurr's family and to recount the status of their land claim. The passage does not elaborate legal entanglements or expand the seeking of support; if it did, further descriptions of support seeking would be needed. Conflicts and resolutions instead take center stage. The conflicts are over killing, stealing, and land; the resolutions have to do with exile, court action, fighting, killing, and arbitration. Three types of advocacy appear in the passage. (1) Brokerage occurs when the freedman Bǫðvarr goes to Atli Hásteinsson and conveys by *handsal* Qzurr's woods in return for protection from a prosecution for sheep stealing (for this and similar examples of land transfer, see chap. 8). (2) Arbitration occurs during resolution when

Ǫnundr bíldr separates the fighters. In so doing he is acting in the spirit of a góðviljamaðr. (3) In the third type of advocacy, information passing, the shepherd supplies the information that brings Hrafn to initiate conflict.

Most of the examples thus far have concerned quarrels over dowries, land, killings, insults, and the division of the produce of land. Yet even in contests between men and supernatural creatures, the Icelanders tended, from evidence in the sagas, to perceive these struggles within the legalistic concepts of feud. The narrations of such incidents when they take place in Iceland usually fall into feud chains formed by clusters containing all three types of feudemes. For instance, a revenant's killings or maimings of persons and animals often provide the reason for conflict, while resolutions are the final laying to rest of the dead. Advocacy occurs usually as brokerage, after the hauntings have caused disturbances in the community. In the two following examples of feud clusters from *Eyrbyggja saga*, we see the extremes to which they can be successfully adapted.

The first example (partly narrated in saga selection 2) concerns the possessions of Þórgunna, a Hebridean woman, who has lived and worked at the farm Fróðá. After an ominous rain of blood falls, she instructs the *bóndi* Þóroddr, who owns the farm, about the disposition of her property, including an order to burn her bed linen. The interdiction is disregarded because the farmer's wife, sister of Snorri goði, covets the beautiful bedding. After her death, Þórgunna, or what is apparently her attendant spirit, revisits the farm in the form of a seal. As a result of Þórgunna's disturbances, people begin to die, including the *bóndi*, who is drowned at sea with his men while fishing. The bodies are not found, but on the night of the funeral feast the farmer and his men come soaking wet into the farmhouse and sit down by the fire. Similar marvels continue throughout the winter, and many persons die. In the autumn thirty servants were living in the household but by the late winter only seven remain. Eighteen died and five ran away. At this juncture (ch. 55):

Cluster 1:

T/A^b: But when these wonders had reached this stage, Kjartan journeyed to Helgafell to meet with his uncle Snorri goði from whom he sought advice about the specters who had descended upon them.

I/T: By that time the priest, whom Gizurr hvíti had sent to Snorri goði, arrived at Helgafell.

T/A^b: Snorri sent the priest to Fróðá with Kjartan along with his son Þórðr kausi and six other men. Snorri advised them that the bed furnishings of Þórgunna should be burned and then all the revenants should be summoned to a *duradómr*. He asked the priest to conduct holy services, to consecrate with water, and to hear confessions.

T/A^b: They then set off for Fróðá and along the way they called on men from the next farms to ride with them.

Cluster 2:

I: They arrived at Fróðá the evening before Candlemas, as the kitchen fires were being laid. By then Þuríðr, the mistress of the house, had taken sick in the same way as the others who had died. Kjartan immediately went inside and saw that Þóroddr and his companions were sitting by the fire, as was their custom.

R: Kjartan took down Þórgunna's precious bed hangings and went into the kitchen. There he took glowing embers from the fire and went outside and burned all Þórgunna's bedclothes.

C: After that Kjartan summoned Þórir viðleggr while Þórðr kausi summoned farmer Þóroddr. They charged these men with going about the dwelling without permission and depriving people of life and health. All those who sat by the fire were summoned.

I: Next a *duradómr* was convened. The charges were announced, and all procedures were followed as if it were a thing court. Witnesses were heard, the cases were summed up, and judgments were made.

R: When sentence was passed on Þórir viðleggr, he stood up and said: "We have sat as long as we could sit it out."

T: After that, he went out a door, other than that before which the *dómr* was held.

R: Then sentence was passed on the shepherd; and when he heard that, he stood up and said: "Now I will leave, though I think that this would have been more fitting earlier." And when Þorgríma galdra-kinn heard sentence being passed on her, she stood up and said: "I stayed here while it was safe."

I/T: Then one after the other, the defendants were called and each in turn stood up as judgment was handed down. All said something as they went out; their remarks indicated that they departed unwillingly.

R: Then sentence was pronounced against farmer Þóroddr; and when he heard it, he stood up and said: "Friendships here are few, I think. Let's flee now, all of us."

T: After so saying, he left.

R: Then Kjartan and his companions entered. The priest carried consecrated water and holy relics through the entire house. Later in the day the priest sang holy services and held a solemn mass. After that all the ghosts disappeared, and the hauntings at Fróðá ceased. Þuríðr recovered from her sickness and became healthy.

I: In the spring after this wonder, Kjartan took on a new servant couple. He lived for a long time afterward at Fróðá and became a most outstanding man.

The above passage is highly legalistic and, in a manner familiar to us, the feudemes follow closely one after the other with the density typical of descriptions of local Icelandic feud. Another example of supernatural disturbance occurring earlier in *Eyrbyggja saga* (ch. 34) shows how the sagaman applied the technique of saga prose to a folkloristic passage with a less legal tone. The passage concerns the hauntings and killings of men and livestock by the revenant (*aptrganga*) Þórólfr bægifótr. Arnkell goði's father. The narrative concentrates less on the action of feudemes than on unusually long descriptions of the landscape and the intricacies of carrying out the reinterment of a revenant. Bits of information are interspersed among the feudemes more intricately than in many other examples. This is because Þórólfr's actions and the resulting reinterment (except for Þorbrandr's remonstrance to his sons) are summarized by the sagaman.

The following clusters display thematic cohesion. Cluster 1 concerns animals and an animal keeper. The mistress of the house is the topic of cluster 2, and the local community is the subject of the third cluster. Þórólfr's reburial and its effect on the community and the animals form the nucleus of cluster 4.

Cluster 1:

I/C: Þórólfr during the summer haunts after sundown. The oxen that were used to pull Þórólfr's body and cattle that came near the grave site went mad. The shepherd from Hvammr was often chased home by Þórólfr. One morning the shepherd is found beaten black and blue with all his bones broken.

R: The shepherd is buried near Þórólfr, apparently to keep the old man company and to mollify him.

I: Some sheep are found dead and the others have run
off. Birds that land on Þórólfr's grave drop dead.
People no longer dare to graze their livestock up in
the valley.

Cluster 2:

I/C: Þórólfr's apparition begins to ride the house. In
the winter he molests the mistress of the house until
she dies.

T/R: The dead woman is taken up to Þórsárdalr and is
buried near Þórólfr's grave.

Cluster 3:

I/T/C: People in the surrounding area begin to flee
their farms as Þórólfr continues his haunting and
killing. Those he kills accompany him. The community is disrupted.

I/T/A[b]: Members of the community go to Arnkell goði
thinking it is up to him to cope with his father's
behavior. Arnkell offers hospitality to all who wish
to stay with him. Whenever Arnkell is present
Þórólfr is never destructive.

Cluster 4:

I: No one traveled during the winter.

I/T/A[b]: After the spring thaw, Arnkell sends to the six
sons of Þorbrandr a request that they help to reinter
the body of Þórólfr farther from the community.

I/C/R: All men in the community are obligated by law
to help bury the dead if asked. But the sons of
Þorbrandr refuse. Þorbrandr points out to them that
they are in the wrong. One son, Þóroddr, says he will
help on behalf of his brothers.

T: The messenger Arnkell has sent returns with the
message.

I/T/R: With eleven men, tools, and oxen, Arnkell
meets Þóroddr and his two men, and all go to
Þórsárdalr to the gravesite of Þórólfr. The undecom-

posed body of Þórólfr is dug up, placed on a sledge, and dragged to Úlfarsfell, where the oxen go mad and head toward the sea. The oxen are spent and Þórólfr is buried on a small headland since called Bægifótshǫfði (Lamefoot's Headland). Arnkell built a wall and Þórólfr lay quietly while Arnkell was alive.

How does this story of Þórólfr's hauntings fit into the saga? Is it simply an isolated folkloristic digression? The principle of integration may be perceived in the aid that Þórólfr gives his son, Arnkell goði. By leaving Arnkell's farm in peace while driving the neighbors out of the locality, Þórólfr increases Arnkell's wealth and status. This aspect of a story which is otherwise a simple tale of hauntings helps us to understand the sagaman's narrative strategy. The strategy becomes clearer when the sagaman (ch. 63) recounts a second series of hauntings by the former viking. This time, Þórólfr returns from his grave to seek vengeance on Þóroddr, one of the Þorbrandssons who, together with Snorri goði, killed Arnkell. Þóroddr is a suitable target for Þórólfr's vengeance, for after Arnkell's death, Þóroddr took possession of the two farms Úlfarsfell and Ørlygsstaðir. The deceased father and son had previously claimed the farms, and the question of their rightful ownership had been the basis for the eruption of feud at least three times before in the saga.

Indeed, Þórólfr's acts of vengeance would hardly be unusual if he were not dead. But Þórólfr is dead, and the hauntings that lead to the death of Þóroddr are not only an interesting variation on a theme, but one that yields insight into the rationale of the sagaman. Þórólfr's acts are explicable and important because Arnkell's killing had never been adequately atoned for. The legal settlement that followed his death had determined a compensation far too low for a great chieftain. Arnkell's wife agreed to the inadequate sum because, at the time of her husband's death, she took up the case herself and was in too weak a position to demand suitable terms. The sagaman specifically comments (ch. 38) on the unworthiness of the initial legal settlements. Then, as in many saga feuds, he follows up the dishonor of an unsatisfactory court settlement with a second violent resolution of blood vengeance. In this instance, Þórólfr, even though dead, is apparently the only family member willing to rescue Arnkell's honor.

So strong is the stamp of the feudemic technique that even the tale of a marriage arrangement, like the following one from *Víga-Glúms saga* (chs. 10–11), is told by a progression of feudemes. The passage (saga selection 6), serving as an interlude in the saga, shows how new alliances of marriage and *vinfengi* are formed. The story in the saga selection and in the part immediately preceding it breaks down into feudemes in the following way:

Cluster 1:

(Glúmr and his family)

I: Glúmr now attained a great reputation in the district. There was a man who lived at Lón in Hǫrgárdalr. He was called Gunnsteinn and was powerful and rich and was counted among the more important men. His wife was called Hlíf. Their son was Þorgrímr; he was called Hlífarson after his mother because she lived longer than Gunnsteinn. Hlíf was a most outstanding woman. Þorgrímr was brought up well and became a powerful man. A second son was Grímr eyrarleggr. Their daughter was called Halldóra. She was a beautiful woman and had a good disposition. A match with her was thought to be one of the very best because of her family connections and her own great qualities and abilities.

A[s]: Glúmr asked for the hand of this woman. He let it be understood that he had little need of his kinsmen to speak of his family background, wealth, or general conduct. "These things will be well known to you; I am intent on this match as long as her kinsmen approve." Glúmr received a favorable answer to his suit.

R: Halldóra was betrothed to Glúmr with much wealth, and the marriage feast went well.

I: And now his position was even more respected than before.

Cluster 2:

(The Esphœlingar family)

I: There was a man called Þorvaldr; he was the son of Refr and lived at Barð in Fljót. He was married to Þuríðr, the daughter of Þórðr from Hǫfði. Their children were Klaufi and Þorgerðr, the woman who married Þórarinn at Espihóll. Þorvaldr krókr from Grund [the brother of Þórarinn at Espihóll] married Þorkatla [Oddkelsdóttir] from Þjórsárdalr. Hlenni the old, the son of Ǫrnólfr tǫskubak, lived at Víðines and was married to Oddkatla, another daughter of Oddkell from Þjórsárdalr.

(Gizurr and his family)

I: There was a man called Gizurr. He was the son of Kaðall and lived at Tjarnir in Eyjafjarðardalr. He was married to Saldís, a worthy housemistress. Gizurr was also counted among the most prominent *bœndr* and owned much property. Of their daughters, two are named, Þórdís and Herþrúðr.

The two were beautiful, elaborately dressed women and thought to be good matches; they grew up at home. The brother of Gizurr was Rúnólfr; he fathered Valgerðr, the mother of Eyjólfr at Mǫðruvellir. Þórdís [Gizurr's sister] was the daughter of Kaðall, who was married to Þórir at Espihóll; their children were named earlier.

(Þorgrímr Þórisson) I: Þorgrímr was the son of Þórir and, although he was born in wedlock, he was not the son of Þórdís. Þorgrímr was strong and manly.

T/I: He rode to meet Gizurr with the intention of asking for the hand of Gizurr's daughter Þórdís.

A^b/I: His brothers and friends were pleaders in this marriage suit. The woman's kinsmen felt themselves close enough to be consulted in the marriage of their kinswoman, and they thought that the offer was a handsome one. Nevertheless, Þorgrímr was denied the woman, though it seemed to all that he had made an equitable proposal.

C: Þorgrímr's brothers and kinsmen were offended.

Cluster 3:

I: The saga now speaks of a man named Arnórr, who was called *rauðkinnr*. Arnórr was the son of Steinólfr, the son of Ingjaldr, and first cousin to Glúmr. He had been abroad for a long time and was highly esteemed. When he was in Iceland, he was constantly with Glúmr.

A[b]: He requested Glúmr to offer a marriage proposal on his behalf, and when Glúmr asked what woman he wanted to marry, Arnórr answered, "Þórdís, the daughter of Gizurr, the one who was refused to Þorgrímr Þórisson." Glúmr said, "To look in that direction seems unpromising, because I think there is no difference between you two as men. But Þorgrímr has a good home, much wealth, and many kinsmen to rely upon, while you own no dwelling and have little wealth. And further, I do not want to offer any *ójafnaðr* to Gizurr and place him in a position where he will not be able to marry off his daughter as he chooses. Gizurr deserves only good from me." Arnórr replied: "Then I'll benefit from good kinship if I get a better match by your pleading my case. Promise your *vinfengi* to him. He will give me the woman, for it would have been called a fair match if a man as good as Þorgrímr had not already been turned away." Glúmr gave in to Arnórr's urging.

T/A[b]: Together they went to Gizurr. Glúmr pressed the case on Arnórr's behalf. Gizurr answered: "It may be, Glúmr, that it will be said I made a mistake if I give my daughter to your kinsman, Arnórr, when I did not choose to give her to Þorgrímr." Glúmr said: "That is correct, and yet there is still something more to be said: if you decide to honor our request, I offer in return my *vinfengi*." Gizurr answered: "I consider that of much worth, but I suspect that in return I will earn the *óvinfengi* of other men. "Well," Glúmr said, "You must see your own way in this matter, but your decision will greatly affect my dealings with you whatever you choose." Gizurr, who replied, "You won't leave this time without succeeding," then extended his hand and Arnórr committed himself to take a wife. Glúmr added that he wanted the marriage to take place at his farm, Þverá, in the fall. Glúmr and Arnórr then took their leave.

Cluster 4:

I/T: Arnórr had some malt stored at Gásar, and he and one houseman set out to fetch it. On the day they were expected back with the malt, Þorgrímr Þórisson rode out to the hot springs. Þorgrímr had with him six of his housemen, and they were at the baths at Hrafnagil when Arnórr returned, expecting to cross the river.

C: Then Þorgrímr spoke up: "Wouldn't it be a lucky chance to meet up with Arnórr now? Let's not lose the malt even if we have lost the woman." Þorgrímr and his men went toward Arnórr and his man with drawn swords, but when Arnórr saw what the odds were, he plunged into the water and made it across the river.

I: His packhorses, however, were left on the other side of the river. Then Þorgrímr said: "Our luck is not all bad; we'll drink the ale but they will decide in the matter of the woman."

T: Þorgrímr then rode to South Espihóll.

I: Þórir, his father, was blind by that time. Þorgrímr's companions were in high spirits and laughed a lot.

A$^{i/b}$: Þórir asked what seemed so funny to them. They said that they didn't know which group would be first to hold its feast, and then they told him of their catch and about the chase—"But the bridegroom took a plunge." And when Þórir heard that, he asked: "Do you think you've done well, since you're laughing so much? And what are your plans now? Do you intend to sleep here tonight, as though nothing else is required? In that case, you do not know Glúmr's temper should he approve of his kinsman's journey. I call it prudent counsel to collect our men; most probably, Glúmr has gathered many men together by now."

I: There was a ford in the river then, which is no longer there. They collected eighty fighting men during the night and waited, prepared, at the bottom of the hill facing the ford in the river.

Cluster 5:

I: But of Arnórr there is this to be told: he found Glúmr and told him of his trip.

A^b: Glúmr answered: "It comes as no surprise to me that they did not remain quiet, but the matter is now rather difficult. If we do nothing, we reap dishonor. Yet it is altogether unclear that we will find honor if we seek to right the wrong. Nevertheless, we will now gather men."

T/C: When it was light the next morning, Glúmr came to the river with sixty men and wanted to cross over. But the Esphœlingar pelted them with stones, and Glúmr was unable to advance. Instead, he turned back, and they carried on the fight across the river with stones and shots.

I: In this way, many were wounded, though none are named.

T/A^b: When men of the local region became aware of what was happening, they rode up during the day and went between the two groups and arranged a truce.

R: The Esphœlingar were asked what satisfaction they wished to offer Arnórr for the dishonor they had done him. But the answer came back that no compensation would be forthcoming even though Arnórr had run away from his own packhorses. Then something new was proposed. Glúmr should seek Gizurr's other daughter Herþrúðr as a wife for Þorgrímr, and the marriage of Arnórr and Þórdís was to be consummated only if Glúmr was able to procure this other woman for Þorgrímr. And she whom Þorgrímr married was considered better matched. Now that so many had a hand in the matter, Glúmr promised his aid.

T/Aᵇ: He went to Gizurr and brought the matter up. "It may appear to you, Gizurr, by asking for wives for my kinsman and the Esphœlingar, that I am overstepping my bounds. In order to put an end to dissension here in the district. however, I think I must offer you my faith and friendship, if you do my will." Gizurr answered: "It seems to me best that you decide what is to be done, for I think my daughter will gain from this good offer."

R: And so both marriages were agreed upon.

I: Arnórr settled at Uppsalir and Þorgrímr at Mǫðrufell. A short time after these events Gizurr died. His wife Saldís then moved to Uppsalir. Arnórr had a son with Þórdís who was called Steinólfr. Þorgrímr also had a boy who was called Arngrímr, who was promising in all things as he grew up.

With the end of this chain, the saga turns to the concerns of the succeeding generation.

The density of clusters in saga narrative lessens only when the saga story shifts focus from primarily social and economic issues to primarily personal and ethical matters. Although a fuller discussion of the effect of personal issues appears in chapter 10, it is useful here to mention the categories of sagas that do not rely on clusters as a means of composition, for by understanding cluster development as the norm, the critic can begin to build typologies. For instance, poets' sagas, like those of Gunnlaugr, Hallfreðr, and Kormákr, are built around largely personal issues such as unrequited love. In these tales the action constantly moves back and forth between conflicts and resolutions but the feudemes, instead of appearing with usual saga density, are spread out and lavishly embroidered with detail. One reason for this difference in narrative arrangement is that the progression of action in the poets' sagas does not pivot on the workings of brokerage and arbitration. These major forms of advocacy are based in the social and economic system, whereas insulting verse, which causes feuds for the poets, is not only highly personal and illegal but has about it an aspect of petty, vindictive criminality.

From the texts it is clear that few brokers or arbitrators were willing to risk their honor and prestige in taking on the defense of a poet who, rather than feuding over land and status, maligns the honor of others for reasons of personal satisfaction. The defense of such a man starts out with little hope of success and offers small chance of profit or of gaining other supporters. Further, publicly confronting the insulted husband or his kinsmen might be dangerous. Partly for these reasons, and partly as a result of their own psychological makeup, the poets usually do not try to settle their feuds but carry with them the mixed emotions of a wounded heart until they die. Because the poets do not bring others into their quarrels through brokerage or arbitration, the resolution of conflict is a private issue between antagonists who must settle their quarrel without availing themselves of the mechanisms for conflict management which otherwise come into play when the social or economic equilibrium of the community is threatened. In a manner not altogether dissimilar from the poets, outlaws such as Gísli and Grettir are also presented as being out of sync with the normative codes of Icelandic society. To such men the services of brokers and arbitrators are usually not available.

Along with the poets' and the outlaws' sagas, *Hrafnkels saga Freysgoða* is a narrative marked by little density of clusters, perhaps because both its formal and its social characteristics set it apart from the majority of sagas about feuding in Iceland. The story turns on an untypical offer of brokerage which includes an unusual folk motif, a princely figure rescuing the downtrodden. The feud progresses according to feudemes but, instead of following closely upon one another, the feudemes are separated by unusually elaborate segments of description and characterization. Apparently the sagaman was strongly influenced by

Christian teachings.[4] He may well have been innovative in the type of tale he was telling, for, in a manner unusual for a saga of feud set in Iceland, the energy of the tale is often concentrated in the embroidery rather than in stark action. It is noteworthy that *Hrafnkels saga* has struck many nineteenth- and twentieth-century critics as an exceptionally successful narrative. The uncluttered flow of its prose, and its intriguing and unsagalike glimpses into the "heart and mind" of its characters, have inspired more than one comparison of this tale with two different written genres, the modern short story and medieval hagiography. It is not surprising, then, to see why the Icelandic school of bookprose used Sigurður Nordal's study of *Hrafnkels saga* as a cornerstone in its theoretical position that the family sagas were not a traditional oral story form.[5]

[4]Hermann Pálsson discusses this probability in his short monograph, *Art and Ethics in Hrafnkels saga* (Copenhagen: Munksgaard, 1971). See also Pálsson's *Hrafnkels saga og Freysgyðlingar* (Reykjavík: Hólar, 1962).

[5]Sigurður Nordal, *Hrafnkatla*, Studia Islandica (Íslenzk fræði) 7 (Reykjavík: Ísafoldarprentsmiðja H. F., 1940). The English version is R. George Thomas, trans., *Hrafnkels saga Freysgoða: A Study* (Cardiff: University of Wales Press, 1958). Although Nordal stresses that he is referring specifically to *Hrafnkels saga*, his colleagues had no qualms about extending his conclusions to the entire genre. See, for example Jón Jóhannesson's introduction to *Hrafnkels saga* in Íslenzk fornrit 11. p. xl.

8 The Importance of Land in Saga Feud

Wise men have also said that Iceland became fully settled in sixty winters, so that no additional settlements were made thereafter. At about this time, Hrafn the son of the *landnámsmaðr* Ketill hœngr became lawspeaker [ca. 930].

— Ari inn fróði (*Íslendingabók*, ch. 3)

One of the most readily apparent ways whereby new societies differ from old ones is that new societies know their origins and how they came into being and old ones do not. This knowledge assumes major importance in the history and mythology of a new nation. One of the first tasks of new nations is to develop unifying myths, a sense of national distinctiveness and nationhood. Americans celebrate the landing of the first pilgrim settlers and the taming of the West, Afrikaners revere the "trekboers" who conquered and occupied the wilderness of South Africa during the eighteenth century, and Argentines respect the freedom of the pampas typified above all by the gauchos. Icelanders celebrate the founding of Icelandic society and the early history of their island, particularly the century around 930–1030 known in Icelandic chronology as the Saga Age.

— Richard Tomasson

Two fundamental questions concerning saga feud must be addressed: (1) Why is land so frequently a source of dispute in saga literature? (2) How is the feudemic technique of prose composition wedded to the movement of medieval Icelandic legal, societal, and economic forces? There is more here than initially meets the eye, for the laws surrounding landownership were complex, and the often circuitous means by which land changed hands necessitated feud both to initiate and to maintain land claims.

Because land and its produce were in short supply in medieval Iceland, it is not surprising that both these forms of wealth should recur as subjects for conflict throughout the family sagas, the Sturlunga sagas, and *Landnámabók*. Approximately sixty years after the settlement began, or about 930, all of Iceland's productive land had been claimed; from that time on, the amount of land available for growing and grazing was not merely fixed, but it even began to decrease. Because the first *landnámsmenn* were unaware of the limitations placed on habitation by the climate, some of the settlers established farms either too far inland or at too high an elevation. Unprotected from the cold winds, or too far from the warmth generated by coastal waters, many initial settlements were abandoned as the years passed and have remained uninhabitable to this day.[1]

Even in the habitable coastal regions and in the nearby low-lying valleys, the amount of productive land decreased after a few generations. The need for firewood and building materials, coupled with destructive overgrazing, soon loosened the virgin topsoil and started a cycle of wind and water erosion which has continued to this day. The inhospitable interior of the island precluded internal expansion; thus, with the rare exception of the one-time colonization of Greenland in 985 or 986, Icelanders had no open territory to move into and develop. As a result the society turned in on itself, a fact that heightened the competition

[1] Jón Jóhannesson, *Íslendinga saga: A History of the Old Icelandic Commonwealth*, trans. Haraldur Bessason (Winnipeg: University of Manitoba Press, 1974), p. 33, names, among many other abandoned areas around the country, Þórsmörk, Einhyrningsmörk, and the upper part of Rangárvellir in Rangárvallasýsla, Þjórsárdalur and Hrunamannaafréttur in Árnessýsla, Geitland in Borgarfjörður, and Langavatnsdalur in Mýrasýsla. Jóhannesson also states that about a fourth of the 600 farmsteads mentioned in *Landnámabók* have been deserted for centuries.

for the island's already limited resources. The needs of the population, along with the finite amount of productive land available, meant that the unutilized property available at any one time was minimal. In Iceland, control of family land was almost the only viable long-term source of income, whereas in other medieval societies tracts of unused land were often available for internal development, or ambitious people could capitalize on the possibility of generating wealth through participation in town life, industry, trade, a military career, or foreign colonization.

The acquisition of land in Iceland was a process that had an especially predatory stamp. A man who wished to increase his wealth would usually have to take all or part of another man's property. In recognition of this harsh reality, landholdings were jealously guarded by families and normally transferred by inheritance. At times a parcel of land would be conveyed as payment for acts of brokerage or put up for sale on the open market, but even these transactions frequently assume an air of contention in the sagas.

Saga selection 3 from *Laxdœla saga* narrates a segment of feud in which the reality of limited resources plays a significant role. Bolli Þorleiksson and his new wife Guðrún want to have a farm of their own; they have been living at the farm Laugar (hot springs) with Guðrún's family, a family that itself, according to the saga, needs more land. Ósvífr, Guðrún's father and head of the family, learns of an opportunity to buy a farm close to Laugar from Þórarinn, with whom Ósvífr has already had land dealings (ch. 32). Bolli and Guðrún are sent off to buy the valuable farm Tunga in Sælingsdalr. Þórarinn wishes to move from the region because he sees a feud brewing between the foster brothers Kjartan Óláfsson and Bolli. As he has connections with both sides, he wants to avoid entanglement in the growing quarrel. Kjartan, hearing about Bolli's purchase of Tunga, acts quickly to nullify it. He tells Þórarinn that the property transaction he just concluded in a gentlemanly manner with Bolli is not legal. According to *Grágás* (Ib,

80), a sale of land, to be binding, must be formalized by *handsal*, a ceremony that normally requires twelve witnesses. Kjartan arrogantly gives Þórarinn a choice: either sell to him instead of to Bolli or remain on the land. Kjartan has come prepared with eleven men, enough to threaten Þórarinn and to witness the new sale to which Þórarinn now agrees. The repercussions of Kjartan's actions are more serious than if he had simply insulted Bolli and Guðrún. Kjartan has blocked one of the young couple's few available avenues to prosperity and has severely limited the future wealth of Ósvífr's children, while at the same time increasing his own authority by demonstrating his control over the limited opportunity to acquire land in the community.

Although the medieval audience presumably had sympathy for Kjartan, who has been betrayed in love by Bolli and Guðrún, he is, as Þórarinn points out, acting immoderately. Kjartan's actions within the context of Icelandic feud have the quality of being *ójafnaðr* and result in disquieting social and economic ramifications. A consideration of the geography of Breiðafjarðardalir, the valleys at the end of Breiðafjǫrðr, helps to assess Kjartan's conduct more accurately. Þórarinn's farm Tunga in Sælingsdalr is a bit more than a kilometer away from Laugar, where Ósvífr's family bases its influence. In fact, Tunga is just across from Laugar in the same valley. On the other hand, Kjartan's family lands at Hjarðarholt (Herd's wood) and Goddastaðir lie about 17 kilometers in a straight line to the south in Laxárdalr (the Salmon River Valley), where Kjartan's grandfather Hǫskuldr Dala-Kollsson and his father Óláfr pái established the family's wealth and influence. It is not unreasonable for Kjartan to buy a piece of property at this distance from his family land, but it is provocative for him to block such an obviously advantageous purchase to the people at Laugar.

The nature of Kjartan's actions may also be judged by Þórarinn's statement when he realizes that he is being threatened, "costly to me are the master's words in this matter" (ch. 47). Þórarinn's use of the word *dróttinn* (lord, master) to address Kjartan is marked by sarcasm. Kjartan is not even a *goði*, but if he were the word is still out of place, for it is almost never used to describe an Icelander. *Dróttinn* is usually reserved for ruling princes of foreign lands, such as the king of Norway, or for God.

Kjartan is protected by his father Óláfr, a calm and politically astute patriarchal figure. In this way Kjartan assumes a role not dissimilar to that of Gunnarr or Skarpheðinn in *Njáls saga*. Both these men are spirited and rash in their dealings with others, but they are able to rely upon the brokering and the advice of the sagacious Njáll.

Underlying the narration of Kjartan's feud is the evidence that he is acting in an unrestrained manner by encouraging enmity in the district over an irreversible event: Guðrún's marriage to his cousin Bolli. The feud falls into the pattern of an overbearing aspiring leader creating havoc in a district. Although goaded, Kjartan oversteps the bounds of permissible action. He acts as a man who allows his desire for the humiliation of his opponent to overshadow his responsibility to act with a degree of restraint. He refuses to accept the overtures of compromise made both by his father and by Bolli; instead, he presses for the political destruction of his foster brother and cousin. By following the clusters and chains in this section of the saga, one sees that the story has a striking similarity to feuds where a temperate man, in this case Bolli, is pushed to the extremes of violence by an *ójafnaðarmaðr*. Bolli is not able to restrain the menacing behavior of Kjartan; nor is he able to control the anger of Guðrún and her brothers. Kjartan is killed because the more passive antagonist Bolli is finally goaded by Guðrún's family to seek vengeance.

Because Kjartan is motivated by passion, rather than by greed, he is a more empathetic figure than most of those who conduct themselves in this overbearing manner. Nevertheless, the pattern in the narrative which includes

Kjartan's death and the ensuing settlement is similar to the patterns of incidents surrounding the death of Brodd-Helgi in *Vápnfirðinga saga* and the death of Arnkell goði in *Eyrbyggja saga*. In both instances the settlement does not befit a man of stature. The killer often gets off easily in the legal settlement, even though blood vengeance and further disruption usually follow the killing of a leader. At this point in feud, as members of the society are primarily interested in stabilizing power within the district, mediators step in.

The conditions of rural life in their country gave medieval Icelanders a ready understanding of the issues of property rights and local politics. From the wealth of details with which the sagaman surrounded such issues, it is likely that the medieval audiences followed closely the intricacies of tales such as Qzurr hvíti's from *Landnámabók* or Kjartan's from *Laxdœla saga* in which the wealth and status of families are at stake.

Heightening the medieval Icelanders' concern with feud over property was the fact that much of the valuable land was held through a system of allodial-type landownership.[2] According to this custom, land remained closely connected with the family that originally owned it. The integrity of

[2]Scholars generally agree on the importance of allodial holdings, but it should be noted that the exact nature and the scope of the practice are not clearly stated in the legal sources. Björn Þorsteinsson and Sigurður Líndal, "Lögfesting konungsvalds," *Saga Íslands*, vol. 3, ed. Sigurður Líndal (Reykjavík: Hið íslenzka bókmenntafélag, sögufélagið, 1978), pp. 77–79, stress the importance of allodial landholding. They point out that from the *landbrígðaþáttr* of *Grágás* one may unequivocally (*ótvírætt*) determine that the original settlers, the *landnámsmenn*, understood the fundamental concept of Norwegian allodial practices. Without doubting these findings, one should, nevertheless, point out that in *Grágás*, at least as it is preserved in the thirteenth-century texts, the term *óðal* (ancestral, allodial property) is not used. On the other hand, the term *aðalból*, which means head estate or hereditary family farm, is spoken of in connection with matters of inheritance (*GG* Ib, 150; II, 226). See also Magnús Már Lárusson, "Odelsrett, Island," *Kulturhistoriskt lexikon för nordisk medeltid*, vol. 12 (Malmö: Allhems förlag, 1967), cols. 499–502, and "Á höfuðbólum landsins," *Saga* 9 (1971):40–90. Sveinbjörn Rafnsson, *Studier i Landnámabók* (Lund: Gleerup, 1974), emphasizes the concept of *aðalból* or *höfuðból* as refer-

family land was guarded by the traditional practice whereby the individual was not free on his own to alienate his property from the family—that is, to sell, exchange, or give it away—unless the expectant heirs agreed to the transfer. Since transfer agreements were often disadvantageous to the heirs, their consent was difficult to obtain. If the family was unimportant and its land of small value, a powerful man would probably have had little trouble bypassing the heirs' claims and acquiring the property. If, however, the land in question was valuable, perhaps even a *staðr* or an *aðalból* (a sizable estate), the heirs would not give up their hopes of ownership easily. Sveinbjörn Rafnsson has argued that allodial-type restrictions made it possible for land to be reclaimed by descendants of the original owner at any time, unless the present possessor could actually prove that he or his ancestors had acquired it in a perfectly legal manner.[3] As a result, the history of ancestors and their possessions was often essential information if the social and economic ramifications of later feuds were to be understood.

These aspects of Icelandic landownership explain in part why so many of the sagas open with extensive histories and

ring to an estate similar to the continental manor. See also A. Ya. Gurevich (Gurevič), "Wealth and Gift-Bestowal among the Ancient Scandinavians," *Scandinavica* 7 (1968):126–138, and "Représentations et attitudes à l'égard de la propriété pendant le haut moyen âge, "*Annales: Économies, sociétés, civilisations*, 27, 3 (1972):523–547, and "Edda and Law: Commentary upon Hyndloliðð," *Arkiv för nordisk filologi* 88 (1973):77–83.

[3]In Part Three of *Studier i Landnámabók*, Rafnsson plausibly argues that the purpose of *Landnámabók* was to verify the actual twelfth- and thirteenth-century possession of land. Rafnsson points out that verification was necessary because of the allodial nature of property ownership. In *Saga og samfund*, P. M. Sørensen also asserts that later heirs had the opportunity to reclaim family property and notes the possible connection of *Landnámabók* and genealogical lists with this practice: "Som antydet ovenfor [on p. 28] kan de lange slægtsrækker i *Landnámabók* også have haft en anden funktion. Der var i islandsk lov uindskrænket vindikationsret, dvs. adgang til at kræve ejendom tilbage, hvis den kunne bevises, at den på et eller andet tidspunkt i fortiden var blevet overdraget eller solgt til andre end de retmæssige ejere eller arvinger. Især for de

genealogies. In some instances, as in *Laxdœla saga*, background information fills more than a quarter of the saga, chronicling the descent of families and their lands. At times such passages provided the audience with background information for the action of individuals who were involved in a feud, whether they were aiding others, defending their own rights and property, or attempting to add to their wealth and status. The heart of many saga feuds lies within a setting of aggressive individuals trying to get at the family lands of others. The ambitious man, especially a *goði*, circumvented the technical complication of the heirs' rights by creating confusion as to just which heir should inherit. The process for a nonfamily member was to acquire a family member's claim, usually by purchase or as payment for the services of a broker. For example, in saga selection 7 from *Eyrbyggja saga*, Þórólfr bægifótr transfers to Snorri goði the ownership of a valuable woodland in return for Snorri's aid in a legal case. Arnkell goði, Þórólfr's heir, was not consulted about this conveyance. Later in the saga Arnkell makes it known that he does not recognize the legality of the transfer of this part of his inheritance. He calls it a case of *arfskot* (fraud or cheating in matters of inheritance), and Snorri and Arnkell dispute the ownership of the property which by then has come under Snorri's control.

An outsider who had acquired a tenuous claim to land that rightly belonged to someone else would next move to take physical possession of the property. The title would then be clouded, the party in possession having the stronger claim. At this juncture all the aspects of Icelandic feud, especially brokerage, arbitration, and different forms

---

jordbesiddende har genealogien altså haft vigtig juridisk funktion" (pp. 33–34). However, as pointed out in n. 2 above, although the concept of maintaining the integrity of family property appears to have been firmly entrenched, the lawbooks offer only sketchy proof. This is an area in which much scholarly work remains to be done.

of resolution, came into play as the new claimant tested the strength of the original family members to see if they had the means and the support to retake the land. Such a ploy was obviously a dangerous, but a necessary, way to acquire land. It is the way Atli Hásteinsson proceeded in the passage from *Landnámabók* (see chap. 7). Qzurr's heirs were plagued by the denial of patrimonial rights, and it fell to the outcome of a blood feud to determine the ownership of the land given to their freedman Bǫðvarr. The ploy is similar to the one Einarr Þorgilsson uses in his attempt to acquire Heinaberg in *Sturlu saga*. Through the same device, Arnkell goði acquires Úlfarsfell and Ørlygsstaðir in *Eyrbyggja saga*, and Eyjólfr Hallsson lays claim to Helgastaðir in *Guðmundar saga dýra*. This maneuver may indeed be one of the principal ways in which powerful men and families, throughout Iceland's medieval centuries, amassed more and more property until, by the thirteenth century, some families had become extremely wealthy. Because the scenario for land acquisition turns up repeatedly in the sagas, it is enlightening to consider more closely the underlying legal aspects of such a story. For instance, the legal issues inherent in the initial conflict in the *Landnámabók* passage over Bǫðvarr's land are clearly defined in *Grágás*: If a freed slave dies without direct issue, any lands given him by the manumitter are to revert to the estate of that person (*GG* Ia, 227, 247; II, 72–73). Although slavery had long ceased to exist by the thirteenth century, when the extant lawbooks were written, the legal aspects of slavery, especially those that concerned matters of property, remained current knowledge. By the thirteenth century descendants of slaves and freemen had so thoroughly intermarried that such entries did much to clarify the origins of inherited property. As a result, the *handsal* transaction by which an outsider, such as Atli, gained a claim to land that was clearly the property of others would have been easily recognizable to the thirteenth-century audience, as it is to a modern reader of *Grágás*, as a case of *arfskot* (*GG* Ia,

247–249; II, 85–87, 100, 127). The instance of *arfskot* from the *Landnámabók* passage and the feud that it inspired take place in one small region of the Southern Quarter. Yet this incident and the series of feud events that follow are similar, for instance, to an *arfskot* and resultant feud in *Eyrbyggja* saga (chs. 30–31) which, taking place on the Snæfells Peninsula in the Western Quarter, concern entirely different characters. The feudemes in the *Eyrbyggja saga* passage are arranged in the following clusters, the last of which is found in saga selection 7.

Cluster 1:
I: Þórólfr bægifótr is reintroduced. He has become *ójafnaðarfullr* (full of *ójafnaðr*).

T/I: Þórólfr rides to the farm Úlfarsfell to find the *bóndi* Úlfarr. Úlfarr (a freedman) is an excellent farmer. He is skilled at growing hay and his livestock thrive.

Ab: Þórólfr asks advice about farmwork. Úlfarr tells him about his own plans and gives Þórólf advice about when to mow.

T/I: Þórólfr returns home. The weather turns out as Úlfarr said it would.

I: Þórólfr and Úlfarr, who jointly own a meadow, cut, dry, and pile their hay in the field. Þórólfr, thinking the dry period is about to end, decides to have the hay brought in.

T/I: Þórólfr and his slaves go up to the ridge and the hay is brought in.

I: Úlfarr considers the weather and decides to wait another day before bringing in his hay from the field.

T/Ai: Úlfarr sends a man up on the ridge. Þórólfr has already brought in his hay and is taking Úlfarr's as well. Úlfarr's man reports the theft to Úlfarr.

T/C: Úlfarr goes to the ridge and confronts Þórólfr. When he realizes that they will come to blows, Úlfarr leaves.

Cluster 2:

T/Aᵇ: Úlfarr goes to see Arnkell goði, Þórólfr's son, and receives support.

T/C: Arnkell asks his father to make up to Úlfarr for the theft; instead, Þórólfr makes it clear that he would rather hurt Úlfarr.

Aⁱ/ᵍ: Arnkell passes this information to Úlfarr. Angered, Úlfarr goads Arnkell into taking a stronger stand.

R: Arnkell himself pays Úlfarr for the hay.

T/C: Arnkell goes again to Þórólfr, but the old man reacts more outrageously than before.

R: In the autumn Arnkell has seven of Þórólfr's oxen driven down the mountain and slaughtered so as to compensate himself for his previous payment to Úlfarr.

C: Þórólfr demands payment of equal value to the oxen from Arnkell, but Arnkell claims the oxen are to cover his loss. Þórólfr declares that this problem is all Úlfarr's doing and that the freedman will have to pay for the trouble.

Cluster 3:

Aᵇ: The following winter, during the Yule festivities, Þórólfr gets his slaves drunk, telling them that in return for burning Úlfarr in his house they will receive their freedom.

T/C: Six of the slaves go to Úlfarsfell and set the farmhouse on fire.

T/R: Arnkell and his guests are feasting at his home, Bólstaðr. They see the fire, rush over to Úlfarsfell, catch the slaves, and extinguish the blaze.

I: The buildings have not been seriously damaged.

R: The next day Arnkell takes the slaves to a promontory and has them hanged.

Aᵇ: In return for a *handsal* of all of Úlfarr's property, Arnkell becomes Úlfarr's *varnaðarmaðr* (protector).

C: The six sons of Þorbrandr, the manumitter of Úlfarr, who is childless, are angered by this *handsal*. They had planned to inherit their freedman's
property.

I: A coolness develops between Arnkell and the Þorbrandssons. They can no longer play ball together as
was their custom. Arnkell was the strongest at the
games and second-best was Freysteinn bófi, foster
child of Þorbrandr. Most people think Freysteinn is
the son of Þorbrandr by a bondswoman.

Cluster 4 (see saga selection 7):

C: Þórólfr is furious with Arnkell and demands
compensation for his slaves. Arnkell refuses.

T/A[b]: Þórólfr rides to Snorri goði's to get support.
Snorri at first refuses, but, after being offered the
forest Krákunes, which Þórólfr calls the greatest
treasure in the district, he changes his mind. He gives
Þórólfr support and takes the case.

T/I: Þórólfr then rode home and was well pleased with
himself, "but the bargain was not much liked by
other people."

As might be expected, the property transaction between
Úlfarr and Arnkell initiates a feud between the Þorbrandssons and Arnkell. Although Arnkell's legal claim to the
property is dubious if not fraudulent, he nevertheless maintains possession, first by acting as the guardian of Úlfarr
and then, after Úlfarr's death, by taking the land as Úlfarr's
heir. The feud is settled many killings later when Arnkell's
rival Snorri goði is goaded into aiding his thingmen, the
Þorbrandssons, in their killing of Arnkell.

Even when the line of inheritance was established and
there was no question of fraud, the transfer of land served
as a magnet for dispute in the sagas. In accordance with
Icelandic procedure, anyone who held even a scrap of a
claim when valuable property was passing to heirs might
bring an action to share in the estate. This practice initiated

a major feud in *Sturlu saga* (chs. 30–36). This feud, called the *Deildartungumál* (the Tunga affair, after one of the main properties), exemplifies the energy important people devoted to feuds over land at the end of the twelfth century. The narrative progresses by means of a dense clustering of feudemes, often repeating advocacy and attempts at resolution. The organization of the narrative is similar to that of feud stories from the family sagas, where, in most instances, a feud escalates from the original parties through advocates to even more powerful advocates, each sharing the potential for profit and loss. This particular feud in *Sturlu saga* is noteworthy for the amount of detail with which it is told and the insight it provides into the manner in which wealthy churchmen participated in feuds.

The feud begins when a man with large landholdings, the priest Þórir auðgi (the wealthy), his wife Þorlaug, and their one child die while abroad on a pilgrimage to Rome. The question arises whether the husband's or the wife's side will inherit the couple's property. As far as the law is concerned, the determining factor is the order of death, for the property falls to the heirs of the possessor who died last. More than one sagaman saw the possibilities that such a mundane but crucial issue offered to a saga of feud. For instance, in *Laxdœla saga* (ch. 18) a boat carrying members of Þorsteinn svarti's family overturns and everyone drowns except a man named Guðmundr. This lone survivor recounts the order of the deaths of Þorsteinn's family, but Þorsteinn's son-in-law Þorkell trefill (fringe) stands to profit by a different order. Þorkell convinces the survivor to change his story so that his own wife will inherit. The feud in *Sturlu saga*, however, blossoms without even a question of fraud. The all-important order of deaths was reliably reported in Norway by two separate individuals.

The news of the deaths of Þórir auðgi and his family was brought to Iceland in 1178 by the newly ordained bishop, Þorlákr Þórhallsson (bishop at Skálaholt, 1178–1193), who reported the information at the Althing. Since the wife,

Þorlaug, died last (hence without a living child), her father, Páll Sǫlvason, a priest and chieftain from Reykjaholt in the Western Quarter, stood to inherit everything. Páll publicly announced the deaths at the same Althing where the bishop first broadcast the news and made sure to point out that the husband had died first and next the boy. At this point, with all legal issues resolved, the feud erupts. The sister of Þórir auðgi feels that she should receive some of her dead brother's riches and turns to a kinsman, Bǫðvarr Þórðarson, and the dispute becomes a contest of strength: Can the sole legal heir hold onto his acquired property in the face of others who wish to take part of his claim? Both sides call in more and more supporters until, among others, Guðmundr dýri is aiding Páll while Bǫðvarr finds a major supporter in the aggressive and at times brutal parvenu, Sturla Þórðarson from Hvammr. (Sturla was the progenitor of the great thirteenth-century family named after him, the Sturlungar.)

Perhaps because of the large amount of wealth at stake and the possibilities for gain to the brokers, the feud drags on for years. At one Althing, the dispute is arbitrated by the powerful and respected chieftain Jón Loftsson, but Bǫðvarr, backed by Sturla, is not pleased with the proposed settlement. The next year at the Althing the case is again taken up, but no resolution is found. A reconciliation meeting at Páll's home at Reykjaholt is, however, set for the autumn. At this meeting the men sit in a field to the south of the house and discuss the issues. Páll and Bǫðvarr cannot agree, when suddenly Páll's wife Þorbjǫrg intervenes. Þorbjǫrg has a violent temper and is unable to control her anger against Sturla, who has become her husband's major antagonist. She thrusts a knife at Sturla, stating that she intends to make him one-eyed like Óðinn. Þorbjǫrg is grabbed before she achieves her goal, but Sturla receives a serious cheek wound. Instead of immediately giving vent to his anger, Sturla, a man famous for his cunning, controls himself and proceeds with exceptional moderation. With Sturla bleeding but remaining in the negotiations, a settlement is reached between Bǫðvarr and Páll over the inheritance. Páll gives in to most of Bǫðvarr's demands, granting him a third of Þórir auðgi's property.

Although the initial feud over Þórir auðgi's property has been settled, Sturla, who entered the case as a broker, now has a claim of his own against Páll. He has a right to demand compensation for the wound given him by Páll's wife, Þorbjǫrg. Páll's friends, aware of the danger in leaving Sturla's injury uncompensated, urge the priest to grant Sturla *sjálfdœmi*. Although Páll is reluctant to follow this advice, other men persuade him that Sturla has already shown great moderation and, it is assumed, will continue to do so. This assumption turns out to be a gross miscalculation. By granting Sturla *sjálfdœmi*, Páll has placed himself in the power of a greedy man. Páll's misjudgment becomes evident the next spring when Sturla awards himself so huge a sum that it would exhaust the wealth of Páll's family. The subsequent choices that the priest Páll now gives to his sons reveal an aspect of feud which was familiar to Icelanders for centuries:

> Páll called his sons together to discuss the matter and inquired what path seemed to them best to choose. "Men will think that if this price is paid then all our money would go with it. The choice is now whether you wish alone to withstand the brunt of the difficulties that will come of Sturla's attacks and waylayings or whether you wish to seek the protection of others by the purchase of support through gifts of wealth." [ch. 33]

Páll's sons decide they will not give up their property without a fight. Páll then sends one of them south to Oddi to seek the aid of Jón Loftsson. Jón promises to support Páll insofar as he can. With Jón's entry into the dispute on Páll's side, Sturla's plan to take Páll's lands is disrupted, although he apparently doubts Jón's willingness to risk a fight with him for the sake of Páll. He sends Bǫðvarr to Jón's booth at the Althing with the message that some of

Páll's friends will lose their heads should Sturla suffer a reverse in this case. This time, however, Sturla has met his match. Jón has no intention of being bullied, and in no uncertain terms he lets Sturla know that he is altogether ready for a showdown. To Bǫðvarr he replies (ch. 33): " 'Men are aware that Sturla is often unrestrained in killing. But more men than Sturla know how to have someone killed. And this I say to you, Bǫðvarr, if Sturla has one of Páll's men killed, I shall have three of Sturla's men killed.' With this they ended their talk.''

In keeping with the standard mechanisms of dispute settlement, third parties now come between the two groups seeking to mediate a solution. At this point the sagaman allows Sturla to recount his own view of the feud. The result is a highly introspective summary of one side of the feud with glimpses into Sturla's supposed motivations and concepts of honor. Like the parable in *Þorgils saga ok Hafliða* (quoted in chap. 6), this story illustrates how the needs of the society dominated the needs of the individual. Like Hafliði sixty years before, Sturla in the end accepts compromise.

> Now a settlement was sought, and Sturla and his followers became aware that Jón intended to aid Páll staunchly at Bishop Brandr's request. Men negotiated between them, requesting that Sturla agree to Jón's judgment in the case and expressing the expectation that he would, through this, reap the greatest part of the honor. On the other hand, it was altogether unclear how things would go if they quarreled. They said that Sturla's side had broken the agreement that Jón had worked out in the Tunga affair, and in this way did him no honor. They also pointed out that this case could nonetheless be arranged even though it had been brought in an abominable manner.
>
> Then one day when most people were coming to the Law Rock, Sturla walked up to the breastwork in front of his booth. It was often his practice to make long speeches about his lawsuits, since the man was both intelligent and smooth-tongued. He also, as always, wanted his reputation to be

widely known. He now spoke: "Men will be aware of my lawsuit with Páll and of that dishonor which was intended for me if it had gone forward. And my luck, rather than the conduct of the case, was more the cause of what happened. Then an agreement in the suit was reached and self-judgment was granted to me by Páll. And now the noblest men in Iceland are sought out so that this suit, which earlier came up for self-judgment, should be placed in arbitration. If a precedent is found that men have done this before then it should be considered. But these men who now enter the case—I name first Jón Loftsson, who is the worthiest man in this land and the man to whom all appeal their cases—well, I don't know whether any other honor is now to be expected than in trying what honor he will grant me. Now it may be that I don't have the intelligence to look after my part in this, but I would want to preserve my honor."

Then Bishop Brandr answered: "No man questions your wits; you are rather suspected in regard to your good intentions."

Jón declared Sturla to be speaking wisely and to be taking many viewpoints into account. "But," said Jón, "for Páll's sake fines must lean toward moderation, since they were inflated and now men will have to deal with me and not with Páll." [ch. 34]

Sturla accepts Jón Loftsson's settlement and in so doing increases his stature; for his part, Jón makes a handsome gesture with far-reaching consequences for Icelandic politics in the thirteenth century and for the country's literature for all time: "But before the Althing ended Jón offered to foster Sturla's son and invited him and his son Snorri home to Oddi for the anniversary of the church there. Sturla accompanied the boy south and received noble gifts from Jón. The fines were greatly reduced." [ch. 34]

In 1181, when the two-year-old Snorri (d. 1241) was sent south to be fostered, Jón Loftsson's home at Oddi was Iceland's major center of learning. Jón was widely respected as the island's most cultured *goði*, a reputation he apparently cultivated. Jón's grandfather was Iceland's first scholastic historian, Sæmundr inn fróði (the wise) (1053–1133). In his youth Sæmundr had studied in Paris, probably in the school of Nôtre Dame, and was esteemed by later writers for his learning. Equally important, Jón was the grandson of King Magnús berfœttr (barelegs) (1093–1103). Jón's mother Þóra was the illegitimate daughter of this violent Norwegian ruler who died at the age of thirty. The men of Oddi, the Oddaverjar, were exceedingly proud of their royal link; Jón was fostered as a boy in Norway, where he tasted noble life. In the ambience of culture and scholarship at Oddi, Snorri learned the crafts by which he was to become the foremost Icelandic politician and one of the greatest sagamen.

9 Two Sets of Feud Chains in Njáls saga

Time now passed into winter, and Christmas was over. Flosi said to his men, "I now intend that we travel from home, for I think from here on we will have little respite. We ought now to go in search of support; and it will be proven true, as earlier I said to you, that we may have to crawl at the feet of many men before this case is over."

—*Njáls saga* (ch. 133)

N*jáls saga* is an intricate network of feud stories. In this chapter I look at two types of feud chains from *Njáls saga* which are representative of the ways feud chains are used in the family and Sturlunga sagas. Since the construction of chains is of primary concern in this chapter, I have excluded cluster divisions.

The first type is a support-seeking chain, composed chiefly of repetitious descriptions of advocacy, usually preceded by units of travel and information. The support-seeking chain forms part of an ongoing feud story by providing an extended link between a particularly serious offense and the attempts at resolution. The decision to employ such a chain is a matter of choice open to the sagaman. If in the telling of his tale he had chosen to move quickly through the brokerage mechanism in order to concentrate on other aspects of the saga, he could have substituted a single feudeme, or several feudemes, of advocacy in place of one or more support-seeking chains. The composer of *Njáls saga*, with his usual narrative skill, chose to do both. At times he elaborated and counterbalanced his narrative with expansive sets of chains; at other times he concentrated on developing the dramatic potential inherent in acts of conflict and resolution.

The second type of chain encompasses the basic elements of feud and forms a small feud in itself. Whole sections of sagas are made up of several of these small chains, interlocked and arranged one after the other until an often long and complex feud is narrated. An example is the quarrel between the two wives Hallgerðr and Bergþóra, a well-developed feud story in *Njáls saga* which might well have become the focal point of a saga in itself. Instead, in keeping with the sagaman's obvious decision to create a longer narrative, it was telescoped and inserted into *Njáls saga*.

Both series of chains are typical of saga construction. They rely on repetition of feudemes arranged in similar clusters and exhibit traditional saga development based on the recurrence of formal elements. The attributes that make these saga passages so valuable to a study of feud and narrative form are the very ones that have caused some modern critics to dismiss these repetitious passages as unnecessary and nonfunctional.

The series of support-seeking chains considered here describes the journeys taken by Flosi, the burner of Njáll and his sons, and his opponent Kári Sǫlmundarson, Njáll's son-in-law who escaped from Njáll's burning farmstead. In these travels (chs. 133–140) both Flosi and Kári gather support for the ensuing case at the Althing, and the chains of the journeys of both men are composed in similar ways. They consist of units of information and travel which combine with the action of advocacy in the form of brokerage to form clusters. The compositional strategy is quite simple. The sagaman repeatedly returns to the feudeme of advocacy, attaching information and descriptions of travel as the protagonists move first around the countryside from farm to farm and later from booth to booth at the Althing. In this way the sagaman draws into the legal case numbers of other men while at the same time focusing the attention of the audience on the coming confrontation in court.

Scholars who tend to find narrations of such travels within Iceland uninteresting have faulted the sagaman on his use of repetition. For instance, in his analysis of *Njáls saga*, Lars Lönnroth classifies the visits of travelers such as Flosi as "traditional episodes" and "stock scenes" and argues that most saga writers developed these

traditional episodes and stock scenes as if they were ends in themselves. These writers would, for example, repeat twenty times that their heroes were "received well" and "given good gifts" each time they visited someone even though the visits are insignificant and uninteresting to the saga as a whole. A force of habit, strengthened by the conventional expectations of the audience, encouraged the inclusion of unnecessary details. This is a weakness inherent in all oral literature and in many written works based on oral tradition. Although the author of *Njála* is more in command of his saga than most other sagawriters, he too suffers from this weakness. He is often much more circumstantial in his treatment of conventional motifs than is warranted by his own "blueprint" for the saga. Subordinate characters are often introduced with long genealogies. Actions easily summarized are presented in dramatic scenes as if the whole plot depended on them.[1]

In arriving at these conclusions Lönnroth ignores that repetitious visits are representative of an indigenous Icelandic type of saga journey, usually to brokers or to the Althing. Lönnroth instead concentrates on the journeys of Icelanders abroad, comparing them to the wanderings and

[1]Lars Lönnroth, *Njáls saga: A Critical Introduction* (Berkeley, Los Angeles, London: University of California Press, 1976), pp. 54–55.

quests of heroes in continental epics and folktales.[2] Rather than assume, as Lönnroth does in the above passage, that an often repeated feature of the literature is a "weakness," a more profitable tactic would be to consider why repetition is so prominent. The repetitions of visits to farmsteads in search of support stimulated the saga audience to assess the reasons for a character's success or failure. The assessment is rooted not so much in any single event in the lives of individuals as in the multitude of transactions and decisions narrated in the saga. A modern writer might have shortened the descriptions of the visits and instead told the results of the journey or examined the thoughts of the hero to indicate the outcome of the trip. The sagaman, however, repeats each leg of the journey in order to show how success comes little by little. The importance of such visits is to show how obligation is bartered. When a character has little or nothing to barter, the appeals for support are often glossed over, as in the story of the failed hero Gísli Súrsson (saga selection 4).

In the series of chains from *Njáls saga* which follow, there are distinctive differences in the methods Flosi Þórðarson and Kári Sǫlmundarson use to gain support on their journeys prior to the meeting of the Althing (see map 4). The unpolitical Kári counts on receiving support from those linked by blood or marriage ties to Njáll and, in a mistaken assessment, thinks he can rely on the justness of his case. On the other hand, Flosi, having committed a heinous crime, chooses to dramatize his position as a supplicant by walking rather than riding through the East Fjords. He visits important man after important man, calling in past obligations, buying support with money, and promising future bonds of friendship. If Flosi cannot gain support by kin bonds or reciprocity, he offers money; if that does not work, he tries goading and flattery. When he fails

[2]Ibid., pp. 71–76.

entirely, he turns to insults. The men Flosi visits are carefully chosen by the sagaman for their differing relationships to him; they represent the varied degrees of interest aroused in the society by his feud. What is significant in this sequence is the type of obligation called upon or created. The men whom Flosi visits are aware that he is an important leader who, though in a dangerous situation, has a strong possibility of succeeding.

Before he begins his walk, Flosi knows he can count on those who were bound to him before the burning, since the burners had previously sworn an oath that anyone withdrawing from the group would forfeit life and wealth. In alliance with Flosi were more than fifteen other leaders, including the Sigfússons, Gunnarr's son, two Lambasons who were cousins of the Sigfússons, Hróarr Hámundarson, and Ingjaldr from Keldur. At the last moment Ingjaldr was dissuaded from joining the burners by his sister; he was in the difficult, but typical, position of being related to both groups of antagonists. Similarly, the visits for support at times focus on the complexities of keeping political and kin ties separate. As support solidifies, many family members find themselves on opposite sides of the dispute or forced to support one party over the other because of a powerful kinsman's preference. Such divisions within a family are often part of the drama of support-seeking chains. For instance, the split that develops among the three children of the chieftain Brodd-Helgi as they are visited in turn by Flosi adds a small but significant source of tension to the tale. The relationship with Bjarni Brodd-Helgason is especially well detailed. Not only does Bjarni willingly offer his support but later, at the Althing, becomes Flosi's companion, and together the two men go from booth to booth seeking support for Flosi. As part of this relationship, Flosi knows that Bjarni will count on him for aid in the future rather than take immediate compensation.

As in *Vápnfirðinga saga*, where the deaths of Brodd-

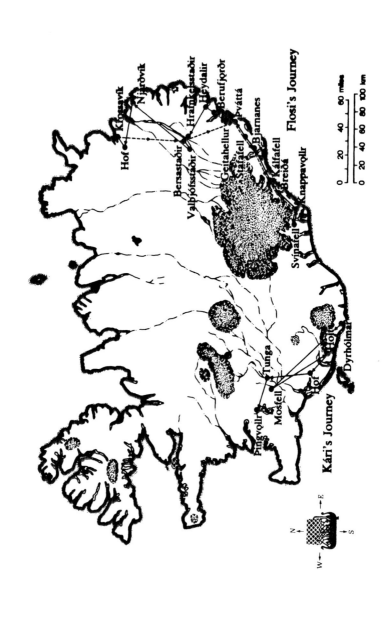

Hof
Kirkjubøur
Njarðvík
Hrafnkelsstaðir
Heydalir
Berufjørð
Þváttá
Bersastaðir
Valþjófsstaðir
Geitahellur
Stafafell
Bjarnanes
Kálfafell
Breiðá
Knappavøllr
Svinafell

Flosi's Journey

0   20   40   60 miles
0 20 40 60 80 100 km

Tunga
Mosfell
Hof
Lón
Dyrhólmar
Þingvøllr

Kári's Journey

N
W ——— E
S

Helgi and Geitir are prefigured in portents, Flosi dreams of the deaths of his supporters (ch. 133) before he sets out on his journey in search of support. Similar metaphysical explanations of events are found throughout the sagas, for instance, in the passages given below where Bjarni Brodd-Helgason foresees the death of any man who acts as Flosi's lawyer and Snorri goði confirms the danger (ch. 138).

The support-seeking chains begin with the passage (ch. 133) quoted at the head of this chapter. In Flosi's long search for support in the East Fjords, conflict comes into play only twice, once when Flosi is refused aid by Sǫrli Brodd-Helgason and retaliates with insults. The sagaman could have picked up this conflict later in the tale, but he does not. The second incident of conflict is Ásgrímr Elliða-Grímsson's attempt to kill Flosi when Flosi, flushed with the success of his journey in the East Fjords, pays a sudden insulting visit to this determined supporter of Kári. Again this specific conflict is left without development. What follows is the text of the saga (ch. 134), divided according to feudemic occurrences.

Map 4. Journeys described in *Njáls saga* as Flosi Þórðarson and Kári Sǫlmundarson prepare for the court case after the burning.

Flosi's journey beginning at his home, Svínafell: 1—Knappavǫllr; 2—Breiðá (Qzurr Hróaldsson, related to Síðu-Hallr); 3—Kálfafell (Kolr Þorsteinsson, related to Síðu-Hallr); 4—Bjarnanes; 5—Stafafell (Starkaðr, Flosi's nephew); 6—Þváttá (Síðu-Hallr); 7—Geitahellur; 8—Heydalir (Hallbjǫrn inn sterki); 9—Hrafnkelsstaðir (Hrafnkell Þórisson); 10—Bersastaðir (Hólmsteinn Spak-Bersason); 11—Valþjófsstaðir (Sǫrli Brodd-Helgason); 12—Njarðvík (Þorkell fullspakr and Þorvaldr Ketilsson); 13—Hof (Bjarni Brodd-Helgason); 14—Krossavík (Þorkell Geitisson); 15—Bersastaðir (Hólmsteinn Spak-Bersason); 16—Þváttá (Síðu-Hallr); 17—Svínafell.

Kári's journey beginning at his home, Dyrhólmar: 1—Mosfell (Gizurr hvíti Teitsson); 2—Holt (Þorgeirr skorargeirr); 3—Hof (Mǫrðr Valgarðsson); 4—Tunga (Ásgrímr Elliða-Grímsson).

Chain 1: Flosi's travels.

I: Afterward they all prepared to leave [from Flosi's home at Svínafell]. Flosi was wearing breeches with stockings attached to them because he intended to walk and he knew that then the others would mind walking less.

T: They traveled first to Knappavǫllr, reached Breið River the next evening, and from there continued on to Kálfafell, in Lón, and from there to Þvátt River to see Hallr of Síða.

I: Flosi was married to Hallr's daughter, Steinvǫr. Hallr received them exceptionally well [*allvel*].[3]

A[b]: Flosi said to Hallr: "I want to ask, father-in-law, that you and all of your thingmen ride to the Althing with me." Hallr replied: "Now it has happened as in the saying, that the hand rejoices in a blow only a short time. And those very same men are in your company, now hanging their heads, who earlier had urged the worst deeds. But I am obligated to give my support, all that I am able." Flosi asked: "What do you advise me to do now, as things stand?" "You shall travel all the way north to Vápnafjǫrðr," Hallr answered, "and ask all the leaders for support. And you will need them all before the Althing comes to an end."

I: Flosi stayed there three days and rested.

T: From there he traveled east to Geitahellur and on to Berufjǫrðr, where he and his men remained overnight. From there they traveled east to Heydalir in Breiðdalr.

I: Hallbjǫrn inn sterki [the strong] lived there. He was married to Oddný, the sister of Sǫrli Brodd-Helgason. Flosi was well received there [*góðar viðtǫkur*]. Hallbjǫrn inquired closely about the details

---

[3]"Hallr tók við þeim allvel." This could also be translated, "Hallr received them with great warmth."

of the burning, and Flosi told him clearly about everything. Hallbjǫrn asked how far north Flosi intended to go in the fjords. He said his intent was to go to Vápnafjǫrðr.

A^b: Flosi then took a bag of money from his belt and said he wanted to give it to Hallbjǫrn. Hallbjǫrn took the money, but said that he was owed no gifts by Flosi—"nevertheless, I want to know how you want me to repay this." "I don't need money," said Flosi, "but I would like you to ride to the Althing with me and support my case, even though I have no kinship claim on you, either by blood or by marriage." Hallbjǫrn replied: "I'll promise to ride to the thing and support your case, as I would if you were my brother." Flosi thanked him.

T: From there Flosi rode to Breiðdalsheiðr and then on to Hrafnkelsstaðir.

I: Hrafnkell lived there. He was the son of Þórir, the son of Hrafnkell, the son of Hrafn. Flosi was well received there [*góðar viðtǫkur*].

A^b: Flosi asked Hrafnkell to ride to the Althing and support him. Hrafnkell refused for a long time, but eventually he promised that his son Þórir would ride with all their thingmen and would grant the same support as the three *goðar* in the district. Flosi thanked him.

T: Flosi left and continued on to Bersastaðir.

I: Hólmsteinn, the son of Spak-Bersi, lived there. He received Flosi exceptionally well [*allvel*].

A^b: Flosi asked him for support. Hólmsteinn said that he had long ago earned his support.

T: From there Flosi and his men traveled to Valþjófsstaðir.

I: Sǫrli Brodd-Helgason, the brother of Bjarni, lived there. He was married to Þórdís, the daughter of Guðmundr inn ríki from Mǫðruvellir. They were received well [*góðar viðtǫkur*].

A[b]: In the morning Flosi hinted to Sǫrli that he might ride to the Althing with him. Flosi offered Sǫrli money to do so. "I can't decide that," Sǫrli said, "while I still don't know where Guðmundr inn ríki, my father-in-law, stands on this matter, because I intend to support him, whichever party he sides with."

C: Flosi said: "I see by your answer that here you are under woman's rule." After this, Flosi stood up and told his men to take their clothes and weapons.

T/I: They departed and received no support there.

T: They traveled below Lake Lagarfljót and across the heath to Njarðvík.

I: Two brothers lived there, Þorkell fullspakr [the sage] and Þorvaldr; they were the sons of Ketill þrymr, the son of Þiðrandi inn spaki [the wise], the son of Ketill þrymr, the son of Þórir þiðrandi; the mother of Þorkell fullspakr and Þorvaldr was Yngvildr, the daughter of Þorkell fullspakr. Flosi was well received there [*góðar viðtǫkur*].

A[b]: He told them the details of his business and asked for support, but they refused until he gave each of them three marks of silver for their backing. Then they agreed to stand by Flosi.

I: Yngvildr, their mother, was present. She wept when she heard them promise to ride to the Althing. "Why are you crying, mother?" asked Þorkell. She replied: "I dreamed that Þorvaldr your brother was wearing a red tunic, and it seemed to me that he was wearing red hose wrapped with shabby ribbons. I thought ill of it to see that he was so uncomfortable, but I could do nothing about it." They laughed and called it nonsense, saying that her babblings would not stand in the way of their ride to the Althing. Flosi thanked them well.

T: From there he journeyed to Vápnafjǫrð, and they came to Hof.

I: There lived Bjarni Brodd-Helgason, the son of Þorgils, the son of Þorsteinn inn hvíti, the son of Qlvir, the son of Eyvaldr, the son of Øxna-Þórir[Oxen-Þórir]. Bjarni's mother was Halla, the daughter of Lýtingr; Brodd-Helgi's mother was Ásvǫr, the daughter of Þórir, the son of Graut-Atli [Gruel-Atli], the son of Þórir þiðrandi. Bjarni Brodd-Helgason was married to Rannveig, the daughter of Þorgeirr, the son of Eiríkr of Goðdalir, the son of Geirmundr, the son of Hróaldr, the son of Eiríkr ǫrðigskeggi [bristle-beard]. Bjarni received Flosi with open arms [*með báðum hǫndum*].

Aᵇ: Flosi offered Bjarni money to support him. Bjarni said: "Never have I sold my valor nor my support for a bribe. And now when you need a following, I will ride to the Althing out of friendship and support you as I would my brother." "Now you are putting all the obligation back into my hands," replied Flosi, "although I had expected this from you."

T: After this Flosi traveled to Krossavík.

I: Þorkell Geitisson was from before a great friend of Flosi's.

Aᵇ: Flosi told him his errand. Þorkell declared that it was his duty to support him in such a manner as he was capable of, and that he would not turn him away in this difficulty. Þorkell gave Flosi good gifts at their parting.

T: Then Flosi traveled south from Vápnafjǫrðr and up into the Fljótsdalr district.

I: He stayed at Hólmsteinn Spak-Bersason's and said that everyone had backed him in his need except Sǫrli Brodd-Helgason. Hólmsteinn said that was because he was no man for violence. Hólmsteinn gave Flosi good gifts.

T: Flosi traveled up Fljótsdalr and from there went south across the mountains by Øxarhraun [lava], then down Sviðinhornadalr and out along the west side of Álptafjǫrðr. He continued on without stopping until he came to the place of his father-in-law, Hallr, at Þvátt River.

I: Flosi and his men stayed there for half a month and rested.

A^b: Flosi asked Hallr how he should proceed and how he should handle his affairs. Hallr said: "I advise that you and the Sigfússons stay at your farm and that they send men to put their households in order. For now, ride home. But when you ride to the Althing, ride all together and don't disperse your company; the Sigfússons should at that time see their wives. I will also ride to the Althing with Ljótr, my son, and with all our thingmen and will give you such support as I am able." Flosi thanked him and Hallr gave him good gifts at their parting.

T/I: Flosi then left Þvátt River. And there is nothing to tell of his journey until he arrived home at Svínafell. He now stayed home for the rest of the winter and the following summer until it was time for the Althing.

Once the sagaman has chronicled Flosi's journey, he turns to Kári, Flosi's opponent, who also undertakes a series of visits to powerful men. Unlike Flosi, Kári has to be told to seek support. He is not a native Icelander and apparently is unfamiliar with the intricacies of the Icelandic system of brokering support. Kári is a Hebridean war leader who rescued two of Njáll's sons from viking marauders off the coast of Scotland; later, after coming to visit the Njálssons, he remained in Iceland and married one of Njáll's daughters. Kári's position as Njáll's son-in-law is his only kin relationship in Iceland, and he relies upon two chieftains, the kinsmen Gizurr hvíti and Gizurr's nephew Ásgrímr Elliða-Grímsson, to put together a legal action. These *goðar* arrange for Gizurr's son-in-law Mǫrðr Valgarðsson and Ásgrímr's son Þórhallr, both lawyers, to direct the case. One major difference between Flosi's and Kári's journeys is that Flosi actively seeks to cement new alliances, whereas Kári visits only those who are already in his corner (Gizurr hvíti, Þorgeirr skorargeirr Þórisson, and Ásgrímr Elliða-Grímsson) and Mǫrðr Valgarðsson, who we know in advance will be forced to join the proceedings against the burners. In constrast with the crafty dealings of Flosi, Kári tells the story of the burning and makes his allies aware of the threat posed by the success of Flosi's swing through the East Fjords. The result is that the sagaman, though relying on similar formal elements to construct these diverse support-seeking journeys, was nevertheless free to develop a sharp contrast between two very dissimilar men with two very different approaches to acquiring the support of others. The importance of this contrast is perceived, and an insight into the sophistication of sagas as a genre is gained, when we remember that neither of the antagonists is a villain. On the contrary, both leaders, as well as their modi operandi, are honorable.

In the following passages, although they are as tightly constructed in the narrative as Flosi's travel sequence, I have summarized the text to avoid quoting long segments of narrative. Through the alternation of these six chains, the sagaman interlocks the journeys of Flosi and Kári. As he involves more and more people in the coming event, he constantly builds tension. In this way he constructs an entire narrative segment of support seeking which fills seven modern chapter divisions in the saga.

Chain 2: (ch. 135) Kári's travels.
　　T: Kári, accompanied by Þórhallr Ásgrímsson, goes to Mosfell where the *goði* Gizurr hvíti lives.
　　I: Gizurr welcomes Kári with open arms. The men discuss the burning, and Kári recounts his grief in verse.
　　A^b: Gizurr provides Kári with a plan of action which will ensure Kári that Gizurr's son-in-law, the *goði*

Mǫrðr Valgarðsson, will take on the prosecution of Flosi in the upcoming case at the Althing. Kári never asks for support; rather, he assumes it.

T: Kári goes to Þorgeirr skorargeirr Þórisson, *goði* and nephew of Njáll.

I: Kári is welcomed with the greatest warmth (with open arms, ms. M).

A[i]: Þorgeirr tells Kári about Flosi's journey and the support he has received in the East Fjords. Kári tells Þorgeirr about Gizurr's plan.

A[b]: Þorgeirr joins Kári and rides with him.

T: They go to Mǫrðr Valgarðsson's farm.

I: The travelers are received well.

A[b]: Mǫrðr is reluctant to prosecute Flosi. Kári then delivers Gizurr's threat that Mǫrðr's wife Þórhalla must immediately be returned. Mǫrðr, who loves his wife, declares himself ready to take on the legal action for Kári. Although Mǫrðr is Flosi's nephew by marriage, he will now head the prosecution of the burners.

C: Mǫrðr calls together his nine nearest neighbors to witness formally that Þorgeirr is assigning to him the action against Flosi for the killing of Helgi Njálsson. Mǫrðr then undertakes the necessary legal formalities and summons Flosi. Mǫrðr completes the legal initiation of the prosecution by summoning his nine nearest neighbors to ride with him to the Althing.

A[b]: Mǫrðr, Þorgeirr, and Kári, pledging themselves to one another, part with *vinátta*. They agree to meet at the Althing.

T: Þorgeirr rides east to his farm. Kári continues west to seek out Ásgrímr Elliða-Grímsson of Tunga.

I: Kári is warmly welcomed.

A[i]: Kári tells of Gizurr's advice, describes Mǫrðr's legal moves, and reports on what he has learned of Flosi's progress in gaining supporters.

I: Ásgrímr's son Þórhallr is described as one of the greatest lawyers of Iceland. He has developed a severe leg inflammation which has left him temporarily lame.

Aᵇ/T: Ásgrímr sends Þórhallr along with twenty men to help Kári set up at the Althing.

The saga now returns to Flosi. On the way to the Althing he pays an unwelcome and taunting visit to Ásgrímr Elliða-Grímsson. Flosi's arrogant behavior during this stopover stands in sharp contrast to the good manners he displayed in the East Fjords.

Chain 3: (ch. 136) Flosi stops at Ásgrímr's farm.

T: Flosi with a hundred of the burners sets off from his home in the east and travels to Fljótshlíð.

I: The Sigfússons see to their farms.

T: In the evening they cross the Þjórs River to Ásgrímr's farm.

I: Ásgrímr recognizes them from a distance and prepares the tables for travelers, as is the custom. Ásgrímr offers no greeting. Flosi and his men are served their meal in silence. Ásgrímr is flushed with anger.

C: Ásgrímr tries but fails to kill Flosi. Flosi prevents his men from retaliating and says to Ásgrímr that the matter is yet to be decided.

T: Flosi and his men go to Laugarvatn and Beitivellir, where they are joined by Hallr of Síða and the supporters from the East Fjords.

I: Flosi gives them a fine welcome.

Aⁱ: Flosi recounts his dealings with Ásgrímr. Some praise him, but Hallr makes it clear that Flosi went too far with Ásgrímr.

T: The men ride to the Upper Plains. There they assemble before riding into the Althing and proceeding to their booths.

I: Flosi's booth is fortified.

Chain 4: (ch. 137) Kári's supporters begin gathering to go to the Althing.

T/I: Þorgeirr skorargeirr and his brothers come from the east with a large following. They pass by Hof and pick up Mǫrðr, who has gathered every able-bodied man in that district.

I: Mǫrðr is confident and determined.

T/I: They all travel west to meet Hjalti Skeggjason, to whom they give a good welcome. Then they all ride off to Reykir in Byskupstunga to meet Ásgrímr. Then they ride west over Brúar River.

A^i/I: Ásgrímr informs them about his visit from Flosi. Þorgeirr is hoping for a fight.

T/I: They ride over to Beitivellir and are joined by Gizurr hvíti, who has a huge following. They talk together for a long time. They ride to the Upper Plains and assemble before riding into the Althing.

I: Flosi and his men take up their arms, but Ásgrímr and his men, refusing to be enticed into a fight, ride to their booths. *Goðar* from every quarter arrive and the Althing is the most crowded within living memory.

Chain 5: (ch. 138) Flosi's visits at the Althing.

I: Background, lineage, reputation, and description of the lawyer Eyjólfr Bǫlverksson are given. Like his kinsmen he is avaricious.

T: Flosi goes to the booth of Bjarni Brodd-Helgason.

I: Flosi is welcomed with open arms.

A^b: Flosi asks advice and Bjarni says that it is time to get a lawyer. Flosi suggests Bjarni's kinsman, Þorkell Geitisson. Bjarni rejects this idea and tells Flosi that whoever takes over the defense of the burners is sure to die. Bjarni's choice is Eyjólfr Bǫlverksson whom he calls the greatest lawyer in the Western Fjords. Bjarni tells Flosi how they will proceed and offers to accompany him to seek support.

T: Bjarni and Flosi go first to see the Øxfirðingar (the people of Axe Fjord).

A^b: Bjarni brokers for Flosi and the Øxfirðingar promise support.

T: Bjarni and Flosi go to see Kolr, son of Víga-Skúta, and Eyvindr Þorkelsson, grandson of Áskell goði.

A^b: Bjarni and Flosi ask for support. Kolr and Eyvindr delay, but finally they agree to enter the case on the side of the burners for three marks of silver.

T: Bjarni and Flosi go to see the Ljósvetningar (the people of Light Water).

A^b/g: The Ljósvetningar are stubborn and Flosi goads them, trying to shame them. He first reminds them of Skarpheðinn's insults and then offers money and flattery. In the end the Ljósvetningar agree to support Flosi, promising to fight if need be.

I: Bjarni compliments Flosi on his style.

T: Bjarni and Flosi go across the Øxar River to the Hlað booth.

I: The lawyer Eyjólfr Bǫlverksson is described as wearing a scarlet cloak and a gold headband; he carries a silver-worked axe. Eyjólfr recognizes Bjarni and receives him well.

T: Bjarni and Flosi take Eyjólfr up through the gorge to a private place where they can talk.

A^b: Bjarni asks for Eyjólfr's help and flatters him. When Bjarni states that he and Flosi want Eyjólfr to take up the case, Eyjólfr refuses, claiming he is under no obligation in the dispute. Flosi offers Eyjólfr a gold arm ring worth the huge sum of 1,200 (1,440 if the long hundred) yards of the finest homespun cloth in return for Eyjólfr's *vinátta* and support. Eyjólfr takes the arm ring and the case. The agreement is witnessed and Eyjólfr and Flosi clasp hands. Eyjólfr tells Flosi and Bjarni to keep quiet for a time about his position as their lawyer, and not to reveal that he has been paid. (Later during the court case the prosecutors use this payment against Flosi and Eyjólfr and accuse them of giving and receiving a bribe.)

T: Bjarni and Flosi go back to their booths; Eyjólfr goes to see his kinsman Snorri goði.

I: Snorri sees the gold arm ring and hopes that it will not cost Eyjólfr his life.

T: Eyjólfr goes to his booth.

Chain 6: (chs. 139–141) Kári's visits at the Althing.

I: Kári, Ásgrímr, Gizurr, Hjalti, Þorgeirr, and Mǫrðr hold a meeting.

A[i/b]: Gizurr provides the information that he has received a message from Snorri goði stating that Flosi has strong support from the north and that Snorri's kinsman Eyjólfr Bǫlverksson received a gold arm ring and is keeping it a secret. Snorri surmises that Eyjólfr is taking up the defense of the burners and that the arm ring was given as payment. Gizurr notes to his allies that his son-in-law Mǫrðr has taken on the most difficult task of prosecuting Flosi and that the rest of them should distribute the other legal actions among themselves. Ásgrímr asks Gizurr to accompany them when they go asking for support. Gizurr agrees and assumes leadership.

T: The prosecutors go first to the booth of the Ǫlfysingar to see Skapti Þóroddsson, the lawspeaker.

I: Skapti greets them well.

A[b]: The prosecutors make a request for support, stating that Skapti will certainly want to lend his support because of blood and marriage ties.

C: Skapti recounts insults which he has suffered in the past and trades further insults with Gizurr and Ásgrímr.

T: They leave Skapti's booth and go to Snorri goði's booth.

I: Snorri bids them welcome.

A[b]: Ásgrímr says he and his kinsman Gizurr have come to ask Snorri for help, especially if there should be a pitched battle. Snorri recounts a possible court scenario, proposing that he not go to the court but draw up his men and await Flosi's party if they should retreat. Snorri also states that the prosecutors should obey his orders if the retreat occurs and should stop fighting when he and his men intervene. Snorri says that this point will be reached when he estimates that they have killed as many of the burners as they can afford to pay fines for without suffering banishment from their regions or loss of their chieftaincies. Gizurr thanks Snorri.

T: The plaintiffs leave Snorri's booth and go next to the Mǫðruvellingar booth and see Guðmundr inn ríki.

I: They are received well and they exchange news.

A[b/i]: Ásgrímr asks for Guðmundr's full support. In response to Guðmundr's question about their other supporters, they inform him of their meeting with Skapti and Snorri. Guðmundr offers the support of himself and his followers. He pledges his life to theirs, saying that he will make up for previous stubbornness. He also promises that his son-in-law, Skapti's son Þorsteinn, will fight on their side. The son-in-law's participation will make Skapti want to stop the fighting. The prosecutors thank Guðmundr and they talk for a long time in private. Guðmundr advises them to stop looking for support but to go about armed.

T: The men return to their booths.

The stage is now set for a tense and potentially bloody Althing session. By the time the case comes to court both sides have gathered so much support that a compromise is clearly in the best interest of everyone. Yet emotions are high, and legal quibblings over jury selection and other such points of law keep the case alive. As one might expect, the feudemes at this point are dominated by advocacy in the forms of information passing and brokerage as the issue is fought out through legal maneuverings. Finally, when the court action goes against one side, a fight breaks out. In time-honored Icelandic tradition, reasonable men (Snorri goði, Skapti the lawspeaker, and Hallr of Síða) intervene after a limited amount of bloodshed and, through compromise, a truce is arranged. This inconclusive attempt at legal resolution is followed by Kári's travels outside Iceland, tracking and killing the outlawed burners until his desire for vengeance is sated. Flosi's consistent refusal to retaliate against Kári's attacks on the other burners allows the feud to come to an end. The two meet when Kári is shipwrecked near Flosi's farmstead and seeks shelter with Flosi. Flosi greets Kári with open arms. He gives him an honored place on the high seat and his niece Hildigunnr in marriage. By this marriage a major stumbling block to peace is removed, for Hildigunnr had been an implacable enemy of Njáll's family after the Njálssons killed her former husband, Hǫskuldr Hvítanessgoði.

The above chains show how the sagaman relied on repetition to construct a portion of his tale. The next series of chains from *Njáls saga* which I consider occurred earlier in the saga (chs. 35–45) and also relies heavily on the skillful use of repetition. This group of chains recounts the feud between Bergþóra, wife of Njáll, and Hallgerðr, wife of Gunnarr. Instead of being the link between an act of conflict and an attempt at resolution, as were the above support-seeking chains, each of the small chains in the following example is a small feud in itself. Like the preceding example, this series consists of alternating chains linked together to form a larger segment of the narrative.

The event that sparks the feud between the two women is an exchange of insults at the autumn feast, shared annually by Njáll's and Gunnarr's families. Hallgerðr is offended

when told by Bergþóra to move down to make room for
Helgi Njálsson's wife. A little later Hallgerðr retaliates by
saying that Bergþóra has deformed fingernails and that
Njáll is beardless.[4] Bergþóra's retort recalls that Hallgerðr
arranged for her former husband's death.[5] When Hallgerðr
calls on Gunnarr to avenge the slight, he rebukes her
instead. The conflict between Hallgerðr and Bergþóra continues, drawing in their husbands in the same way two
farmers might draw in local chieftains or chieftains might
draw in other chieftains. Gunnarr sums up the point suc-
cinctly when he tells Hallgerðr that she may decide her own
actions, but he has to deal with the consequences.

Throughout the relationship Njáll acts as a broker for
Gunnarr much as he does for his own sons, and Gunnarr
values this relationship. Njáll, too, values the friendship,
and the husbands consistently seek to settle their differences through compromise even though this constantly
leads to conjugal conflict. This method is not the weakness
of lamb-husbands, but is mature and reasonable conduct
from heads of households hoping to maintain stability and
to resolve disputes. The wives, like *bœndr*, exercise certain
rights: they hire workers for the farms and get others to kill
for them and, in Hallgerðr's case, to steal. The women
respond to insults by ordering their servants to kill for
them, while the men settle legally at the Althing by direct
compromise. In each instance the wives demand personal
vengeance. They ignore the possibilities of legal action and
cast aside the previous settlements reached by their husbands. This part of the action falls into the familiar pattern

---

[4]At other crucial points in the saga (chs. 41, 44, 91), feud is fueled by
Hallgerðr's calling Njáll and his sons derogatory names.

[5]Hallgerðr had her first husband killed after he slapped her (ch. 11). Her
second husband, Glúmr, also slaps her (ch. 16) and, although she does not want
him killed, her foster father kills the husband (ch. 17). The famous third slap (ch.
48), by Gunnarr, causes her to refuse to give him strands of her hair when he is
attacked. Without the strands Gunnarr is unable to make a bowstring and is killed
at his farm.

of double resolution—first blood vengeance, then a formal settlement—and the feud between the two women is composed of remarkably symmetrical chains. The enmity between the two women fills ten chapters of the saga and escalates into a series of killings, and the cost of resolving the dispute mounts as the feud rises through the social ranks. This specific feud is especially important as it illustrates the depth of the friendship between Gunnarr and Njáll. Also a series of other relationships, such as the tie between the Njálssons and Gunnarr, the animosity between the Sigfússons and Gunnarr, and Hallgerðr's hatred of many people, including her husband, are either defined or begun. All these relationships and emotions figure significantly in successive feuds.

Perhaps of equal importance for the success of *Njáls saga* as a long tale is the way the feud between Bergþóra and Hallgerðr forms a contrast with succeeding feuds in the saga. The quarrel between the wives is kept within bounds by compromise and rationality; it serves to counterbalance the next few feuds, which are not so controlled and thus breed unrestrained violence. In the feuds following the quarrel between the two women, Gunnarr's killings move beyond the realm of his and Njáll's households. The new killings result not only in court actions, which are often manipulated by Njáll, but also in revenge acts, which are not. These acts of vengeance then cause Gunnarr to continue killing and lead first to his death and then to the burning of Njáll and his family. T. M. Andersson, who places the feud between the wives under his category of introduction, takes a very different position about the function of this story in the saga:

> The rivalry between Hallgerðr and Bergþóra has ultimately no function in the plot, but is simply a bit of unattached prefatory matter. The fact that it is so elaborately worked out actually misleads the reader into seeking some function for it which it does not possess. It does not even contribute anything essential to the characterization of the two women; Hallgerðr

is fully delineated elsewhere and Bergþóra's character does not play an important part in the saga.[6]

It is questionable to explain the feud between Bergþóra and Hallgerðr as a narrative slip on the part of the sagaman, for its inclusion is indicative, not of a weakness in the literary nature of *Njáls saga*, but of the tale's compositional technique. The repetition of clusters and chains enabled the sagaman to compose without having to expend a great deal of energy on form. Through this device the mind of the sagaman was freed to concentrate on the details of the individual feudemes and the arrangement of the tale to come.

An outline of the feud between Hallgerðr and Bergþóra follows. I have entitled each of the chains according to the compensation paid for the dead man, which is pegged to the victim's social standing.

Chains 1 and 2: Silver compensation at slave value

Chain 1:

I: Gunnarr prepares to leave for the Althing. Before riding off he speaks with Hallgerðr.

C: Hallgerðr insults Gunnarr. (She is still angry that he took Bergþóra's side in the quarrel instead of hers.)

T: Gunnarr and Njáll leave for the Althing.

I: Background of Gunnarr and Njáll's joint ownership of land. Information about Svartr, one of Bergþóra and Njáll's favorite farmhands. Bergþóra sends Svartr to chop wood.

T: Svartr goes to chop the wood on the jointly owned property.

A[i]: Hallgerðr learns from passing beggars of Svartr's activity.

C: Hallgerðr decides that Bergþóra is stealing from her.

---

[6]Theodore M. Andersson, *The Icelandic Family Saga: An Analytic Reading* (Cambridge: Harvard University Press, 1967), p. 46.

A$^{i/g}$: Hallgerðr tells her overseer Kolr about the perceived theft and goads the man to take action.

T/R: Kolr goes to the woods and avenges the insult to Hallgerðr by killing Svartr.

T/A^i: Kolr rides home and tells Hallgerðr of the killing.

T/A^i: Hallgerðr sends a messenger to Gunnarr at the Althing.

T/R: Gunnarr goes to Njáll's booth and offers *sjálfdœmi*. Njáll awards himself twelve silvers, a standard slave payment.

T: All ride home from the Althing.

C: Bergþóra complains to Njáll that the payment received for Svartr was inadequate while, at Hlíðarendi, Gunnarr and Hallgerðr quarrel over the fact that Gunnarr has compensated Njáll for the loss of the thrall.

Chain 2:

T: Njáll and his sons go up to Þórólfsfell, one of their farms.

T/A^b: While the men are away, a man named Atli arrives at Bergþórshváll. He has come to ask Njáll for work. Bergþóra hires him after asking him if he would be willing to kill for her.

T: Njáll and his sons return home.

I: Njáll learns of the hiring of Atli as a new farmhand. Njáll expresses doubt about the new man. Skarpheðinn gets on well with him.

T: Njáll and his sons ride off to the Althing.

I: Njáll has a pouch of silver with him. Skarpheðinn inquires about this silver, and Njáll tells him it is the previous payment for Svartr.

A^b: Bergþóra asks Atli that day to kill Kolr.

T/R: Atli finds and kills Kolr. The act is to avenge Svartr's death.

A^i: Atli reports the death.

T/A[i]: Hallgerðr sends a messenger to Gunnarr at the Althing; Gunnarr, in turn, sends someone to inform Njáll.

R: Njáll goes to Gunnarr's booth and offers *sjálfdœmi*. Gunnarr places an equal value on Svartr and Kolr and awards himself twelve silvers.

I: Njáll takes out a pouch of silver. Gunnarr recognizes that this is the same money he previously paid to Njáll for the killing of Svartr. The friendship between Njáll and Gunnarr remains strong.

T: All ride home from the Althing.

C: Njáll reproaches Bergþóra. Hallgerðr scolds Gunnarr for making a settlement.

Chains 3 and 4: Silver compensation at freedman's value

Chain 3:

I: Njáll warns Atli to leave but he chooses to stay. Atli asks Njáll not to take slave payment for him if he is killed. Njáll makes Atli a member of the household and promises to seek a freedman's compensation.

T/I: Without informing Gunnarr, Hallgerðr sends to the west for her kinsman Brynjólfr to become overseer. Brynjólfr, who is nicknamed the scoundrel, arrives. Gunnarr keeps his distance but is not unfriendly.

T: Gunnarr and Njáll ride to the Althing.

T: Bergþóra sends Atli to Þórólfsfell to make charcoal.

A[g]: Hallgerðr asks, then goads, her kinsman Brynjólfr to kill Atli.

T/R: Brynjólfr finds and kills Atli in order to avenge the killing of Kolr.

T/A[i]: Brynjólfr rides home and reports the killing.

T/A[i]: Hallgerðr sends one messenger to Bergþóra and another to Gunnarr at the Althing.

T/R: Gunnarr goes to Njáll's booth and offers him *sjálfdœmi*. Njáll awards himself 100 silvers.

T: All ride home from the Althing.

C: Bergþóra says that the money alone is not sufficient compensation. At Hlíðarendi, Hallgerðr calls Gunnarr and Njáll cowards.

Chain 4:

T: Gunnarr and Njáll leave for the Althing.

I: Þórðr leysingjason (freedman's son), foster father of the Njálssons, is introduced.

A^g: Bergþóra goads this peace-loving man to kill Brynjólfr.

T/A^i: Þórðr goes to Hlíðarendi and Hallgerðr tells him where Brynjólfr is. She thinks he is too peaceful to kill Brynjólfr, but Þórðr is resolved and rides on.

R: Þórðr kills Brynjólfr.

A^i: Þórðr reports Brynjólfr's death to Hallgerðr's shepherd.

T/A^i: Þórðr rides back to Bergþórshváll and tells Bergþóra.

I: The news reaches Njáll at the Althing.

R: Njáll is shocked. He talks the matter over with his son Skarpheðinn and they go to Gunnarr's booth. Gunnarr is granted *sjálfdœmi* and awards himself a hundred (120) silvers.

Chains 5 and 6: Double silver compensation

Chain 5:

I: Sigmundr, Gunnarr's kinsman, and Skjǫldr, his Swedish companion, are introduced. Gunnarr advises Sigmundr to temper his rowdy and arrogant behavior.

C: Hallgerðr tells Gunnarr she is dissatisfied with the compensation for Brynjólfr and swears to avenge him. Gunnarr walks away from his wife.

T: Gunnarr sends his brother to Njáll at Bergþórshváll.

A^i: The brother tells Njáll to warn Þórðr to be on his guard.

I: Þórðr and Njáll are outside when Þórðr sees his fetch, a goat. Njáll prophesies Þórðr's death.

T/A[b]: Hallgerðr goes to Þráinn Sigfússon, her son-in-law, to get him to avenge Brynjólfr's death. They develop an elaborate plan to kill Þórðr. The plan depends on tricking Gunnarr.

T/I: Njáll sends Þórðr to the Eyjafell district. Þórðr's return is delayed by the rising of a river.

T: Njáll is unable to wait and rides to the Althing without Þórðr.

T: Þórðr returns from the east and is sent by Bergþóra to the farm at Þórólfsfell.

A[i]: Hallgerðr learns of Þórðr's movements and tells Þráinn and the others.

T/I: Þráinn, Sigmundr, and Skjǫldr leave and lie in wait for Þórðr. Þórðr rides toward them a little later.

I/R: Sigmundr tells Þórðr that he is about to die, and Þórðr invites Sigmundr to single combat. Sigmundr refuses. Þórðr states that his fosterson Skarpheðinn will avenge him. The fighting begins; Þórðr defends himself vigorously against Sigmundr and Skjǫldr while Þráinn stands by.

I: Þráinn states that they have done a vile deed, and the Njálssons are going to be angered.

T/A[i]: The three ride home and inform Hallgerðr. She is delighted to hear of Þórðr's death.

I: Gunnarr's mother warns Sigmundr that if he does such a thing again it will cost him his life.

T/A[i]: A messenger is sent to Bergþóra and another to Gunnarr at the Althing.

T/R: Gunnarr goes to Njáll's booth and offers *sjálf-doemi*. Njáll grants himself double compensation of 200 silvers.

A[i]: Njáll tells his sons of the killing of their foster father and asks them not to break the settlement.

T: All ride home.

C: At Hlíðarendi Gunnarr berates Sigmundr.

Chain 6:

I: Gunnarr's friendship with Njáll and his sons remains
strong but the rest of the two households have little
to do with each other.

A^i: Some beggarwomen arrive at Hlíðarendi from
Bergþórshváll. They pass information concerning
the activities of Njáll's family.

C: Sigmundr, at Hallgerðr's behest, composes an insulting poem about Njáll and the Njálssons, attacking their manhood. Gunnarr, who overhears the rec-
itation, threatens anyone in the room who repeats
the verse.

I: The beggarwomen discuss among themselves that
they would be rewarded by Bergþóra for this
information.

T/A^i: They go to Bergþóra and tell her of the insult.

A^g: Bergþóra uses the information to goad her sons
into killing Sigmundr.

T: The Njálssons go to Fljótshlíð, stay the night, and in
the morning continue to Hlíðarendi.

I: Skarpheðinn explains to his half-brother Hǫskuldr
that he should stay out of the fight because he often
travels alone.

R: The Njálssons attack and kill Sigmundr and
Skjǫldr.

T/A^i: The Njálssons send one of Hallgerðr's shepherds
with Sigmundr's head to Hlíðarendi and ride home.
The shepherd throws the head down. On their way
home the Njálssons meet some men and announce
the killings.

A^i: At home the Njálssons tell their father the news.
At Hlíðarendi the shepherd tells Hallgerðr of the
incident, and she says that he should have brought
the head.

A^g: Hallgerðr tries to goad Gunnarr into avenging his
kinsman's death.

I: Three Althings pass without Gunnarr's taking any

action to avenge the death of Sigmundr.

T/I: Gunnarr goes to see Njáll at Bergþórshváll. Njáll greets him warmly.

A[b]: Gunnarr asks for advice on another matter.

R: Njáll tells Gunnarr that he should set compensation for Sigmundr; Gunnarr makes it 200 silvers. The settlement is announced at the district assembly, and Gunnarr publicly tells how Sigmundr caused his own death. Gunnarr and Njáll pledge their friendship.

With the pledge of continued trust the feud between the wives has run its course, and the saga turns to an entirely different story. Tested in this series of feud chains were bonds of friendship, obligation, and marriage, while the seeds of future alliances and dissensions have been sown. Here and elsewhere in the sagas, there are instances of conflict which do not lead to further plot incidents. Had the sagaman wished to do so, he might have expanded the saga by developing these embryonic conflicts, such as that between Gunnarr and his kinsman Sigmundr, into feuds. But he did not do so, and, though the sagaman may simply have forgotten, it is equally likely that he was being selective. In choosing to drop or expand such an incident, a skillful narrator would have to consider not only the length of the entire tale but the social aspects that would come into play. For instance, the sagaman may have decided that it would not be in keeping with Gunnarr's character to kill this kinsman. Gunnarr's anger at Sigmundr, however, does serve several functions in the story. It shows that Gunnarr's loyalties lie with Njáll rather than with his wife Hallgerðr and her circle, and it furnishes an occasion for Gunnarr to foretell Sigmundr's death at the hands of the Njálssons. Such predictions occur throughout the sagas.

As the above two sets of saga chains illustrate, repetition of form is not a failing on the part of the sagaman, but a key to his art. Within the details of the support-seeking visits of Flosi and Kári, the sagaman explores not only the characters and actions of these two men, but the range of power available at the Althing. Certainly, for much of the medieval audience, this was a point of interest. In the highly stylized small feud between Hallgerðr and Bergþóra, the sagaman relies on repetitions of similar actions to examine the psychology of certain characters, especially Hallgerðr, and to illustrate the personal and often emotionally charged relationships between husbands and wives, friends, and enemies. At the same time the tension that mounts as killings move from unimportant thralls to foster fathers and then to kinsmen is a direct result of the compositional technique of relying on repetition. The same mounting of tension is seen in other feuds, and the reasons for it are quite clear: as the action moves closer and closer to the center of the family or of political power, the consequences and complications become more serious. Over and over the importance of kinship, which is often exaggerated at the time when conflict occurs, is offset by other ties and obligations created or relied upon during resolution.

10 Saga Narrative with Low Cluster Density

Genres, like any other institution, reveal the constitutive traits of the society to which they belong.

The necessity of institutionalization makes it possible to answer another question that one is tempted to raise: even if one concedes that all genres result from speech acts, how does one explain why all speech acts do not produce literary genres? The answer is that a society chooses and codifies the acts that most closely correspond to its ideology; this is why the existence of certain genres in a society and their absence in another reveal a central ideology, and enable us to establish it with considerable certainty. It is not chance that the epic is possible during one era, the novel during another (the individual hero of the latter being opposed to the collective hero of the former): each of these choices depends upon the ideological framework in which it operates.

—Tzvetan Todorov

Feud clusters occur but do not dominate saga narrative (1) when the narrative concentrates on an individual, such as an outlaw, who does not abide by the sanctions of Icelandic society, and (2) when the action takes place outside Iceland. In a third instance, typified by *Hrafnkels saga*, the narrative follows the logic of feudemic composition, but the feudemes are expanded by unusual elaboration and description. I am not saying that clusters of feudemes are absent in such narratives, nor is it my point to make a black-and-white issue of the presence or absence of feudemes. It may be said, however, that the prose shows a lower density of traditional units of action when saga narrative concentrates more on the biography, personality, and psychology of a major character than on the intricacies of Icelandic feud. When the prose does center on the legal and political maneuverings that underlie the progression of Icelandic feud, the saga story, as we have seen, concentrates more on the action of feud itself than on the personality of individuals.

In the outlaw sagas the story concentrates on Icelanders who live for long periods of time outside the sanctions of their society. These men, such as Grettir Ásmundarson and Gísli Súrsson, have often been compared with epic and tragic continental heroes. Because they live outside normal societal intercourse, they have little to offer in a reciprocal relationship. They become isolated, tragic individuals. Their tragedy is heightened by their deep awareness of failure in Iceland's complex world of family and political obligation.

Since Grettir and Gísli are outlawed early on in their sagas, the narratives focus on their lives as hunted men. They are in sharp contrast with men who succeed in feud—Flosi Þórðarson, Kári Sǫlmundarson, Snorri goði, Guðmundr inn ríki, Víga-Glúmr, Guðmundr dýri—and retain wealth, honor, and life. The saga of Gísli Súrsson is the psychological exploration of a socially inept individual, whereas Flosi's tale is the description of a successful brokerage campaign. Like Flosi, Gísli resorts to killing but, unlike Flosi, he does not know how to employ the social tools available to him. It is not by chance that *Gísla saga* contains a mere handful of brokerage visits. The traditional progression whereby a man saves his life, property, and honor by appealing to others for support in *Gísla saga* is truncated (see saga selection 4). Unlike Flosi (see chap. 9),

Gísli is unable to turn a dangerous situation to his own advantage.

Behavior that is inconsistent with the current norms of a society is often considered irrational, even dangerous. Gísli follows the traditional Norse code of family honor which was no longer appropriate to the settled conditions of Icelandic society. The change from a viking to an agrarian ethic has escaped him. Even his brother and sister recognize his conduct as irrational and destabilizing. They offer only minimal help to him during the years of his outlawry.

Gísli's troubles begin in Norway where his sister is seduced—a recurring event—and the honor of his family is called into question. Gísli responds by killing the seducers, only to arouse the anger of his sister, who loses her lovers, and of his brother, who loses friends. Similarly, to avenge a friend, Gísli kills his own chieftain, who is also his brother-in-law. Thus he loses his political leader and the support of his kin group. An outlaw without means, Gísli has little to offer or to bargain with, and so his visits to chieftains are of little avail. In *Gísla saga* Gísli's failure to gain brokerage is telescoped into the few lines of the saga selection, conveying the vital information that Gísli has no resources. The passage makes clear that Gísli has no hope, and after it the saga becomes an exploration of the character and the actions of a doomed man whose death is attributed to a curse.

The curse as a metaphysical explanation for Gísli's lack of success is reminiscent of the dying outlaw's curse on the young Brodd-Helgi in *Vápnfirðinga saga* (ch. 2), which brought strife for two generations. In the sagas, a curse, a literary device of anticipation, usually means that a tragedy will follow. The time between the curse and its ultimate effect is explained, however, in social rather than in metaphysical terms. Thus tragedy is seen as stemming from an exaggerated social flaw. In Gísli's case it is idealized honor; in Brodd-Helgi's, greed. Although the characters themselves proceed in such a way as to bring about their own deaths, the curse provides the saga author with a thread of expectation to weave into an already well-known tale.

Only when a character is an outsider does saga literature abandon its concentration on the individual's social ability. Then the tale turns inward and examines in some depth the outsider's psychological makeup. An intermediary stage is seen in the descriptions of two other Icelandic heroes, Gunnarr and Skarpheðinn in *Njáls saga*. Both of them are famous fighters but political liabilities. Because both Gunnarr and Skarpheðinn continue to take part in ongoing feuds and legal decisions, their stories are told with a high density of feud clusters, and the seeking of support is often elaborated. Gísli and Grettir, unlike Skarpheðinn and Gunnarr become isolated early in their stories. For a long time Njáll with his cunning and ability as a broker remains Gunnarr's and Skarpheðinn's link with the political system. He demands no payment for his help to Gunnarr and Skarpheðinn, and he never denies them assistance, even though both of them fail to hold to his advice. They respond to breaches of honor by trying to right wrongs, as Grettir and Gísli do, rather than by trying to balance claims in arbitration.

Without regard for his own gain, Gunnarr challenges men to individual combat (*hólmganga*) on behalf of a kinswoman and, later, of an old man. Finally, disregarding Njáll's warning, he kills two men in the same family, one over an insult, one over the honor of a woman (chs. 54, 72). His exaggerated sense of justice sometimes overshadows his ability to act reasonably. Gunnarr's intent, like Gísli's, is clearly honorable, but on many occasions he lacks the control exhibited by more socially adept Icelanders. Gunnarr never quite fits into his community. As Gunnarr's tale develops, it focuses less on his actions and more on his revulsion over the necessity to kill in response to insults. This kind of internal conflict is rare in saga literature.

Skarpheðinn, the eldest of the Njálssons, lacks almost entirely his father's political subtlety; he seems to enjoy ignorance of the ways in which men gain support. He insults not only his enemies, but also those who promise not to oppose him and his brothers. His leering grin and his constant insults contribute to a psychological picture of a menacing, lonely outsider who nevertheless, through his family, retains his connections with the social processes of his society.

The poets' sagas such as *Hallfreðar saga*, *Gunnlaugs saga*, and *Kormáks saga* deal principally with outsiders and concentrate on the psychological state of the protagonist. These stories primarily resort to exaggeration in speaking of love that is never quite realized, often because the poet himself rejects the woman. The poets conduct themselves very differently from another victim of unrequited love, Kjartan Ólafsson in *Laxdœla saga*. Like Gunnarr and Skarpheðinn, Kjartan continues to be guided by the socio-economics of his society. In fighting his feud he uses land and power as well as insults, in contrast with the poets, most of whom use scurrilous, erotic, and insulting verse. As such poetry is illegal, the poets are consistently in the wrong. Principally because his father Ólafr pái acts in the background as his advocate, Kjartan participates in political and social exchange, and the narrative of his tale shows a high density of feud clusters. The poets Gunnlaugr, Hallfreðr, and Kormákr cannot rely on similar politically astute advocates and as a result do not participate in the decision-making processes of the society. They are lonely men whose conduct provokes dispute and who seem to prefer continuing conflict to resolution. In a society that has organized feud so as to be profitable to those who master its intricacies, activities of the poets are not socially productive. Almost no one gains from their feuds. Like the sagas of outlaws, these tales turn inward, groping for a psychological explanation of often tragic social deviants. As one would expect, the narratives are characterized by a low density of feud clusters.

Like the sagas of outlaws and of poets, other family sagas
and *þættir* about Icelanders who wander abroad concentrate largely on biography, personality, and psychology.
The disputes are among persons involved in the competition that surrounds hierarchical positions of authority.
Often loyalty to the king, especially by retainers and vas-
sals, is particularly important. In *Egils saga*, for example,
the norm of Icelandic social behavior is not central to the
saga since the tale concentrates on the activities of Egill's
ancestors and of Egill himself in Scandinavia, England, and
the Baltic lands. Egill often battles as a mercenary for
foreign kings. The descriptions of his exploits are not unlike
continental epics about warrior-heroes who depend upon
kings and leaders to retain them. When Egill returns to
Iceland for the final time (ch. 76), the construction of the
narrative changes and the density of feudemes and clusters
increases. The saga turns from recording the wanderings of
an epic poet and mercenary warrior to narrating events
familiar to the family saga: dispute, brokerage, arbitration,
and alliance through marriage, kinship, and political
friendship.

Gradually the focus shifts to Egill as broker for his son
Þorsteinn, who enters into a dispute with a neighbor,
Steinarr Qnundarson, over land. The sequence of clusters
which develops out of this confrontation is similar to many
others in the sagas: conflict over a shared parcel of property
giving rise to a number of other conflicts. Not that Egill
becomes any more gentle in his role as a *goði*. Indeed, even
after he becomes feeble in his old age, Egill denies his
children his treasure by burying it and killing the slaves who
helped him carry it. Yet his dealings as an Icelandic chieftain with freemen are characterized by his skillful use of the
controlled power that leads to success in the Icelandic legal
system. The old warrior does not mistake the fact that in
Iceland men gather supporters, not simply for a physical
fight, but to gain strength in ensuing court cases. Egill,

showing his mastery of the system, at first pretends to take no part in Þorsteinn's case. His posture is believable because it is well known that little love is lost between father and son. But Egill's son is in trouble. Þorsteinn's opponent Steinarr has purchased the support of two powerful brokers, the chieftains Einarr from Stafaholt and Tungu-Oddr.

Egill decides to intervene. Quietly he gathers information and assembles men. At precisely the right moment, during the spring assembly, Egill impressively enters with eighty fully armed men (saga selection 1). Playing on the potential for violence which underlies the pragmatism of Icelandic justice, Egill assumes the defense of his son. He calls out his old neighbor and traveling companion, Ǫnundr, to help stop this quarrel. Ǫnundr forces his son Steinarr to hand over the case to him, and he then gives Egill the sole right to arbitrate it. Meanwhile, Steinarr frees from obligation the two *goðar* whose support he has paid for. After recounting the history of Steinarr's land, originally owned by Egill's father, Egill announces his unexpectedly harsh verdict: Steinarr will lose his farm, Ánabrekka, and will be outlawed from the district. Ǫnundr lets it be known that he will hinder Þorsteinn wherever he can (ch. 81).

The episodes at the end of *Egils saga* are composed through the use of clusters (many of them nuclear) and are quite different from the first three quarters of *Egils saga*, the sagas of outlaws and of poets, and a few family sagas such as *Hrafnkels saga*. All these sagas are constructed with feudemes, but the central role played by brokerage in so many of the sagas whose stories are about feud within Iceland is missing. The relative unimportance of brokerage is also a marked feature in the sagas translated into Icelandic prose from continental epics. For example, antagonists such as Gvitalín and Rollant or Karlamagnús and King Agulandus gather support almost without brokerage in the

Norse *Karlamagnús saga*, a translation of several chansons de geste.[1] In contrast with a saga of feud taking place in Iceland, *Karlamagnús saga* is an epic set within a hierarchical social order, and the way feud takes form in this essentially continental tale is at variance with the elements of feud evident in stories in the family and Sturlunga sagas.

In *Karlamagnús saga*, behavior turns to a large degree on knightly loyalty or disloyalty. Hero and villain are often distinguished by their willingness or unwillingness to do their duty and to follow their leaders. Reward, in such a situation, is often the consequence of loyalty, and the audience is given a standard by which to judge the characters' actions. Karlamagnús gathers support by summoning his *stórhǫfðingjar* (lords) to aid him against the pagan King Agulandus (Pt. IV).[2] They agree to follow their leader without question. In other instances men are enlisted for similar purposes: earlier, Karlamagnús gathers men to

---

[1]*Karlamagnús saga* is a compilation of translations from several French sources. According to E. F. Halvorsen, *The Norse Version of the Chanson de Roland*, Bibliotheca Arnamagnæana 19 (Copenhagen: Einar Munksgaard, 1959), the original texts may be envisioned as including the following items: a nonextant *Vie Romancée de Charlemagne*; a chanson de geste similar to *La Chevalerie Ogier de Danemarch*; the Pseudo-Turpin chronicle (French material in Latin); *Chanson d'Aspremont*; a chanson de geste about the war with the Saxon king Guitalin; a *Chanson d'Otinel*; the *Pèlerinage Charlemagne*; a *Chanson de Roland* that includes the war in Libya; and a *Moniage Guillaume* (pp. 64–66). The original translations were probably done by two or more Norwegians or Icelanders in Norway during the reign of Hákon Hákonarson (1217–1263) (pp. 75–76). Four incomplete manuscripts taken from two originals survive. The A group (MSS from around the fifteenth century) contains a fairly literal translation of the Pseudo-Turpin chronicle and the *Chanson d'Aspremont*; the B versions, both seventeenth-century manuscripts, are based on a manuscript whose editor tried to clear up the inconsistencies that are evident in A (pp. 32–34, 37). The edition used is Bjarni Vilhjálmsson, ed., *Karlamagnús saga og kappa hans*, 3 vols. (Iceland: Íslendingasagnaútgáfan, Haukadalsútgáfan, 1954).

[2]Part IV of the saga is a combination of the Pseudo-Turpin chronicle and the *Chanson d'Aspremont*. Peter Foote presents a detailed analysis of the sources of the Pseudo-Turpin section of *Karlamagnús saga* in *The Pseudo-Turpin Chronicle in Iceland: A Contribution to the Study of the Karlamagnús Saga*, London Mediæval Studies 4 (London: University College, 1959).

protect him at his coronation at Eiss, because Reinfrei is planning to kill him (Pt. I); the pope brings in supporters for the same coronation; Basín and Geirarðr of Numaia gather men to support Karlamagnús (Pt. I).[3] When Karlamagnús is trapped in a castle, Hermoen volunteers to ride to Rollant for help in the fight against Gvitalín. Once Hermoen has volunteered to undertake the mission, Karlamagnús promises to reward him with command over the castle and region if they are victorious in wresting the area from Gvitalín (Pt. V).[4] The enemies of Karlamagnús also gather their forces for these conflicts. Instead of brokerage, a system of loyalty to one's leader prevails, and the structure of the narrative differs widely in the two types of tales.

Issues such as Gvinelún's betrayal or Rollant's defense of the state are central considerations in sagas adapted from continental epics. In the native sagas about feud in Iceland, duplicity is not a social evil to the extent that it is in continental epics, partly because the Icelandic state was not founded on the need to maintain a strong military organization. In Iceland betrayal of one's leader or an ally has an aspect of business double-dealing—a slightly disreputable yet cunning manipulation that does not carry with it the onus of military treachery or betrayal of the state. Acts that would be deemed treacherous or villainous in the chansons de geste are, in the setting of the sagas, neither evil nor

[3]Constance Hieatt discusses the various possible sources of Part I in *Karlamagnús Saga: The Saga of Charlemagne and His Heroes*, 2 vols. (Toronto: Pontifical Institute of Mediaeval Studies, 1975), 1:42–52. Names of the traitors seem to come from *Berte aus grans pies* and *Mainet*. There are some details similar to those in *Renaud de Montauban*. The story of the fathering of Rollant has parallels in *Tristan de Nanteuil*, the Chronicle of Weihenstephan, and the *Roman de Berte*. Chapters 38–42 of the saga correspond to parts of the chanson de geste, *Girart de Vienne*. Hieatt agrees with Paul Aebischer's idea that Part I must have had a single French source, Aebischer's lost *Vie Romancée de Charlemagne*. Halvorsen (*Norse Version*, pp. 45, 64) also accepts Aebischer's theory.

[4]Part V was translated into Icelandic from an unknown source, although there exists a French work, Jean Bodel's *Chanson de Saisnes*, which may have derived from a similar, or identical, source.

socially destructive. Rather, they fall within the rough-and-tumble competitiveness of the society, and double-dealing by an Icelandic chieftain or leader is, in accordance with its success, seen as a virtue. Revered men such as Hǫskuldr Dala-Kollsson, Njáll Þorgeirsson, Óláfr pái, and Snorri goði are famous for their ability to connive to win legal cases and to get the upper hand in feuds. Even a deceitful chieftain, such as Mǫrðr Valgarðsson in *Njáls saga*, is not denied the success of his double-dealings. Mǫrðr incites the Njálssons with false stories which arouse their jealousy of their foster brother, Hǫskuldr Hvíta-nessgoði, and drive them to kill him. Mǫrðr's reason for doing so is that many of his thingmen are shifting their allegiance to the more popular Hǫskuldr. Having engineered his rival's death, Mǫrðr then changes sides, partly as a ruse, and supports Flosi, who is leading the avenging party against the Njálssons for the killing of Hǫskuldr. Although Mǫrðr's actions have initiated a new stage in the long feud chain, later on Mǫrðr again changes his allegiance. This time he turns against Flosi and becomes the lawyer for Kári, who is seeking vengeance for the burning of Njáll and his sons. Although Mǫrðr is not an honorable character, he is not a clearly delineated villain. Within the world of the sagas he is a man who skillfully uses the political tools of his society to his own advantage. There are few utterly villainous characters in the sagas.

Resolutions of feuds in *Karlamagnús saga* are also different from those in sagas about Iceland. In *Karlamagnús saga* the enemy must either be destroyed militarily or incorporated into the structure of command through conversion or an oath of fealty. In Part IV, for example, each side offers to end the war; Karlamagnús sends messengers to Agulandus, Agulandus sends messengers to Karlamagnús, and the offers are repeated later. All proposals are based not on arbitration or balancing of strengths but on the enemy's willingness to capitulate. Since these are religious wars, Karlamagnús demands conversion to Christianity by defeated opponents. In Part I young Rollant tries to act as an arbitrator by asking Bernarður of Averna to help him effect a settlement between Karlamagnús and Geirarður of Vienna. Bernarður refuses because he knows his relative Geirarður will not agree if the settlement requires him to give up Vienna and become a follower of Karlamagnús. The war must go on. In Iceland, the object of the extensive court system was to ensure that feuds did not turn into small wars and that resolutions, if possible, did not allow the destruction of one side or the too great aggrandizement of the other. The Icelanders' long-term concern for the successful regulation of feuds accounts for the resolution of so many disputes in socially acceptable and sensible compromises.

In a few instances in the family sagas, as in *Hrafnkels saga*, the narrative shows a highly creative and individualistic usage of traditional units of action. *Hrafnkels saga* relates five unusual events, connected with one another by feudemes. As a result its overall structure resembles one long nuclear cluster instead of a series of clusters. *Hrafnkels saga* has more epic and folkloristic pretensions than most of the other family sagas that narrate feud in Iceland. Perhaps because of these enriching literary elements, critics have viewed this saga as a masterpiece of saga writing. Ironically, it is one of the few tales of feud set in Iceland which cannot be taken as an exemplar of traditional saga narration.

In *Hrafnkels saga* the feud is engendered by a religious interdiction, a highly folkloristic element and an unusual cause of saga conflict. Hrafnkell is a worshiper of the god Freyr and has given his horse Freyfaxi to the god, swearing that he will kill anyone who rides the animal. The shepherd Einarr, however, disobeys; he rides Freyfaxi hard while trying to herd Hrafnkell's sheep. The horse is sweating and spent when it returns on its own to Hrafnkell.

Because of his oath to Freyr, Hrafnkell kills the shepherd. The father of the shepherd, a poor neighbor of

Hrafnkell's, seeks atonement. Hrafnkell usually does not award compensation for his killings, but because he feels badly about this one, he does make an offer. The shepherd's father, however, wants arbitration, but Hrafnkell rejects the proposal out of hand because the two are not at all on an equal footing.

The father goes to his nephew Sámr, a good lawyer, for aid. At first Sámr refuses because Hrafnkell is a *goði* and has a reputation of being a dangerous opponent. Finally the father succeeds in persuading Sámr to prosecute the case. The second unusual event then occurs: Sámr ignores the potential for brokerage with local leaders and instead goes to the Althing on his own. With his plans to prosecute a chieftain, Sámr, who is an unimportant farmer, seeks support from every chieftain there, but they all refuse because of Hrafnkell's reputation, the risk of failure, or the lack of obligation to Sámr. Hrafnkell, finding Sámr's actions highly amusing, treats them lightly. The third event unusual within the normal course of Icelandic decision making is then described: a distinguished stranger appears on the scene and induces his brother, who is administering the chieftaincy they own jointly, to support Sámr.

Little in this narrative is typical of Icelandic feud. Unlike the normal brokerage procedures, rooted in preexisting obligations among farmers and chieftains, the process in *Hrafnkels saga* is truncated. It leaps from a poor farmer from the eastern part of the country who is unsupported in his struggle against a *goði* to an alliance between the farmer and a princely stranger from the distant West Fjords. This imposing stranger, Þorkell Þjóstarsson, is an Icelander who has just returned from service in Byzantium, where he was a liegeman of the Greek emperor. Holding a sword in his hand, he strolls about the Althing in a colored kirtle. A man of nobility, Þorkell acts in terms of chivalric ethics instead of Icelandic political survival. He quickly decides, for reasons neither of obligation nor of payment, to embroil himself in a feud on behalf of a small farmer from the other side of the country. As if in a folktale the stubborn peasant, through tenacity and cunning and luck, locates a donor-benefactor. With the backing of his new protector, Sámr successfully pleads his case. Hrafnkell is barred from presenting a defense by the large number of people assembled by the sons of Þjóstarr. At this point the fourth unusual event takes place: political strength is ignored. Instead, a weak farmer with no resources is completely successful and the *goði* is outlawed. In the fifth unusual act, the stranger and his brother, without regard for payment and on their own volition, ride all the way across Iceland to help Sámr carry out the sentence of outlawry, including confiscation of Hrafnkell's property.

Sámr, despite his success thus far, does not realize that if he is going to contest a chieftain he will have to act like a chieftain. Hrafnkell, who has been caught, is too dangerous an enemy to let live, but Sámr is compassionate and does not kill his rival. He only banishes Hrafnkell from the district, thus permitting him to set up a new household. Sámr takes over Hrafnkell's old chieftaincy, but in his new location Hrafnkell thrives and again becomes powerful. Eventually Hrafnkell seeks revenge; he kills Sámr's brother (see chap. 5 where the washerwoman goads Hrafnkell) and retakes his *goðorð*. The situation returns to the status quo before the feud, except that now Sámr is of even lower status. Again a farmer, he has to live under the thumb of Hrafnkell.

The feud in this saga has the three feudemes of conflict, advocacy, and resolution, but they do not form tight clusters, as feudemes do in most tales of Icelandic feud. As a narrative entity *Hrafnkels saga* is less dependent upon traditional conventions than most other family sagas. Its characterizations are so embroidered with Christian ethics, folkloristic elements, and epic heroic attributes that it is hard not to see it as the product of a highly literate sagaman consciously innovating a traditional narrative form and subject. Indeed, in few other places in Iceland's vast medieval literature is the union between foreign and native modes of storytelling so thoroughly integrated and so successfully harmonized.

11 Conclusion

W HEN I began working on this book my purpose was to illustrate how feud in medieval Iceland stemmed from the island's limited resources and how the sagas presented this basic reality. The achievement of this double goal seemed a reasonable objective, since there exists a body of legal and historical information about medieval Iceland. Moreover, the sagas, although largely fictional, are a traditional literature about life in a rural country, and plausible characters and events tend to dominate the narratives. Although much is known about early Icelandic history and law, I soon became aware that relatively little analysis has been directed toward determining how medieval Iceland functioned as a societal entity. As the task grew larger, the book became a study of how feud worked in the society and in the literature.

The Icelandic state did not even pretend to have the means or the mandate to enforce its authority. Instead, the tenth-century Icelanders created a complex court apparatus to endorse resolutions arrived at by private parties. As I followed the development of feuds in the sagas, I became aware that middlemen or brokers, over and over again, joined in the disputes of others, usually for a fee or for an advantage to be gained, or because of an obligation owed. It was soon apparent that brokers, and the process of brokerage, were necessary ingredients in saga feud; brokers provided the means, and the force, to initiate, maintain, and resolve disputes. Working within the skeletal frame of the three active elements of saga feud, the feudemes, I charted the ways in which conflicts, advocacies, and resolutions took place, and I began to discern the variations of each. I came to realize that feudemes occur as formal narrative units whether or not they are of major importance in a specific story. For example, one instance of advocacy in a cluster may be highly elaborated because it is fundamental to the story, whereas the same feudeme in another cluster may be a simple device enabling the sagaman to pass quickly from one event to another. Besides the three active elements, I found that repetitive devices employed by the sagaman in constructing his feud chains included two major nonactive units: information and travel.

The fact that these units, both active and nonactive, which make up saga narrative are not governed by a sequential order lies at the heart of the technique of saga construction. The conclusion that the sagaman substituted a limited number of elements for one another opens the way for further inquiry; in particular, it raises the question of whether we can determine with greater precision the narrative strategies of individual sagamen.

Recording the arrangement of feudemes and units of travel and information provides the raw data of saga construction, allowing us to approach saga prose in line with the way it was composed. By using these data we can avoid developing theories based on the careers of heroes; the data also constitute an important tool that will enable us to make the needed distinctions between epic and saga. In so doing, we may reinforce conclusions arrived at by other researchers, thus supporting earlier theories and assumptions about certain sagas. If new conclusions are reached, we have moved a step closer to understanding a significant form of medieval storytelling. Much work needs to be done, however, before we can determine with certainty how feudemes form clusters and whether or not patterns underlie the formation of feud chains in different sagas.

Inquiries could take a number of directions, but some questions are crucial. Are some formations of feudemes used more than others? Did a particular sequence of feudemes evoke the recognition in the medieval audience of what was to come? Did the listeners know what forthcoming actions would be emphasized? Such questions are all the more important when we remember that surprise was not a major factor in these tales and that sagamen were working with quasi-historical material. If we break down large blocks of information scattered throughout feuds, can we discover narrative codes there as well?

A study of the placement of these blocks in the narrative would shed light on the informational needs of the medieval audience and would also help us to distinguish the different prose styles used by sagamen to communicate information. Common sense tells us that portents and genealogies suggest who will be important in the coming actions and what will befall major characters. But a further question must be asked: What else is contained in these descriptive passages? And to answer that question we need more than a passing acquaintance with the attributes of the society portrayed in the sagas and the institutions and laws of the Icelandic Free State. Here too an awareness of feudemes is a help, for identifying feudemes provides a basis for understanding the process by which members of the community became embroiled in and then extracted themselves from feuds. The method supplies information on how the legal and social systems worked to promote compromise and to condone and channel necessary violence.

In exploring the functions of feud in the sagas, I have not assumed that saga narrative is a mirror of actual events. I have, however, relied on the premise that repetitive stories of feud written in different parts of the country, at different times, by different people, give an idea of the ambience of medieval Icelandic dispute settlement. Even problems with ghosts in the sagas have an air of reasonableness about them and, with a few notable exceptions, are solved by plausible rather than fantastic means. The ways of aggression, the means of defense, and the anxieties apparent in saga after saga arise less from the caprices or fantasies of an individual author than from centuries-old social and economic forces.

Appendix A

A Brief Account of Legal and Social Terms

T HE sagas tell primarily the tales of chieftains and farmers, who as landowners controlled the major source of wealth and power in Iceland's rural society. In order to provide the reader with needed social and legal information about medieval Iceland, this appendix defines terms and concepts used throughout the book. Instead of giving exhaustive definitions, I have grouped the material thematically so that terms can be understood in conjunction with related information. A number of socioeconomic issues are treated in greater depth in chapter 5.

Iceland was an independent country from the end of the ninth century to the years 1262–1264, a period traditionally called the age of the Old Icelandic Commonwealth or Free State. The period of settlement (*landnámatíð*) began around 870 and lasted approximately 60 years. Before the settlement, Iceland's only occupants were a few Irish hermit-monks who either were driven out of Iceland when the Norse colonists came or left voluntarily. Beginning in the settlement period, the Icelanders developed an extensive system of laws, maintained orally for several centuries; not until 1117 were the first sections written down. The law of Free State Iceland is called *Grágás*, the "gray-goose" law (abbreviated here as *GG*). All extant manuscripts of *Grágás* are private compilations, commissioned, it seems, to record the official law. It is not clear whether official compilations were ever written down. The two most important of the private lawbooks are *Konungsbók* (ca. 1260) and *Staðarhólsbók* (ca. 1280). Although specific entries are often detailed, the laws are casuistic and give only limited information about the operation of the society. *Grágás* gives basic information about the two major groups of landholding farmers, the *goðar* and the *bœndr*, and their responsibilities to the judicial and social order.

The *goðar* (sing. *goði*) were chieftains who originally performed both leadership and religious functions. The word *goði* seems to have been derived from the Old Norse *goð* (god), thus reflecting the early role of *goðar* as temple chieftains responsible for sacrifices and other religious rituals. As the office of chieftaincy, the *goðorð* (pl. *goðorð*), could be bought, inherited, or traded; it was accessible to men of ambition. Successful farmers or their sons often became chieftains, and during much of the Free State's history the difference between prosperous farmers and chieftains was not great.

When the government was first formed in 930, leadership was divided among thirty-six chieftaincies or *goðorð*. Around 965 the number of *goðorð* was increased to thirty-nine, the country was divided into quarters, and the quarter courts at the Althing were established. The Southern, Eastern, and Western Quarters each had nine chieftaincies; the Northern Quarter, because of its demography, had twelve. In the early eleventh century the number of *goðorð* was finally expanded to forty-eight. At the national assembly, the Althing, the relative strength of the different chieftains was balanced by complex voting rules, and the Northern Quarter, with its extra chieftaincies, enjoyed no advantage as a political bloc.

Because control of a chieftaincy was often shared (*GG* Ia, 38, 43, 141), at any time approximately fifty men may have been claiming all or part of a *goðorð*. In order to ensure stability the minimum tenure for each *goði* was set at three years. Nothing in the judicial apparatus or in the *goðorð* system could be changed without the consent of the main legislative organ of government, the *lǫgrétta*. This national legislative council was convened as part of the Althing, which met yearly between mid-June and the first week in July at Þingvǫllr (the Thing Plain) in the southwestern part of the country. The *lǫgrétta* was empowered to make new laws and to alter old ones. Only *goðar* had voting rights in the *lǫgrétta*, although each chieftain took with him two *bœndr* from his thing district as advisers. The composition of the *lǫgrétta* as set in the early tenth century remained intact until the early twelfth century, when the final governmental reform of the Free State seated two bishops as full voting members of the *lǫgrétta*.

By the time the bishops were seated, Iceland had been Christian for more than a century. The country had been converted through negotiation at the Althing in the year 999, although for many years thereafter the Church's organization was rudimentary. The first permanent bishopric was created at Skálaholt in the south. Skálaholt was the family farm of the chieftain Ísleifr Gizurarson, who apparently at a meeting of the Althing was elected Iceland's first native bishop. In 1056 he journeyed to Bremen, in northern Germany, to be consecrated. Ísleifr, who died in 1081, had willed his farm to the Church to be the seat of the bishop; his son Gizurr was consecrated bishop in 1082. In 1106 a second bishopric was created at Hólar in the north. The early bishops and priests behaved in accordance with the secular traditions of their countrymen, participating in feuds, killings, and legal cases. In many instances, despite occasional attempts at reform by a bishop (the two bishops seldom acted in concert) and the warnings of the distant archbishop in Norway, such conduct continued in the thirteenth century.

The farmers were called *bœndr* (sing. *bóndi*). Among the *bœndr* the most important were the *þingfararkaupsbœndr* (the thingtaxpaying farmers). Members of this large group, 4,000–5,000 heads of households at the end of the eleventh century, qualified for full rights as freemen by owning a certain minimum amount of property—a cow, a boat, or a net for each person in their charge (*GG* Ia, 159–160; II, 320–321; III, 173, 431–432). Each *bóndi* was required by law to establish a formal relationship with a chieftain. The *bóndi* would then be known as a follower, a thingman (*þingmaðr*), of his chieftain. Thing bonds, along with kin bonds, were the underlying ties of reciprocal obligation in the Icelandic system. The laws give a good deal of information about the legal nature of this relationship. According to *Grágás*,

> If a man wants to declare himself out of the thing [relationship with his *goði*], it is the law that he declare himself so at the springtime thing, if he enters into a thing relationship with that *goði*, who is a *goði* of the same district. So also if he enters into a thing relationship with that *goði* who has a thing within the boundaries of the same district. It is the law that he declare himself out of the *þriðjungsþing* [three-chieftain assembly] of the *goði* at the high court at the *Lǫgberg* at the Althing, if the *goði* listens. If the *goði* does not listen, then he must say it to him, and it is the law that he declare himself out of the thing

with witnesses for himself. And on the same day he must declare himself to be in a thing relationship with another *goði*.[1]

The relationship between a chieftain and a farmer was designed to be mutually beneficial. Much of a *goði*'s power depended on his ability to hold on to the support of his thingmen, whose number varied according to the chieftain's popularity; the farmers, in turn, looked to their *goði* for protection. One of every nine farmers was required to follow his *goði* to the Althing, although when important cases were pending a chieftain might press more of his thingmen to ride with him. In order to underwrite the expenses incurred in taking supporters to the Althing, a *goði* collected the thing tax, *þingfararkaup*, from the *þingfararkaupsbœndr*. Because it covered only actual expenses, this tax was not a lucrative source of income for chieftains. The money was paid to the supporting farmers after their arrival at the Althing, where they carried out judicial responsibilities and supported their chieftain in legal cases.

The *bóndi* was legally free to ally himself with any chieftain in his quarter and had to renew the bond annually (*GG* Ia, 136–139, 140–141; II, 272–276, 277–278). The right to choose a leader, highly unusual in medieval times, was possible because the thingmen of one chieftain could, and often did, live interspersed with the followers of another chieftain. When a chieftain became overbearing, a thingman was free to move away from the area.[2] For his part, a

---

[1]The Icelandic text reads (*GG* 1a, 140): Ef maðr vill segiaz or þingi, oc er rett at hann segiz or avarþingi ef hann fer i þess goða þing er samþingis goðe er við hin. sva oc ef hann fer við þan goða iþing er þing á ieno sama þingmarke. Rett er at hann segizc or þriþiungi goða a alþingi at háðom domum at lǫgbergi ef goði heyrir. Ef goði heyrir eigi oc scal hann segia honom til enda er rétt at hann segizc brott með vatta fyrir honom siálfom. en in sama dag scal hann segia sic iþing við anan goða. For editions of *Grágás* see chapter 2, footnote 7.

[2]Although the move of a freeman was a drastic act, it is nevertheless attested to a number of times in the sources. *Sturlunga saga* relates many instances of the

chieftain could refuse to accept a *bóndi* as a thingman (*GG* Ia, 141; II, 278–279; III, 427). Although a *bóndi* could shift his allegiance from one chieftain to another, such changes were infrequent because of personal and family loyalties or proximity to a particular *goði*.

The courts in Iceland, which met yearly at legally established dates, were not convened in response to individual requests to hear special cases. They provided a readily accessible and relatively neutral forum for airing and resolving disputes. Each quarter of the island was divided into local thing districts; the Southern, Eastern, and Western Quarters each had three, and the Northern Quarter had four. Three chieftains were jointly responsible for holding the district assemblies, the most important of which was the *várþing*, or springtime thing. This local assembly was a political gathering whose functions were both regulatory and judicial. It dealt with local disputes and defined the prevailing alliances. Each *bóndi* was required to attend the *várþing*, which met toward mid-summer approximately five weeks before the meeting of the national Althing. The Althing was convened at the end of the ninth week of summer; after 999 this was changed to the end of the tenth week. Later, toward fall, another local assembly, the *leið*, was held; it was attended by district farmers and chieftains. Unlike the *várþing*, it had no judicial function; it was simply a forum where new laws and information from the Althing proceedings were announced.

Conflicts that could not be resolved at the *várþing* or cases in which the prosecution desired a wider, and perhaps more impartial, hearing were taken to the courts at the

---

buying and selling of land and of moving: *Hrafns saga Sveinbjarnarsonar*, I, 214; *Guðmundar saga dýra*, I, 166; *Sturlu saga*, I, 65, 68, 72, 96, 100; *Íslendinga saga*, I, 234, 239, 243, 260, 266, 303, 304, 309, 314, 345, 346, 448, 478. These examples from *Sturlunga saga* indicate that a farmer could move away at his own discretion, even at a time when chieftains' power over freemen was growing. In the earlier period, when a chieftain's claim to territorial overlordship was less advanced, the *bœndr* probably had even more freedom of movement and choice.

Althing. The national assembly, besides conducting the serious business of the *lǫgrétta* and the judicial courts, had a lighter side. It attracted all manner of people: tradesmen, peddlers, storytellers, ale brewers, even young men and women looking for spouses. The assembly thus served the island as a national concourse where information was passed and business was transacted.

The Althing was an open-air assembly, as the site at Þingvǫllr lacked fixed buildings, though after the conversion a small church was built. Most people pitched tents, but chieftains and other important men maintained from year to year turf booths roofed with sailcloth for the two weeks of the assembly. On a grassy slope near the center of the assembly was an outcropping of rock called the *lǫgberg* or lawrock, where charges, decisions, and summonings were publicly announced. The Althing opened on a Thursday and the *goðar* were required by law to arrive before sunset. At the *lǫgrétta*, the holders of the original or "ancient" thirty-six *goðorð* appointed farmers to the four quarter courts of justice, the *dómar*, which had been established at the time the island was divided into quarters. Each chieftain named four judges, and it was decided by lot in which of the four quarter courts each judge would sit. This method of selection guaranteed impartiality, insofar as possible, and minimized regional biases. Also the fact that *bœndr* from one quarter took part in making decisions about cases from other quarters helped to standardize judgments and to bring farmers from the entire country into the arranging of settlements. On Saturday the appointed judges could be challenged; kinship relationships to litigants and other evidence of partiality might be disqualifying.

Cases of first instance as well as cases on appeal from the *várþing* were heard. In about 1005 a *fimtardómr*, or fifth court, was instituted at the Althing as a court of appeals. Cases that were not clearly decided at the quarter courts could be referred to the *fimtardómr*. Establishment of this court of last instance, which required only a majority for a verdict, was the final reform in the judicial structure of the Old Icelandic Free State. As in the quarter courts, farmers could serve here as judges (*GG* Ia, 77).

The things in Iceland attended to legislative and judicial but not executive matters. The only official in this loose governmental structure was the *lǫgsǫgumaðr*, or lawspeaker. Elected for a three-year term, he recited a third of the law every year at the lawrock. In this manner the law was preserved orally for several centuries. The lawspeaker made decisions concerning fine points of the law and proclaimed rulings, but when necessary he could consult five or more legal experts (*lǫgmenn*). Despite his official position, he was free to participate in disputes as a private citizen and to take sides. The most famous lawspeaker was Skapti Þóroddsson, called Lǫg-Skapti; he served for twenty-seven summers. The names and dates in office of the lawspeakers from about 930 until 1271, when the position was abolished with the introduction of the first Norwegian laws, are reliably preserved in the medieval sources. As a form of dating the Icelanders often recorded events according to who was lawspeaker at the time.

The court system was directed toward maintaining the balance of power rather than meting out justice to the individual. Court cases, which were open to all comers, were very public affairs. Onlookers scrutinized the proceedings and could criticize them publicly. Witnesses (*vætti*) testified to what they had seen or heard; a jury of neighbors (*kviðr*) testified to what its members thought.[3] Failure to follow correct legal procedure could mean losing an important case on a technicality.

---

[3]*Grágás* has a great deal of information concerning the composition of the courts: *GG* Ia, 36, 40, 51–52, 143; Ib, 134, 139, 146, 161, 200–201, 212–213; II, 45, 56, 195, 219, 236, 310, 327–329, 369, 506, 536; III, 41, 52, 53–54, 431. In cases of insulted honor a court of five property owners could be called in instead of the usual *tólftarkviðr*, a panel of twelve chieftains, to testify that they heard the insults from the summoned man (*GG* Ib, 181–183; II, 390–391).

The judicial, political, and social structures of Iceland were designed to benefit property owners, the *goðar* and the *bœndr*. Other groups were slaves, minors, indigents, individuals unable to take care of themselves, and free but landless tenant farmers and laborers. The majority of the population, estimated variously at 30,000 to 60,000, lived under the nominal control of a *bóndi*, or head of a household, on the lands of the *þingfararkaupsbœndr*. As each *bóndi* was tied to a *goði*, almost all inhabitants had a defined place in the decentralized social system of Iceland.

Because medieval Icelandic alliances, both social and political, relied to a large extent on reciprocal arrangements between peers, the formalization of agreements was of the utmost consequence. The standard way to seal an agreement was the *handsal*, (verb, *at handsala*) a handshake or a handslap. To be recognized as legally binding, a *handsal* had to be witnessed. *Handsal* agreements could be entered into for many reasons: to arrange a marriage and dowry, to transfer land, to bind a resolution to a feud. A transfer of land by *handsal*, in which one man gave over his land, perhaps to a *goði* in return for protection, sometimes violated Iceland's inheritance laws. A man who transferred land without consent of the heirs was guilty of *arfskot*, or the cheating of an heir (*GG* Ia, 247–249; II, 85–87, 100, 127).

Political alliances were often formed through contractual friendship agreements called *vinfengi* or *vinátta*. Such agreements, found widely in the sagas, extended a person's sphere of influence beyond kinship and the standard *goði-bóndi* relationship. Most *vinfengi* arrangements were expected to bring political or financial gain to both parties to the agreement. Breaking *vinfengi* was a breach of faith and, as shown in examples in this study, signaled severe consequences.

A man who ignored the terms of his contractual agreements, or who aggressively imposed his will on those around him, was often called an *ójafnaðarmaðr* (overbearing man). He consistently flouted the norms of moderation and compromise in social, legal, and financial dealings. His conduct, marked by greed and ambition, went beyond acceptable limits. The behavioral code revealed by the sagas was based on the standard of *hóf*, meaning moderation or measure. A man of power, such as a *goði*, was expected to curb his ambitions. *Hóf* was more than an ethical judgment; it specified the kind of conduct looked for in those who held power.

The standard of *hóf* was frequently reinforced by the intervention of third-party arbitrators, often called *góð-viljamenn* or *góðgjarnir menn*, men of goodwill or good intentions. In negotiating solutions acceptable to both parties, the *góðviljamenn* were also serving their own best interests. Disruption in the district could destabilize their own alliances, impair their reputations, and disturb the balance of power.

Ideally, two men resolved their differences by direct compromise. One party to a dispute could offer *sjálfdœmi*, or self-judgment, allowing the other party to fix the terms of the settlement. *Sjálfdœmi* was granted when the party offering it assumed that the other party would act with moderation, or when the opponent was so powerful that he demanded the right to set the terms.

A *hólmganga*, or duel, was a less peaceful way of directly resolving a dispute. Old men sometimes had to give up their lands because they declined a challenge to a *hólmganga* or lost the fight. The duel was eventually outlawed in Iceland, probably because it embodied outdated values not compatible with the carefully developed system of negotiation and compromise.

When a conflict could not be settled directly, the parties usually went to court. Anyone with a claim could bring a case. The wronged party or his family had the right to prosecute, but that right could be given away, often to a more powerful man who had a better chance of success. The claim entitling one to prosecute could also be sold, often to a *goði* assembling a group of cases against one particularly troublesome opponent.

Most conflicts in Iceland were finally resolved by arbitration. A legal term for arbitrator was *sáttarmaðr* or *sættarmaðr*. The arbitrators took up the work of the *góðviljamenn* and could be the same people. A man who was more intent on destroying his opponent than on settling a dispute sought the extreme judgment of outlawry. Outlawry could be part of a private or a court settlement. Two types of outlawry are prevalent in the sagas. A "lesser outlaw," a *fjǫrbaugsmaðr*, had three summers after the judgment to find passage out of Iceland. He had to ask at least three shipowners for passage each summer; a shipowner who refused was fined three marks of silver. While the outlaw stayed in Iceland, the *fjǫrbaugsgarðr*, which is best translated as sanctuary, was in effect. It meant that the outlaw was limited to three domiciles not more than a day's journey apart. He could travel the roads between them, but if people came along he had to leave the road for a distance greater than a spear's throw in order to remain *heilagr*, or protected by the sanctity of the law. Once abroad, he had to stay for three years, during which he enjoyed the same rights as other traveling Icelanders. If the *fjǫrbaugsmaðr* did not leave Iceland after three summers, he became a *skógarmaðr*, or full outlaw.

A man could also be declared a full outlaw by a court sentence or a private sentence sanctioned by the *lǫgrétta*. A *skógarmaðr* was not to be harbored by anyone, nor could he be helped out of the country. When the settlement was a private one, there were sometimes mitigating circumstances. For instance, a man might be given a certain amount of time to settle his affairs before leaving the country. If the normal *skógarmaðr* did manage to leave Iceland, he lived without the rights of a traveling Icelander and could never return. He could not have a Christian burial and his children had no inheritance rights.

An outlaw who did not abide by the terms of his outlawry

was considered *óheilagr* (unprotected by the law) and could
be killed or wounded with impunity. Similarly, a man could
be declared by a court to be, or to have died, *óheilagr*
(*óhelgr*), literally unholy or profaned. Being in the state of
óhelgi meant that an individual's protection under the law
was forfeited and that heirs would be left without the right
to seek legal redress.

In cases of outlawry a court of confiscation (*féránsdómr*)
was held, usually on the outlaw's lands, fourteen days after
the end of the court session at which the judgment was
made or, in a private settlement, fourteen days after the
next Althing. The *féránsdómr* consisted of twelve judges
selected by the prosecutor's *goði*. This group gave the
outlaw's creditors what was owing them from his holdings.
From what was left, the *goði* received a cow or an ox. The
rest of the property was confiscated; half of it went to the
prosecutor and the other half to the men of the quarter
(*GG* Ia, 83 ff., 108, 112 ff., 118, 120, 125; II, 359). Since the
system was profitable for them, prosecutors may have
pushed many cases of outlawry simply to obtain valuable
land. If the outlaw gathered supporters and successfully
blocked the judgment of the *féránsdómr*, his outlawry
might be renegotiated and reduced to a fine. Again, the
settlements reached depended on relative strength. Winning in court was only part of the suit; the rest was imple-
menting the verdict without the aid of a police mechanism.
This arrangement proved to be a highly conservative and
stabilizing force in the society.

Other sentences besides outlawry were handed down.
An *útlagi*, though the term technically means "outlaw,"
denoted a man on whom a fine was levied. Fines were
originally assessed in silver, but beginning in the eleventh
century, as a result of the growing scarcity of silver, the
chief currency became homespun cloth, *vaðmál*. The basic
monetary unit was the *lǫgeyrir* (law ounce, pl. *lǫgaurar*)
which equaled six ells of homespun cloth two ells wide (an
ell was about 49 cm.). In the period of settlement the law

ounce was probably equal to an ounce of pure silver; over the years the ratio varied from about four to one around the year 1000, to eight to one around 1100, to six to one around 1300. The modern reader is seldom sure which value is being used in a specific saga. Prices of goods were calculated in *þinglagseyrir* (standardized ounce). These standardized ounces were set at the *várþings* and varied from district to district. Usually they were equal to three or four ells of homespun cloth.

Appendix B

Examples of Conflict

THE feudeme of conflict centers primarily on the scarcity of resources. The scarcity caused competition for supplies and possessions and raised anxiety within the insular state. Conflict in the sagas is usually tied to material wealth in one way or another, or to the maintenance of power. It is sometimes difficult to distinguish different types of conflicts from one another, but the following examples provide a basis for understanding what people in the sagas feuded about. Issues of wealth often blend into issues of power, and at times a conflict over property is or becomes a matter of insult. For instance, in *Laxdœla saga* (see chap. 8), Kjartan buys the land of Þórarinn Þórisson sælings primarily to insult Bolli. In *Vápnfirðinga saga* (ch. 7), Brodd-Helgi takes Þormóðr Steinbjarnarson's timber in order to harass Þormóðr and his chieftain Geitir. Because of the wide variety of reasons for conflict, the following categories are meant to be guidelines, not hard-and-fast delineations. Some examples used earlier in the book reappear in the appendixes so that they can be placed within the context of a particular feudeme. Some feuds are mentioned in all three appendixes as the action progresses to different feudemes.

The examples suggest a number of tentative conclusions. One is that saga characters confronted each other regularly over mundane matters such as ownership, produce, and protection of property. The examples in Appendixes C and D suggest that recurring acts of brokerage were the usual type of advocacy, and that arbitration was the primary form of resolution.

Material Sources of Conflict

Desired land.—Forests, workable land, and meadows, sharply limited in medieval Iceland, were constant sources of contention. Fields such as "Sure-giver" in *Víga-Glúms saga* and "Rich-giver" in *Egils saga* were so productive that they were recognized by name. Other parcels of desired land were haggled over, and sometimes one party would buy land that another party had already claimed. Final ownership depended more on strength than on legitimacy.

In *Hrafns saga Sveinbjarnarsonar* (ch. 13), Loftr Markússson buys land at Mýrar from Mǫgr Mǫgsson, a thingman of Hrafn Sveinbjarnarson's (it is stated, however, in the index to *Sturlunga saga* [1946] that Mǫgr owned part of a *goðorð*). Despite the fact that Hrafn has an option on the land, he is not consulted about the sale. When Loftr sets up his household on the land, after making insults about Hrafn and his thingmen, Hrafn goes to Mýrar with Þorvaldr Snorrason and other supporters. Loftr is unwilling to settle, but when he realizes they mean to burn the farm he changes his mind. Sighvatr Sturluson is chosen to arbitrate the dispute, but the conflict continues until Loftr is eventually banished.

The feud discussed earlier in this book (chap. 8) between Kjartan and Bolli in *Laxdœla saga* escalates (ch. 47) when Kjartan approaches Þórarinn Þórisson with the objective of buying a piece of land that Þórarinn has already promised to Bolli. Kjartan convinces Þórarinn to convey the land to him by *handsal* for the price that Bolli would have paid. Kjartan points out he would prevent Þórarinn from selling the land at all if it is not sold to him.

In *Eyrbyggja saga* (ch. 31; see saga selection 7), Snorri goði accepts a valuable forest, Krákunes, from Þórólfr bægifótr as payment for prosecuting Þórólfr's son, Arnkell, who killed some of his father's slaves. The slaves had been sent by Þórólfr to burn the farm of Úlfarr, a freedman under Arnkell's protection. After the death of Þórólfr (ch. 33), Arnkell decides he wants the forest that he would have inherited, had it not been transferred to Snorri (ch. 35). When Arnkell's men inform him that Snorri is having wood cut in the forest, he kills Snorri's follower Haukr and seizes the cut wood. This final incident in the feud leads to Snorri's killing of Arnkell (ch. 37).

Shared land.—In a sequence in *Hávarðar saga Ísfirðings* (ch. 14), Hólmgǫngu-Ljótr, a most unjust man, and Þorbjǫrn at Eyrr share a meadow. Ljótr first dams up a brook flowing over his land to the meadow; then he claims all the land for himself. Þorbjǫrn is afraid of Ljótr and buys the land back. The sons of Þorbjǫrn, understandably upset, kill Ljótr. They are then sent by their father to his friend, the powerful chieftain Steinþórr at Eyrr, with a gold ring to gain his support. Steinþórr sends the sons to Hávarðr. Because Ljótr was an *ójafnaðarmaðr* and because Steinþórr takes on the case, Þorbjǫrn is awarded the meadow when the case is tried at the thing (ch. 22).

Fóstbrœðra saga (ch. 12) tells the story of Helgi Snorrason, who refuses to sell a meadow he owns to Þorsteinn Egilsson. Þorsteinn attacks and wounds Helgi as Helgi is taking in his hay. After men of goodwill step in and arbitrate, Þorsteinn pays Helgi for the field and for the wounds he inflicted on Helgi.

A sequence of feud clusters in *Víga-Glúms saga* (ch. 5) narrates a struggle over land which escalates to feud. In this feud (see chap. 7) the protagonists are a widow, Ástríðr, and her supposedly backward son, Glúmr, on one side, and on the other their neighbors, Þorkell and his son Sigmundr. These latter are related to a very powerful family, the Esphœlingar. Ástríðr is unable to protect herself against the aggressiveness of her neighbors, who want her land. At one point Ástríðr's land is divided between the contending parties, the widow receiving the half without the buildings. Although she has powerful relatives, as a woman she lacks the means to win their support.

Later, another conflict starts when two heifers belonging to the neighbors are missing and Ástríðr's thralls are summoned for stealing them. Ástríðr goes to her eldest son Þorsteinn and asks him to defend the thralls, for she fears she cannot continue to work the farm without them. She tells Þorsteinn that, rather than having the thralls outlawed, she would pay a fine for them if no other solution is possible. Because of the strength of the opponents' relatives, the Esphœlingar, Þorsteinn proposes that he and his mother pay what Þorkell and Sigmundr want. Ástríðr knows, however, that the father and son will want property that she and her younger son, Glúmr, cannot do without. Ástríðr, with no one else to turn to, follows Þorsteinn's advice; she lets Þorkell and Sigmundr decide how the case shall be settled. They want *sjálfdœmi* or outlawry for the thralls. Þorsteinn and Ástríðr choose the former. Ástríðr is forced to accept the *sjálfdœmi* settlement; Þorkell and Sigmundr award themselves full ownership of a valuable piece of property, a field called "Sure-giver," which the two families had always shared. Even when the heifers are found the field is not returned, although Þorkell and Sigmundr offer to pay for it. Ástríðr refuses because she would rather have the field than the money. When Glúmr, who has been in Norway, returns, Ástríðr goads him into action and the feud escalates. Glúmr goes to the field "Sure-giver" and there kills Sigmundr. Then, beginning to act as the responsible son of a chieftain, he gains the support of powerful relatives. Since it is decided at the local assembly that Sigmundr was in the wrong, no fine is assessed on Glúmr for killing him. Then Glúmr brings the case against Þorkell for fraudulent acquisition of land. When Þorkell, Sigmundr's father, is given the choice of being outlawed or selling the land back to Glúmr, Þorkell's friends convince him to settle, and Glúmr gets the land back (chs. 7–9). This sequence of feud clusters sets the stage for a feud between the Esphœlingar and Glúmr.

Inherited land.—In an inheritance case in *Laxdœla saga* (ch. 18), Þorsteinn surtr and several of his relatives drown. Þorsteinn's daughter, Guðríðr, inherits from her father. She could inherit more, depending on who drowned last. Her husband, Þorkell trefill, secretly bargains with the sole survivor of the accident, apparently altering the order in which the deaths occurred. In this way he is attempting to inherit more property than he would otherwise be entitled to. The intricate detail in which this situation is described reflects the concern of saga literature with realistic portrayal. The order of deaths is worked out as follows: first, Þorsteinn surtr, about whose estate there is no dispute; second, his son-in-law Þórarinn, which would make Þórarinn's daughter, Hildr, the heir; third, Hildr, whose heir would be her mother, Guðríðr's sister; finally, Guðríðr's sister, which would make Guðríðr heir to the property. Þórarinn's relatives, somewhat doubtful of the truth of the order in which the deaths are recounted, arrange an ordeal to test Þorkell's veracity. He manages, however, to get through the ordeal by a trick and takes all the property.

In *Njáls saga* (ch. 60), Ásgrímr Elliða-Grímsson has a suit at the thing against Úlfr Uggason over an inheritance. Ásgrímr calls only five witnesses when he should have had nine, but Úlfr pays when Gunnarr acts on Ásgrímr's behalf and challenges Úlfr to single combat. Ásgrímr says he will thereafter always support Gunnarr.

Land whose ownership is changing through inheritance is insecurely held and therefore often becomes the subject of a dispute. *Laxdœla saga* (ch. 26) offers the case of Hǫskuldr Dala-Kollsson, who intends to leave a third of his estate to his bastard son, Óláfr, a portion equal to the share of each of his two legitimate sons. When one of the latter refuses to agree, he is tricked by Hǫskuldr, who gives Óláfr the family luck and great treasures in the form of the sword and the golden bracelet he had received from King Hákon. Óláfr becomes a rich and powerful chieftain.

In *Sturlu saga* (ch. 28), the inheritance rights to Birningr Steinarsson's property are bought by Einarr Þorgilsson from Birningr's daughter by his first marriage. Einarr strengthens the daughter's inheritance rights by claiming that Birningr's second marriage is unlawful. Einarr is willing to give the second wife Guðbjǫrg and her sons something, if Birningr will give up his farm and move to Einarr's. Birningr refuses. Einarr has seventy sheep of Birningr's slaughtered. In order to protect himself Birningr conveys all his property by *handsal* to Sturla Þórðarson, who is better able to contend with Einarr.

Dowry.—Land also changes hands through dowry. In the event of a divorce, the dowry is not always returned, and when it is, the return is often made only after a fight. This situation occurs in *Vápnfirðinga saga* (ch. 6) where Brodd-Helgi and Geitir quarrel over Halla Lýtingsdóttir's dowry.

In *Njáls saga* (ch. 8), Mǫrðr gígja and his son-in-law, Hrútr Herjólfsson, dispute over the divorce settlement between Hrútr and Mǫrðr's daughter, Unnr. Hrútr challenges Mǫrðr to a *hólmganga*, and when Mǫrðr, who is old, refuses to fight, Hrútr keeps the dowry. Later in the saga (ch. 21) Unnr asks her kinsman, Gunnarr Hámundarson of Hlíðarendi, to retrieve her dowry for her. The case goes to the thing, where Hrútr wins it on a legal technicality. Gunnarr then challenges Hrútr to single combat, and Hrútr chooses to pay (ch. 24).

In *Droplaugarsona saga* (ch. 9), Þorgrímr skinnhúfa asks Þórarinn moldoxi to represent him in the division of goods

between himself and his wife Rannveig, who is divorcing
him. Rannveig has already enlisted the support of her
relative Helgi Droplaugarson. Þórarinn moldoxi sends
Þorgrímr with news of Helgi Droplaugarson's travels to
Helgi Ásbjarnarson, since Helgi Droplaugarson has been
outlawed by Helgi Ásbjarnarson and Þórarinn knows that
Helgi Ásbjarnarson is looking for a way to get at the other
Helgi. This conflict is one of a series between the two
Helgis.

In *Eyrbyggja saga* (ch. 17), Þorgrímr Kjallaksson and his
sons set themselves against Illugi svarti at the thing over the
marriage settlement and dowry of Illugi's wife.

Produce of the land.—This term may include foodstuffs
for the household and fodder for farm animals, firewood
or timber cut from the valuable forests, and wool or
homespun.

In *Hœnsa-Þóris saga* (ch. 5), in a dispute that sets the
action of the saga in motion, Hœnsa-Þórir and Blund-
Ketill quarrel over some hay. Blund-Ketill asks Hœnsa-
Þórir for hay for some of his farmers who have not planned
well for the winter. Hœnsa-Þórir, although he has plenty of
hay, repeatedly turns down Blund-Ketill's generous offers
of payment. Finally Blund-Ketill takes the hay and leaves
some money, which infuriates Hœnsa-Þórir. Hœnsa-Þórir
gains the support of Þorvaldr Oddsson and burns Blund-
Ketill in his house (ch. 9).

As a part of the long-standing feud between Vémundr
Þórisson (Fjǫrleifarson) and Steingrímr Ǫrnólfsson narrated in *Reykdœla saga* (ch. 9), Vémundr, in order to insult
Steingrímr, buys timber from a Norwegian which Steingrímr has already bought. Steingrímr has Vémundr's thralls
killed and takes the wood. Not long afterward (ch. 11) a
similar problem arises when Steingrímr arranges to buy two
oxen from Ǫrnólfr rella. Vémundr, hearing about the
transaction, tells Ǫrnólfr that he wants to buy the oxen for
his uncle Áskell. Although Ǫrnólfr informs him that Steingrímr has already bought the animals, Vémundr manages

to get them anyway. He orders his thrall Svartr to watch them overnight. Steingrímr, finding out what has happened, sends his servants after the oxen. They kill Svartr and take the animals. Vémundr then borrows a tracking hound from Konáll of Einarsstaðir and sets out with several followers to find the oxen. In the ensuing fight Vémundr cuts off the heads of the beasts. Later the dispute is settled by the arbitration of Áskell and Eyjólfr Valgerðarson, another chieftain, who often arbitrates with Áskell.

In *Qlkofra þáttr* (ch. 1), the beer seller Qlkofri accidentally burns his own woods and a woodland belonging jointly to six *goðar*. The chieftains had bought the woods to use at the Althing. The first chieftain to hear of the burning, Skapti the lawspeaker, recognizes the potential profit to the owners in the case and sends word to Guðmundr inn ríki Eyjólfsson, another of the chieftains. During the winter messages are sent among the six, and it is agreed that Skapti should prepare the case, as he lives closest to Qlkofri. Skapti summons Qlkofri, intending to have him outlawed. At the thing Qlkofri has little luck finding supporters until he meets Broddi Bjarnason (ch. 2). With Broddi's backing, Qlkofri is fined only a small amount (ch. 3). This *þáttr* is similar in plot to *Bandamanna saga*.

In *Eyrbyggja saga* (chs. 30–31) one of the early conflicts between Snorri goði and Arnkell goði originates when Þórólfr bægifótr and Úlfarr the freedman quarrel over the cutting of hay in a jointly owned field. In *Reykdœla saga* (ch. 1), Áskell Eyvindarson's thingman Mýlaugr wants redress from the *ójafnaðarmaðr* Eysteinn Mánason, who took firewood from Mýlaugr's farm when Mýlaugr refused to sell it. Eysteinn has taken wood before without paying. Because he is the foster father of one of Áskell's nephews, Hávarðr Þórisson (Fjǫrleifarson), Mýlaugr tells Hávarðr of Eysteinn's thieving, and Hávarðr reports to Áskell. When Áskell says he will bring the case against Eysteinn, Eysteinn lets Áskell arbitrate and a settlement is reached.

Finally, I have included beached whales in the category of produce of the land. Stretches of coastal land were especially valuable because of driftwood, beached whales, and the collection of eggs from seabirds. Because of the value of a whale, the question of who would claim this enormous resource at times caused contention among the men of a whole region.

In *Reykdœla saga* (ch. 8), Máni is the watchman for Áskell Eyvindarson's jetsam. Áskell tells Máni that he may sell what the current washes ashore. Vémundr Þórisson (Fjǫrleifarson) travels to Grímsey to take what has not been sold. When Máni tells him he has sold it all, as arranged with Áskell, Vémundr takes a whale from Þorbjǫrn and his son Steinn at Árskógr, so as not to have made the trip in vain. Vémundr offers Áskell part of the whale, but Áskell wants no part of stolen goods. Steinn goes to meet his brother-in-law Steingrímr Ǫrnólfsson and complains of Vémundr's theft. Steingrímr tells him they should ask Áskell for his judgment and let the incident lie quiet. Steinn supports Steingrímr in later conflicts against Vémundr.

In *Hrafns saga Sveinbjarnarson* (chs. 16–17), a whale washes ashore on Hrafn's land. The man who finds the whale tells Þorvaldr Snorrason, Hrafn's enemy. Þorvaldr tells the finder to say the whale beached on common land so that Þorvaldr will have a legal claim to it. Þorvaldr then has the whale cut up and taken to his farm. When Hrafn hears of this, he sends to his brother-in-law, Hallr the lawspeaker, and Hallr's brother for advice on how to conduct the case against Þorvaldr. These two men recommend that Hrafn prepare prosecutions against Þorvaldr and all the men who had taken part and present the case at the Dýrafjǫrðr assembly. Þorvaldr and nine others are outlawed.

In *Fóstbrœðra saga* (ch. 7), Þorgils Másson and his companions claim a whale that has beached on common land. When Þorgeirr Hávarsson and Þormóðr Bersason hear about the claim, they go to the place where Þorgils is cutting up the whale and say they want part or all of it. The two sides fight. Þorgils is slain and Þorgeirr is later outlawed for the deed.

Chattels.—Sheep and cattle sometimes led to conflict. In *Sturlu saga*, Einarr Þorgilsson steals sheep from Birningr as part of his effort to obtain Birningr's property by purchasing inheritance rights (see details above). It is told in the same saga that Brandr Jónsson has in the past let Einarr Þorgilsson slaughter sheep on his land. Einarr Helgason, when he marries Guðný, Brandr's daughter, wants the slaughtering to cease. Einarr Þorgilsson intends to continue, however, and while moving sheep, his man, the priest Ljúfini, wounds a farmer who refuses to let Einarr's men use his boat. When Einarr Helgason and his stepfather Sturla Þórðarson slaughter Einarr Þorgilsson's sheep in retaliation, a long feud between the two Einarrs is started (ch. 11).

In *Reykdœla saga*, Eysteinn Mánason has Bjǫrn, a relative of the Fjǫrleifarsons, plant sheep on the property of Háls Þórisson (Fjǫrleifarson) because he wants people to think that the animals have been stolen. Háls is outlawed because his uncle, the *goði* Áskell Eyvindarson, will not take his case and instead advises him to go abroad (ch. 2). Áskell later does take the case when he is convinced that Háls was not involved, and Eysteinn is outlawed (ch. 3).

An example from *Droplaugarsona saga* (considered in chap. 2) occurs when two farmers, Þorgeirr at Hrafnkelsstaðir and Þórðr at Geirólfseyrr, dispute over sheep that Þórðr has sold to Þorgeirr. The two farmers involve Helgi Ásbjarnarson and Helgi Droplaugarson. This instance is just one of the many in which the two Helgis are in dispute. Each has his strength: Helgi Ásbjarnarson is a chieftain; Helgi Droplaugarson is extremely knowledgeable in the law and is a fine warrior.

In *Hrafns saga Sveinbjarnarson*, Galti, a friend of Loftr Markússon's, refuses to sell a horse to Gísli Markússon and Guðmundr Hallsson but gives it to Loftr. When

Guðmundr tries to steal the horse, Loftr and four other men kill him; all five are then banished from the district and fined (ch. 13). In *Sturlu saga* (ch. 18), in a long-running feud, Einarr Helgason drives holes into three of Einarr Þorgilsson's boats; he also goes to Staðarhóll while Einarr Þorgilsson is at the thing and takes some livestock, which is, however, later returned. Einarr Þorgilsson steals sheep from Ingjaldr, Sturla's son-in-law (ch. 20).

Cheating and stealing.—Many of the cases concerning chattels involve stealing. The following examples are cases that are not simply construed as stealing and cheating but are so named in the sagas.

Oddr Ófeigsson, in *Bandamanna saga* (ch. 4), when missing sixty sheep suspects that Óspakr Glúmsson, with whom he has had a falling-out, has taken them. So as to avert trouble, Oddr's foster brother, Váli, goes to Óspakr to determine whether Óspakr has really stolen the sheep. When he feels certain of Óspakr's guilt, he offers to bring about a settlement without dishonor, but Óspakr refuses. After the winter is over, Oddr rides with twenty men to Óspakr's farm to summon Óspakr. Váli is killed, bringing on a new conflict.

In *Njáls saga* (chs. 47–49), Gunnarr, Kolskeggr Hámundarson, Þráinn Sigfússon, and Lambi Sigurðarson go to Otkell Skarfsson to buy meat and hay. Otkell refuses to sell them either of these commodities, but he does sell his troublesome thrall Melkólfr to Gunnarr. Later, Hallgerðr, Gunnarr's wife, has Melkólfr steal cheese from Otkell. Through a cunning scheme devised by Mǫrðr Valgarðsson, Hallgerðr is identified as the thief. When Gunnarr offers Otkell self-judgment, he is refused because Otkell would rather prosecute.

In *Ljósvetninga saga* (A, ch. 6; C, ch. 14), Guðmundr inn ríki pursues cases against Þórir Helgason's thingmen because of an insult by Þórir. Guðmundr has succeeded in outlawing Þórir Akraskeggr (also called Þorgils Akrakarl), a wealthy thingman of Þórir Helgason. While Guðmundr's men are collecting Þórir Akraskeggr's livestock at the *féránsdómr* held on his farm, Guðmundr's shepherd discovers ten (almost thirty, according to version C) goats inside a sheepfold. The goats are all freshly marked with the sign of Þórir Helgason. When Guðmundr confronts Þórir Helgason with this information, Þórir claims that Þórir Akraskeggr gave him the goats, at the time of summoning, for supporting him. Þórir (in C) says he had marked the goats before the *féránsdómr*. Guðmundr summons him, along with witnesses, for stealing the goats. Guðmundr later gets *sjálfdœmi* from Þórir, who is fined and outlawed for three years (C, ch. 17).

An example of cheating a merchant in *Ljósvetninga saga* (ch. 1) is reminiscent of Brodd-Helgi and Geitir's (*Vápnfirðinga saga*) cheating and killing of a Norwegian merchant. The example from *Ljósvetninga saga* concerns a Norwegian merchant, Sigurðr, who sells goods to the *ójafnaðarmaðr* Sǫlmundr Víðarsson. When Sigurðr demands payment, he is refused. Later he and fourteen others go to summon Sǫlmundr, and he is killed by Sǫlmundr's brother, Sǫxólfr.

In *Sturlu saga* (ch. 25), Sturla Þórðarson buys meal from the farmer Þorvarðr and feels cheated because it is of poor quality. He gives Þorvarðr the choice of being summoned or of taking in Sturla's son Halldórr. Þorvarðr chooses the latter option. When Þórhallr Svartsson, an old friend of Þorvarðr's, hears about the fosterage, he takes Halldórr and brings him back to the boy's mother's relatives. Sturla is displeased. When he subsequently sends men to buy food from Þórhallr Svartsson, they are refused. Sturla's son, Sveinn, now talks with Þórhallr's son-in-law, Þorsteinn drettingr, with whom Þórhallr is on bad terms, and Þorsteinn gives Sveinn a large sum to get Þórhallr out of the way. Sveinn then summons Þórhallr for not paying the full tithe and for using false weights and measures. These charges are levied because Þórhallr is interfering with the way in which Sturla and his family want to run the district.

The matter is settled when Þórhallr, on the advice of Þorleifr beiskaldi, offers Sturla *sjálfdœmi*.

Thievery is frequently an issue in the sagas. In *Vatnsdœla saga* (ch. 28), men tell Þorsteinn Ingimundarson, their chieftain, that Þórólfr sleggja is stealing goods in the area. (There is also a suggestion of sorcery about him; he has twenty large cats.) Þorsteinn calls up men against Þórólfr, who runs away. In the pursuit Þórólfr and one of Þorsteinn's men perish in a quagmire. Þorsteinn keeps Þórólfr's money as compensation for his follower.

Nonmaterial Sources of Conflict

Iceland was a small country, and cross-country rumors, gossip, and discussions of events marked the yearly meetings of the Althing. An individual's power depended on retention of wealth as well as on retention of reputation. One source of status was the ownership of a *goðorð*. In *Njáls saga* (ch. 97), Njáll connives to obtain a *goðorð* for his foster son since otherwise the chosen bride will refuse him as a husband. In *Bandamanna saga*, Oddr becomes wealthy as a merchant but, to settle the question of his importance, he purchases a *goðorð* (ch. 2).

Power was also dependent on adequate response to the seduction of a kinswoman, the killing of a kinsman, or an insult to self or family.

Goðorð.—In *Droplaugarsona saga* (ch. 4), the machinations for retention of power are shown in the case of Hrafnkell Þórisson, who wants his share of his *goðorð* from his uncle Helgi Ásbjarnarson. He goes to Helgi Droplaugarson and they concoct a scheme to expose Helgi Ásbjarnarson's acceptance of bribes at the thing. Together they convince Án trúðr, a farmer, to give Helgi Ásbjarnarson seven horses as a bribe. The latter then names the farmer to the honor of being a judge in the court. Helgi Ásbjarnarson has the farmer wear a felt hood to conceal his identity and tells him not to talk much. Helgi Droplaugarson thrusts the hilt of his sword under the hood and uncovers Án. He and Hrafnkell now make a legal charge for bribery against Helgi Ásbjarnarson which they use in the contest for the *goðorð*. In the settlement it is agreed that Helgi Ásbjarnarson and Hrafnkell are to hold equal shares in the *goðorð*.

In *Bandamanna saga* (chs. 3—4), Oddr Ófeigsson goes abroad and leaves Óspakr Glúmsson in charge of his farm and *goðorð*. At first Óspakr does not want the *goðorð*, but he fares well at the assembly in the summer and, in the fall, makes a match with the close relative of a chieftain. When Oddr returns, Óspakr is reluctant to relinquish the *goðorð*, but he promises to do so at the thing. He manages, however, to get to the thing without Oddr, who arrives too late. Finally, under threats, Óspakr gives the *goðorð* back to Oddr by *handsal*.

Seduction.—In cases of seduction, women are basically treated as property, and the resultant conflicts generate the same kind of brokerage and resolution as do those over land or other forms of property. Seduction is rather more than an insult to the woman's husband or other kin; it is damage for which compensation must be paid. In *Vatnsdœla saga* (chs. 37—40), Óttarr at Grímstungur summons Ingólfr Þorsteinsson to the Húnavatn assembly for having seduced and spoken insulting verses about Óttarr's daughter Valgerðr. Ingólfr, threatening violence after the summons, is given the *goðorð* by his father. No settlement for the seduction is made at this time because Ingólfr and his uncle break up the court with a fight. Óttarr sells his land and moves away. Ingólfr marries Valgerðr's young aunt, but then he continues to see Valgerðr. A few years later Óttarr sends an outlaw to kill either Ingólfr or his brother Guðbrandr. In exchange for the killing Óttarr has promised the outlaw protection. Ingólfr will not take the man in and sends him away, but Guðbrandr allows him to stay for some time. When Guðbrandr and the outlaw are out riding one day, the outlaw attacks him. Guðbrandr, however, kills the outlaw. The brothers, suspecting that Óttarr is behind the attack, confront him, and Óttarr denies having sent the outlaw. Finally a settlement is made. Óttarr pays 100 silvers, but Guðbrandr does not pay for killing the outlaw because it is agreed that the outlaw fell without the right to compensation. Ingólfr also will fall *óheilagr* if he continues to visit Valgerðr. Óttarr sends another man, Svartr, to cut off Ingólfr's hand or foot or to kill Guðbrandr should he not get at Ingólfr. Again Ingólfr sends him away, but Guð-brandr takes him in. This time Guðbrandr and Svartr kill each other, and Ingólfr prepares the case for the thing. In the arbitration the final settlement is 300 silvers for the killing of Guðbrandr. Also, the case against Ingólfr for breach of agreement in continuing to see Valgerðr is voided. In the same saga (ch. 45), Hermundr Ávaldason kills Galti Óttarsson, whose brother has seduced Her-mundr's sister Kolfinna. Þorkell krafla, Galti's *goði*, rushes to avenge him, but he is delayed at Hermundr's booth by Hermundr's mother. Instead of taking vengeance, how-ever, Þorkell decides that it is wiser to settle than to kill.

In *Hrafns saga Sveinbjarnarsonar* (ch. 14), Jón Þorsteins-son seduces the mistress of Símon Bjarnason, a servant of Hrafn's. Jón is outlawed by Hrafn after he kills Símon, but he is eventually pardoned by Hrafn. Later Hrafn offers compensation to Símon's relatives. *Droplaugarsona saga* (ch. 6) offers an example of seduction which contributes to the series of conflicts between Helgi Droplaugarson and Helgi Ásbjarnarson. A case is brought against Bjǫrn, foster father of Helgi Ásbjarnarson, because he has been visiting Þórdís, the wife of Þorsteinn at Desjarmýrr. She is related to Helgi Droplaugarson. Þorsteinn asks Helgi Droplaugar-son to speak to Bjǫrn about these visits. When Bjǫrn refuses to stop the visits, he is killed by Helgi Droplaugar-son and then is summoned, so that he will have fallen *óheilagr*. Both Helgis bring cases against each other at the thing: Helgi Ásbjarnarson summons the other for disposing of Bjǫrn's body by dumping it into the sea instead of burying it; Helgi Droplaugarson has a case of seduction against Bjǫrn, whom Helgi Ásbjarnarson represents. Helgi Droplaugarson has witnesses to the burial of Bjǫrn and thus quashes the case against himself, while putting forward his own case to have Bjǫrn declared an outlaw. Helgi Ásbjarnarson offers to pay to prevent the outlawry and Helgi Droplaugarson agrees.

A number of seduction cases are described in *Sturlu saga*. Þorsteinn Ásbjarnarson and his son Eiríkr have Gils Þormóðarson outlawed for fathering a child on Ásný, the sister of Þorsteinn tittlingr (ch. 5). Sturla Þórðarson offers money on behalf of his relative Gils, but it is refused and the case goes to court, where it is settled by payment of fines. In another case, in response to rumors that Þorvarðr Þorgeirsson has seduced Yngvildr Þorgilsdóttir, Þorvarðr goes through the iron ordeal; when he is successful, the accuser, Einarr Þorgilsson, Yngvildr's brother, is forced to pay. Not long afterward the lovers leave secretly for Norway (ch. 9). Sigurðr kerlingarnef, Einarr Þorgilsson's thingman, has a mistress, Arngerðr, whom Einarr Helgason visits. After Sigurðr lets Einarr Helgason's horse loose, he is wounded by Einarr, who sends to the *goði* Sturla Þórðarson for help; Sigurðr goes to his *goði*, Einarr Þorgilsson. Since Sturla has thirty men and Einarr Þorgilsson has only nine when they meet, Einarr agrees when Sturla offers to settle; Sturla arbitrates (ch. 13).

Guðmundar saga dýra (ch. 10) tells of the wounding of Ǫgmundr sneis by the sons of Þórðr Þórarinsson for seducing Þórðr's wife, Margrét. Although the case ends in arbitration, neither side keeps the agreement and the feud continues. In *Njáls saga* (chs. 71–74), Mǫrðr Valgarðsson sets Þorgeirr Otkelsson to seduce a kinswoman of Gunnarr of Hlíðarendi in hopes that Gunnarr will kill him; Gunnarr would thus have killed two members of the same family, an offense Njáll had warned him not to commit. When Þorgeirr Otkelsson and Þorgeirr Starkaðarson ambush Gunnarr and Þorgeirr Otkelsson is killed, Gunnarr is outlawed for three years. He is then killed because he does not leave Iceland (ch. 77).

Killing.—In the sagas, an earlier issue leading to conflict often remained unresolved to the satisfaction of at least one party, and a killing resulted. This killing in turn might lead to further conflict, such as the killing of Gunnarr mentioned above. A clear example is found in *Eyrbyggja saga* (chs. 35–37): the killing of Haukr, Snorri's man, leads to the killing of Arnkell. In *Hávarðar saga Ísfirðings* (chs. 11–12), Hávarðr kills the *ójafnaðarmaðr* Þorbjǫrn, who has killed Hávarðr's son Óláfr, and Hávarðr kills Þorbjǫrn's brother Ljótr. In *Valla-Ljóts saga* (ch. 3), Halli Sigurðarson demands 50 silvers from Valla-Ljótr for breaking the law by dividing up an inheritance on Michaelmas, a legal holy day. Ljótr pays, but later he kills Halli (ch. 4).

In *Fóstbrœðra saga*, Ingólfr sviðinn and Þorbrandr, his son, both *ójafnaðarmenn* (chs. 3–5), steal from farmers around Jǫkulsfirðir. Their chieftain, Vermundr inn mjóvi, protects them because they have given him good gifts. The widow Sigrfljóð particularly is harassed. She takes advantage of the presence of the two foster brothers, Þorgeirr Hávarsson and Þormóðr Bersason, after they arrive at her farm during a storm, by having them kill both father and son. Sigrfljóð immediately goes and offers compensation to Vermundr, which is accepted.

In *Laxdœla saga* (chs. 54–55), Bolli is killed after a settlement is reached at the Þórsnessþing for his and others' killing of Kjartan. Some of Kjartan's supporters, however, are not satisfied with the settlement, and Halldórr Óláfsson and Barði Guðmundarson gather men to kill Bolli. The feud then continues.

In *Droplaugarsona saga* (ch. 13), Helgi Ásbjarnarson is killed in his house by Grímr Droplaugarson, after a fight in which Helgi Droplaugarson (who had been previously outlawed) was killed (ch. 10). In *Njáls saga* (chs. 109–111), Mǫrðr Valgarðsson brings about the death of Hǫskuldr Hvítanessgoði when he convinces the Njálssons that

Hǫskuldr, their foster brother, is plotting against them. Skarpheðinn Njálsson eventually agrees to kill Hǫskuldr, but only if Mǫrðr will accompany the Njálssons. Later Mǫrðr does not acknowledge that he himself inflicted a wound on Hǫskuldr.

In *Guðmundar saga dýra* (chs. 5–6), Hrafn Brandsson is killed by Hákon Þórðarson, lover of Hrafn's wife, Guðrún Þórðardóttir. Hákon is the nephew of the chieftain Guðmundr dýri, who takes his case. Guðmundr sends for Erlendr, Hrafn's brother, and tries to settle the matter. Erlendr, well disposed toward settlement, sends for Hákon's father, Þórðr Þórarinsson, but Þórðr will settle only if Guðrún pays half the fine. Guðmundr and the priest Flosi arbitrate the dispute and make a substantial award, including two pieces of land, to the dead man's kinsmen. Gifts are exchanged and Guðrún and Hákon marry.

In *Bandamanna saga* (chs. 4–5), Oddr Ófeigsson believes Óspakr Glúmsson has stolen some of his sheep. Óspakr will not admit his guilt and Oddr intends to summon him. Váli, Oddr's relative, goes to Óspakr to try one last time to promote an arbitration. Óspakr, thinking Váli is Oddr, attacks him in the dark and strikes a fatal blow. Before he dies, Váli counsels Óspakr to notify Oddr, who is waiting a short distance away, that the arbitration has been completed. By this ruse Oddr is tricked into riding off and Óspakr goes into hiding. When Oddr finds out about Váli's death, he prepares a case against Óspakr.

Insult.—Insults frequently engendered further contests that led to killings. An example is seen in the sequence from *Njáls saga* (ch. 35) between Hallgerðr and Bergþóra (see chap. 9).

In *Laxdœla saga* (chs. 46–47), Kjartan, after the disappearance of his special sword and his wife's headdress, locks Bolli and Guðrún and all their household inside their house for three days, during which they have no access to a privy. Later Bolli kills Kjartan (ch. 49). In *Njáls saga* (chs. 91–93), when the Njálssons and their brother-in-law Kári go to Þráinn Sigfússon to complain about Víga-Hrappr, a man under Þráinn's protection, the men exchange insults and Þráinn is later killed. Atonement is made when Ketill Sigfússon, Þráinn's brother, goes to Njáll, his father-in-law, who pays the sum Ketill sets. Ketill fosters Hǫskuldr Þráinsson (later Hvítanessgoði after he acquires the chieftaincy). This fosterage is later taken over by Njáll.

In *Þorsteins saga hvíta* (chs. 3−7), Einarr Þórisson and Þorsteinn fagri travel as partners to Norway; when Þorsteinn falls ill, Einarr mocks him. Einarr divides the goods unfairly and travels back to Iceland, adding to his insults by convincing Þorsteinn's betrothed and her father, among others, that Þorsteinn is dead. Einarr then marries the girl. When Þorsteinn returns, he demands payment from Einarr; Einarr refuses and Þorsteinn kills him. This deed leads to further conflict and eventually Þorsteinn is outlawed.

In *Valla-Ljóts saga* (ch. 1), Torfi, a thingman of Eyjólfr Einarsson's, wants to marry Halli Sigurðarson's mother. When Halli goes to pick up a pig from Torfi, of whom he has never had a high opinion, there is an exchange of insults. Halli lies in wait and kills Torfi on his way to visit Halli's mother. Halli then goes to his relative, Ingjaldr Hrólfsson, who then seeks assistance from Víga-Glúmr. Ingjaldr and Víga-Glúmr go to Eyjólfr Einarsson, Torfi's chieftain, and offer to give him 100 silvers and also to drop the case against him for Torfi's insulting of Halli. Eyjólfr agrees, as he is related to Halli, and their friendship continues.

In *Reykdœla saga* (chs. 12−13), Steingrímr Ǫrnólfsson is insulted by having a sheep's head thrown at him at the instigation of Áskell Eyvindarson's nephew, Vémundr. Áskell tries to placate Steingrímr with generous gifts, but Steingrímr refuses to accept them. Two years later Steingrímr has Herjólfr, brother of Vémundr, killed. The killing is followed by arbitration, but the conflict continues.

In *Hávarðar saga Ísfirðings* (chs. 5, 7), after Hávarðr's

son Óláfr has been killed by Þorbjǫrn Þjóðreksson, Hávarðr, an elderly man, goes to the killer for atonement but
is offered only an old horse, an insulting gesture. Þorbjǫrn
continues to mock Hávarðr at the thing. When a third man,
Gestr, tries to bring about a settlement, Þorbjǫrn throws
Óláfr's teeth at Hávarðr, who becomes angry and refuses to
settle. Later Hávarðr kills both Þorbjǫrn and his brother.

In *Droplaugarsona saga* (chs. 3–4) the woman Droplaug
is insulted by Þorgrímr, a guest of Þórir's at Mýnes and a
freedman of Helgi Ásbjarnarson's. After her sons, Helgi
and Grímr, kill Þorgrímr, fines are imposed upon them at
the thing.

In *Eyrbyggja saga* (ch. 18), when Þorbjǫrn digri is unable
to find his horses for slaughter in the fall, he sends a man to
Spá-Gils, a seer, to get information on their whereabouts.
Þorbjǫrn interprets the seer's answer to mean that the
horses are at Þórarinn svarti's farm, where he goes and
announces that he wants to conduct a search. After an
exchange of words, Þórarinn tells Þorbjǫrn to do as he
likes. Þorbjǫrn proceeds to summon Þórarinn for horse
theft. Þórarinn's mother, Geirríðr, is angered by the insult
and goads her son into confronting Þorbjǫrn. The ensuing
battle is stopped by the women, led by Þórarinn's wife,
Auðr. When Þórarinn discovers that Auðr has lost a hand
in the fighting, he pursues Þorbjǫrn. When he approaches
Þorbjǫrn's group he overhears another insult by one of
Þorbjǫrn's men. According to this new slander Þórarinn is
accused of cutting off his own wife's hand. Another fight
follows with more killings.

At a wedding feast in *Ljósvetninga saga* (A, chs. 5–9; C,
chs. 13–19), Guðmundr inn ríki's wife is told by Geirlaug,
wife of Þórir Helgason, that Þórir and Þorkell hákr have
insulted her husband. Guðmundr goes to his foster father,
Einarr Konálsson, for advice. Einarr tells him to bring all
the cases he can against the thingmen of Þórir Helgason,
and Einarr will hold the goods he will thereby receive until
Guðmundr has assembled enough wealth to move success-

fully against Þorkell hákr. In response to Einarr's advice,
Guðmundr summons a thingman of Þórir's for cheating a
merchant. The thingman wants a compromise to be arbitrated by Þórir and Guðmundr. Guðmundr, however, refuses to accept compensation, because he wants the outlawry of Þórir Akraskeggr (Þorgils Akrakarl), who is allied
to Þórir Helgason. Such a judgment would bring dishonor
and loss of power to Þórir Helgason. Guðmundr then summons Þórir Helgason for stealing some of Þórir's goats,
which would then be part of the goods confiscated in the
féránsdómr, and manages to get *sjálfdœmi*. Guðmundr and
his men later kill Þorkell hákr, an action stemming from the
original insult, and compensate the kinsmen of the dead
man.

Harboring outlaws.—Harboring an outlaw put one in
direct conflict with the party who outlawed the man and
thus resulted in a confrontation if the prosecution pursued
the matter.

In *Laxdœla saga* (chs. 14–15) the poor, but able, Þórólfr
kills Hallr, the brother of Ingjaldr Sauðeyjargoði, after
Hallr seizes Þórólfr's share of their fishing catch and takes
over the boat they share. He flees to Vigdís, his distant
relative and the wife of Þórðr goddi. Þórðr does not want
him to stay, but Vigdís insists he will remain through the
winter. Ingjaldr travels to Þórðr goddi and offers to give
him three marks of silver and to drop the charges against
him for harboring an outlaw, if Þórðr will surrender
Þórólfr. Þórðr agrees, but Vigdís foils his plans and gets
Þórólfr away.

In *Íslendinga saga* (ch. 55), Sturla Sighvatsson is in conflict with the Hrafnssons for harboring their outlawed relative. There is immediate payment and resolution.

In *Heiðarvíga saga* (chs. 5–6), Víga-Styrr brings cases
against two farmers for harboring a man named Einarr,
whom Styrr has prosecuted and who has been heavily
fined. Styrr has taken possession of Einarr's farm and
Einarr moves about, staying with different farmers. The

next spring Styrr confronts Einarr as he is moving away from the district. Styrr says he could bring a case against Einarr for moving and that he has good grounds to kill Einarr, which he proceeds to do. No fine is paid when Styrr kills Einarr. The farmers must pay fines for their breach of law.

Refusal to return compensation.—In the case from *Víga-Glúms saga* (mentioned above), the father and son, by refusing to give up the field "Sure-giver," even though the heifers have been found, are committing a breach of law and can therefore be prosecuted. In *Njáls saga* (chs. 67–68), Kolskeggr Hámundarson acts on behalf of his mother, claiming from Þorgeirr Starkaðarson part of Móeiðarhváll. This land was previously given to Starkaðr's father in compensation for the loss of another son. Gunnarr, Kolskeggr's brother, has advised him to pay rather than to give up this particular piece of land. Following the advice of Mǫrðr Valgarðsson, Þorgeirr says that such payment would break the settlement and thus constitute a breach of law. Kolskeggr is successful in this case at the thing, but Gunnarr's enemies, claiming that he broke a settlement by offering money instead of conveying the land, plan an attack.

Other less frequent causes of conflict include horse-fighting, witchings, and hauntings.

Horsefighting.—In a dispute during a horsefight in *Víga-Glúms saga* (chs. 13–14), Víga-Glúmr's horse and over-seer, Ingólfr, are struck by Kálfr from Stokkahlaða. When Kálfr is later killed, Ingólfr is accused. Víga-Glúmr is really the killer but he manages to make it appear that Ingólfr is. In *Njáls saga* (ch. 59), Gunnarr is also involved in a dispute over a horsefight. He strikes Þorgeirr Starkaðarson, who has struck Gunnarr's fine fighting horse, causing it to lose an eye. Njáll tries to settle the dispute, but Þorgeirr does not accept his offer and the feud escalates. In *Þorsteins þáttr stangarhǫggs*, the *ójafnaðarmaðr* Þórðr and Þorsteinn Þórarinsson come into conflict at a horsefight. Þórðr strikes Þorsteinn on the brow. Þorsteinn binds his wound and acts as if nothing has happened. He asks the men present not to tell his father that the injury was caused by Þórðr. In the winter, however, his father hears about the blow and brings the matter up. Þorsteinn says he saw no honor in calling it a blow rather than an accident. His father replies he wasn't aware that he had a cowardly son. Þorsteinn then takes up his weapons and goes to find Þórðr to ask him whether the blow was accidental or intentional. As Þórðr's response implies that the blow was not an accident, Þorsteinn kills him.

Witching.—In *Eyrbyggja saga* (ch. 20), Katla is stoned for practicing witchcraft, and her son Oddr is hanged for cutting off Auðr's hand in the fight mentioned earlier. In *Laxdœla saga* (chs. 35–37), Kotkell and his wife meet a similar fate for sorcery. Although several men have been killed by Kotkell's spells, he is still practicing under the protection of Hallsteinn goði at Hallsteinsnes and then under that of Þorleikr Hǫskuldsson, to whom he had given some horses. After Kári Hrútsson is killed by Kotkell's spells for the benefit of Þorleikr, men gather and stone Kotkell and his wife.

Haunting.—Like witchery, hauntings brought an other-worldly element to the community. Hauntings usually resulted in killings, drownings, beatings, and abandonment of farms (see the discussion of the hauntings at Fróðá in chap. 7). In his saga, Grettir Ásmundarson cleanses a region of monsters, but usually revenants are dealt with by the survivors in a rational way, which itself may be the cause of a conflict. In *Eyrbyggja saga* (ch. 34), Þórólfr bægifótr's ghost engenders a conflict. Þórólfr's son Arnkell, responsible for laying the ghost, calls upon the Þorbrandssons, otherwise his enemies, for help. They are obliged by law to assist Arnkell, and although at first they refuse, one of them goes to help for the sake of keeping the law. Later Þórólfr returns from his grave (see chap. 7). Þórólfr's undecayed body is finally exhumed and burned by men of the area (ch. 63).

Appendix C

Examples of Advocacy

SINCE advocacy, used both aggressively and defensively, was so common in the sagas, the following examples are offered to show how advocacy, like conflict, fits as a feudeme into clusters and chains and is defined by the specifics of a particular feud.

Brokerage.—Many of these specifics fall into categories based on what the support cost—payment, fosterage, *vinfengi*, or a *goðorð*—or what induced brokerage—greed, blood vengeance, aggressive claims to tenuously held lands, or a desire to reclaim land or a *goðorð*.

There were a number of ways to seek and pay for support in the Old Icelandic society portrayed in the sagas. Some men could depend on the help of a friend, as Gunnarr depended on Njáll. But most brokers acted on behalf of someone else because of kinship ties or in exchange for payment or the promise of future alliance. A broker who was not paid might not be available on the next occasion when help was needed, a situation that occurs with some frequency in the sagas. Brodd-Helgi's refusal to pay Guðmundr inn ríki in *Vápnfirðinga saga* (ch. 10) proved to be fatal. Guðmundr was angered and later lent his support to Brodd-Helgi's rival Geitir when he moved to kill Brodd-Helgi.

Cases of seeking the support of others, especially powerful brokers, are common in the sagas. In most cases help was sought from local men who had a reputation in the district; but in cases that could not be resolved on the district level and had to go to the Althing, the backing of chieftains and powerful men, who lived in other parts of Iceland, was sought. The following are typical cases of brokerage as a means of strengthening a contender's position in legal matters.

In *Droplaugarsona saga*, Hrafnkell Þórisson brings a case to get his share of the *goðorð* held by his uncle, Helgi Ásbjarnarson. Hrafnkell seeks the support of Hólmsteinn Bersason, who refuses because he is Helgi's brother-in-law. Hólmsteinn does, however, send Hrafnkell to Helgi Droplaugarson, who is knowledgeable in the law and has previously opposed Helgi Ásbjarnarson (ch. 4). In *Hávarðar saga Ísfirðings* (chs. 8–9), Hávarðr's wife gathers forces to go with Hávarðr to the thing, since Hávarðr appears incapable of pulling together the necessary men to win a case. She wants their son Óláfr to be avenged. She and Hávarðr's relative Þórhallr go to her three brothers and arrange to borrow nets and a turf-cutting axe, to be collected later. She then rouses Hávarðr, who dresses himself for battle and along with Þórhallr calls on the wife's brothers to collect the promised goods. They understand this procedure as a request for support, which they give.

In *Reykdœla saga* (ch. 13), Steingrímr Ǫrnólfsson goes to Eyjólfr Einarsson (Valgerðarson), his chieftain, for support. Steingrímr's men have killed Herjólfr Þórisson (Fjǫrleifarson) in revenge for insults Herjólfr's brother, Vémundr, had made against Steingrímr two years earlier.

Eyjólfr wants Steingrímr to settle, and Steingrímr agrees. Eyjólfr then acts as Steingrímr's broker and sends for Áskell, Herjólfr's and Vémundr's uncle, who negotiates for atonement for Herjólfr. The settlement reached determines the payment of 100 silvers for the killing of Herjólfr, life banishment for some of Steingrímr's men, and banishment for three years for others.

In *Njáls saga* (chs. 98–99), the Njálssons kill Lýtingr's brothers to avenge Lýtingr's killing of Hǫskuldr Njálsson, which stemmed from Skarpheðinn Njálsson's killing of Lýtingr's brother-in-law Þráinn Sigfússon. Lýtingr asks Hǫskuldr Hvítanessgoði, Þráinn's son and Njáll's foster son, to intercede with Njáll so that Lýtingr will not be outlawed and can keep his farm. Hǫskuldr acts as broker on behalf of Lýtingr and offers Njáll *sjálfdœmi*. Njáll awards himself 200 silvers for Hǫskuldr Njálsson and advises Lýtingr to move away. Lýtingr's brothers and Lýtingr's wounds are not compensated. Later in the saga (chs. 112–114) the Njálssons go to Ásgrímr Elliða-Grímsson after they kill Hǫskuldr Hvítanessgoði. He promises to support them, although with a heavy heart. Ásgrímr hopes to have the assistance of Guðmundr inn ríki, as they are friends, and he also seeks help from Snorri goði, another powerful friend.

Ties and obligations shifted according to the variety of factors governing the standard of reciprocity. Often the web of bonds crossed kin lines. At times a broker who refused to support either side was available to arbitrate or to come between the fighting men. One of the most elemental aspects of brokerage was that the process usually encouraged resolution. As the number of persons on each side mounted, instability and therefore anxiety increased.

Fictitious kinship bonds.—A way to gain protection either before or during a feud was the creation of ties between families. Fosterage, a bond of fictitious kinship, was especially common. In *Reykdœla saga* (ch. 4), Hánefr fosters Vémundr Fjǫrleifarson's daughter, Þorkatla, and gives the father valuable gifts. Vémundr is thus obligated to take Hánefr's part in a case against him for sheep stealing, which comes up a short time later. In *Hœnsa-Þóris saga* (ch. 2), Hœnsa-Þórir offers to foster Arngrímr goði's son Helgi and to give half of his goods to Helgi in exchange for this chieftain's *vinátta*. Nevertheless, Arngrímr refuses to help Hœnsa-Þórir when Blund-Ketill "steals" Þórir's hay (ch. 6). Þórðr goddi, in *Laxdœla saga* (ch. 16), fosters Hǫskuldr Dala-Kollsson's illegitimate son Óláfr pái as a means of gaining Hǫskuldr's support. Þórðr goddi is involved in a case over the dowry of his wife, who has divorced him. Þórðr promises that Óláfr will inherit from him. In the same saga, after Hǫskuldr's death, Óláfr fosters Bolli Þorleiksson (ch. 27) to placate his half brother, Þorleikr Hǫskuldsson. The latter has objected to Hǫskuldr's wish to have Óláfr share equally in his estate with the legitimate sons. Þorleikr Bollason (ch. 57) of the next generation goes to Þorgils Hǫlluson to be fostered and taught the law. Another famous example is Njáll's fosterage of Hǫskuldr Þráinsson because Skarpheðinn Njálsson has killed Hǫskuldr's father (ch. 94). Njáll also fosters Þórðr Kárason, who dies in the burning, and Þórhallr Ásgrímsson, who becomes the third-best lawyer in Iceland (chs. 27, 109).

Similar to fosterage is an incident in *Vatnsdœla saga* (ch. 42). Þorgrímr Hallormsson offers an axe and kinship recognition to his illegitimate son, Þorkell krafla, if Þorkell will kill Þorkell silfri to keep this opponent from acquiring a *goðorð*. When Þorkell silfri gets the *goðorð* by using magic in a drawing of lots, Þorkell krafla kills him; Þorgrímr takes the *goðorð* and sends Þorkell abroad.

Another tie of fictitious kinship was marriage. As pointed out in an earlier example from *Hœnsa-Þóris saga*, the son of Blund-Ketill is better able to avenge his father's death because he deviously becomes the husband of the powerful Þórðr gellir's foster daughter (ch. 11). Throughout the sagas, when marriage proposals were made, offers were usually accepted or rejected on the basis of whether the ties would strengthen or weaken one's political or legal position. At times, when families faced the problem of divided loyalties, divorces were declared. For example, in *Laxdœla saga* (ch. 16), Vigdís Ingjaldsdóttir divorces Þórðr goddi over the issue of a vagrant relative. In *Gísla saga Súrssonar* (ch. 37), Gísli's sister defies her husband because he is entertaining Gísli's killer. She tries to kill her brother's killer. Her husband stops her and offers the wounded man *sjálfdœmi*. She then declares herself divorced and moves away.

Vinfengi.—Cases of support seeking in return for political friendship are found throughout the sagas. In *Ljósvetninga saga* (A, ch. 6; C, ch. 14), Guðmundr inn ríki asks his brother Einarr, with whom he is not on good terms, to swear *vinfengi*, a common occurrence during brokerage. (In C, Guðmundr goes to Einarr and gives him good gifts, and they agree to support each other before Guðmundr summons Þórir Akraskeggr.) Einarr is not aware that Guðmundr plans to summon Þórir Helgason, a friend of Einarr's, and that Guðmundr is trying to ensure that Þórir will not have Einarr's support. After Þórir has been summoned, Einarr goes to meet Guðmundr and is asked to support him. Einarr wants Þórir and Guðmundr to compromise, but that solution is not part of Guðmundr's plan. He reminds Einarr of his vows of support. When Þórir asks Einarr for his help, Einarr says that he cannot go against Guðmundr but that he will go to the thing with Þórir, as he wants to arbitrate between the two men.

In *Víga-Glúms saga* (ch. 19), Halli Þorbjarnarson goes to his foster son Einarr Eyjólfsson to ask him to take the case against Vigfúss Glúmsson for the killing of Halli's son Bárðr. Together they go to Einarr's relative Þórarinn Þórisson and swear *vinfengi* for support. In *Vatnsdœla saga* (ch. 20), Sæmundr inn suðreyski goes to Ingimundr Þorsteinsson after Sæmundr's nephew, Hrolleifr, is outlawed from the district. Sæmundr asks Ingimundr to take in Hrolleifr and his mother because Ingimundr and he are foster brothers.

Payment in wealth.—Giving wealth in exchange for support is often described in the sagas. In *Hávarðar saga Ísfirðings* (ch. 14), Þorbjǫrn at Eyrr sends his sons to Steinþórr, a chieftain and friend, with a gold ring after they kill Hólmgǫngu-Ljótr. Steinþórr takes the ring and the case. Ljótr was an *ójafnaðarmaðr* who took possession of a meadow he had shared with Þorbjǫrn and then sold the land back to Þorbjǫrn, so Þorbjǫrn has a good case. In *Víga-Glúms saga* (ch. 25), Einarr Eyjólfsson is offered Glúmr's farm at a reasonable price if he will take the case against Glúmr for the killing of Þorvaldr. The proposal is based on the expectation that Glúmr will be outlawed and will lose his farm. Glúmr, who killed Þorvaldr Þórisson, has earlier managed to convince his man Guðbrandr Þorvarðsson that he, Guðbrandr, killed Þorvaldr. Guðbrandr has been outlawed and Glúmr has sent him abroad (ch. 23).

In *Njáls saga*, in the feud discussed earlier (see chap. 9), Flosi offers bags of money, silver, and future support to gain strength for his case at the Althing. In *Ljósvetninga saga*, Eyjólfr Guðmundarson solicits the support of other chieftains for his case at the thing against Þorvarðr Hǫskuldsson. The feud began when Þorvarðr's friend Brandr Gunnsteinsson seduced a woman named Friðgerðr, the daughter of Eyjólfr's thingman Ísólfr. It has since escalated, and Eyjólfr's brother has died from wounds inflicted in a fight between the sides. Eyjólfr offers one ounce of silver for each man and half a mark of silver for each chieftain who comes to the thing on his side. He also gives Hrafn Þorkelsson half an ounce of gold to terminate his connection with Þorvarðr. At the same time Þorvarðr sends his son-in-law Hárekr, a thingman of Skegg-Broddi's, to Skegg-Broddi with the offer of a gold ring should the chieftain support Þorvarðr. Skegg-Broddi has said that he will support the side that has the fewer men (A, chs. 15–16; C, chs. 25–26).

In *Egils saga* (ch. 81), Steinarr Qnundarson offers to give money to *goði* Einarr Teitsson in return for support in his case against Þorsteinn Egilsson. Steinarr makes a similar offer to the *goði* Tungu-Oddr. Both chieftains support Steinarr. Þorleikr Hǫskuldsson, in *Laxdœla saga* (ch. 36), is given some horses he desperately wants by Kotkell, a sorcerer, on the understanding that he will find Kotkell and his family a place to live and guarantee them future protection.

Besides building a legal case, brokerage was used to dismantle a case. Paying off opponents often gave them the financial reward they were anxious for but saved the one who pays them from losing a farm, a *goðorð*, or his reputation. In *Bandamanna saga* (chs. 7–9), Oddr Ófeigsson, a wellborn trader, purchases a *goðorð* (ch. 2). Jealous of his wealth and popularity, eight chieftains band together to proceed against Oddr until he either is outlawed or surrenders to *sjálfdœmi*, at which point they can divide up his property. They prosecute Oddr for bribing the judges in the case against Óspakr for Váli's killing. When the case was first overridden, Oddr's father, Ófeigr Skíðason, had resorted to bribery to obtain the decision of outlawry against Óspakr. Oddr finds out from his father about the band of chieftains planning his outlawry. Following the plan of his father, a free farmer, Oddr gives Ófeigr the handling of the case. Although not a chieftain, Ófeigr possesses a keen understanding of how brokerage works. Secretly he approaches two of the chieftains, Gellir Þorkelsson and Egill Skúlason, and tells them that Oddr will not abandon his rights and intends to fight. In fact, while the chieftains were haggling at the Althing, Oddr loaded all his chattels onto his ship and put out to sea. Ófeigr points out to the two chieftains that they have not thought the matter out carefully. If the *goðar* manage to outlaw Oddr, in the court of execution half of Oddr's goods will go to the men of the quarter, leaving only a sixteenth share for each of the eight chieftains. In return for this small acquisition, Ófeigr continues, the chieftains will run the risk that Oddr

will turn sea raider and destroy their farms. Apparently the
chieftains have not considered this possibility. Ófeigr also
plays on their greed. He tells Gellir and Egill that if they
turn on the other chieftains, financially advantageous
arrangements can be made. Ófeigr gives Egill 200 silvers
and Gellir Þorkelsson 400 silvers for their support. He also
offers that his son Oddr will marry Gellir's daughter Ragnheiðr. Thus Ófeigr succeeds in breaking up the opposition
to Oddr. When the chieftains follow his advice, the prosecution falls apart. Ófeigr uses a very cunning approach to
brokerage in this sophisticated narrative, knowing that vic-
tory without attached wealth is basically meaningless in
Icelandic society.

In *Guðmundar saga dýra*, Guðmundr decides to pay the
fines he owes, and a little more, to Qgmundr sneis, as he
does not want Qgmundr to go against him in the case of the
burning of Qnundr and Gálmr. Qgmundr gladly accepts
the money (ch. 15) and later (ch. 23) actively supports
Guðmundr.

Payment in goðorð.—Another exchangeable source of
support was the *goðorð*. In *Vatnsdœla saga* (ch. 37), Þorsteinn Ingimundarson gives his *goðorð* to his son, Ingólfr
Þorsteinsson, so that the son can handle a case of seduction
brought against him. The *goðorð* had been given to Þorsteinn in exchange for relieving his brother of his *berserkr*
fits. Þorsteinn dies shortly thereafter, and the *goðorð*, as
agreed, remains with Ingólfr.

In *Íslendinga saga* (ch. 56), Abbot Hallr asks Sturla
Sighvatsson to support the Hrafnssons against the chieftain
Þorvaldr Snorrason. Þorvaldr is fining and harassing the
thingmen of the Hrafnssons. Sturla agrees to bring about a
reconciliation between the parties in exchange for the
Hrafnssons' *goðorð*. In another example cited earlier in
this study, Jón and Ásgrímr Ketilsson hand over their
goðorð for support from a more powerful chieftain
(*Guðmundar saga dýra*, ch. 4).

Refusal of support.—One difficulty in brokerage is the

possibility that support will be refused. In *Eyrbyggja saga*, Snorri consistently refuses to help the Þorbrandssons act against Arnkell (ch. 32), and in *Vápnfirðinga saga* Geitir is chastised by his thingman for the same unwillingness to confront his enemy, Brodd-Helgi (ch. 11). In *Gísla saga Súrssonar* (ch. 21), Gísli spends three years traveling throughout Iceland asking chieftains for support after his outlawry. At times it seems as if some of them will support him, but in the end none of them do.

In *Reykdœla saga* (ch. 3), Þorkell Þorgeirsson refuses to support Eysteinn Mánason against Áskell goði Eyvindarson because Áskell takes only just cases. In *Hávarðar saga Ísfirðings* (ch. 7), Hávarðr rides to the thing to seek recompense from Þorbjǫrn Þjóðreksson, for the killing of Hávarðr's son Óláfr. In search of support at the thing, Hávarðr first approaches Steinþórr from Eyrr. Steinþórr turns him away, calling Hávarðr old and capable of nothing. Hávarðr, as is his wont, lies down and doesn't get up until aroused. One morning Steinþórr comes to him and asks why he is lying there. Hávarðr explains he wants compensation for his son, but he expects only injustice from Þorbjǫrn. Steinþórr sends Hávarðr to Gestr Oddleifsson, Þorbjǫrn's brother-in-law, for Steinþórr believes Hávarðr will get better treatment from Þorbjǫrn if he approaches him with Gestr's support. Unfortunately only Þorbjǫrn is in his and Gestr's booth and he insults Hávarðr. When Gestr hears about the incident, he sends for Hávarðr and attempts to settle the case, but Þorbjǫrn further insults Hávarðr by throwing Óláfr's teeth at him, and the conflict continues. In *Ǫlkofra þáttr* (chs. 1–2), after Ǫlkofri has accidentally burned a forest jointly owned by six chieftains, he asks support from friends who have bought his beer at the Althing in the past. Nobody wants to support him because his opponents are too strong. He finally asks Þorsteinn Síðu-Hallsson, who at first refuses on the same grounds but then is chided by his brother-in-law, Broddi Bjarnason, for taking this stand. Þorsteinn then says he will

support Qlkofri if Skegg-Broddi will. With these two arbi-
trating for him, Qlkofri pays only a small fine and is not
outlawed.

In *Droplaugarsona saga* (ch. 9), Þorgrímr skinnhúfa asks
Þórarinn moldoxi to support him against Helgi Droplaugarson, who is aiding his wife Rannveig in their divorce
case. Þórarinn moldoxi, however, sends Þorgrímr to Helgi
Ásbjarnarson, who has more interest in cases against Helgi
Droplaugarson. In *Laxdœla saga* (chs. 37–38), Hrútr
Herjólfsson asks Óláfr Hǫskuldsson for men to help him
against Þorleikr Hǫskuldsson, Hrútr's nephew and Óláfr's
half brother. Óláfr refuses because he wants to maintain
peace. Þorleikr had Kotkell cast spells which killed Hrútr's
son Kári. Later, Óláfr convinces Þorleikr to go abroad to
keep peace in the family.

The same saga (ch. 35) implies that Þorkell hvelpr and
his brother Knútr have gone to different chieftains and
have been refused; they cannot follow through their case
against Þórðr Ingunnarson, who had divorced their sister
Auðr to marry Guðrún Ósvífrsdóttir, because they can get
no support. In *Sturlu saga* (ch. 27), Bárðr Álfsson is ru-
mored to have seduced Klemet Karlsefnisson's wife, Kjartan Þorvaldsson, Klemet's relative, wounds Bárðr. Bárðr's
father, Alfr, goes to the chieftain Einarr Þorgilsson. Einarr
refuses to support Álfr because Kjartan and his father
Þorvaldr are his friends and his thingmen. Finally, Álfr
goes to Sturla Þórðarson, who takes the case. The case is
settled with a fine, and Álfr becomes Sturla's thingman.

Self-advocacy.—A man could buy cases or they could be
given to help him develop an attack on a rival. In *Njáls saga*,
so that Gunnarr can proceed against Starkaðr Barkarson, Njáll gives him a seduction case, involving Þorgeirr
Starkaðarson and a kinswoman of Njáll's. Njáll, in addition
to giving Gunnarr another case pertaining to the theft of
wood, advises him how to carry out his own case and how to
obtain still another case. In *Ljósvetninga saga* (A, ch. 5; C,
ch. 13), Guðmundr inn ríki begins to gather cases against

Þórir Helgason and Þorkell hákr because they have insulted him. In *Reykdœla saga* (ch. 15), Vémundr Þórisson (Fjǫrleifarson) offers to buy for half a mark of silver Ǫrnólfr rella's case against Steingrímr Ǫrnólfsson over the value of some oxen, but Ǫrnólfr will agree only if Vémundr's uncle, the chieftain Áskell, approves. Vémundr and Ǫrnólfr go to Áskell to ask his opinion. Since Áskell does not want the trouble between Vémundr and Steingrímr to continue, he buys the case himself for two marks of silver. Undaunted, Vémundr presents himself as a wanderer named Bjǫrn to the farmer Þórðr at Vǫðlar, where a local assembly is held. Bjǫrn (Vémundr in a hat) wants hospitality from Þórðr while waiting for the thing to assemble. When Þórðr offers him food in exchange for Bjǫrn's sword, Bjǫrn says he will cut turf in exchange instead. Þórðr decides he wants his field enclosed so that it will not be grazed bare by the animals of the men coming to the thing. Þórðr leaves Bjǫrn to work. Bjǫrn goes to Steingrímr's booth, knocks down a gable-end, and drives some cattle into the deserted booth. When Steingrímr's servants arrive to prepare the booth, they have no tools with which to repair it. Bjǫrn offers to lend them his tools to clear the turf and remove stones. As they gratefully accept, he tells them they should take turf from the field he is enclosing for Þórðr. They do so and repair the booth. On his return Þórðr is not pleased. Bjǫrn removes his hat, is recognized as Vémundr by Þórðr, and asks to take the case against Steingrímr over the turf cutting. The land in question is transferred by *handsal* to Vémundr's management, along with the case.

Besides being a defensive tool, advocacy was used aggressively in order to gain a foothold in obtaining a new piece of property. In such instances of self-advocacy someone usually insinuated himself into an ongoing or potential feud. Since self-advocacy often preceded conflict in this situation, the development of feud clusters differs from saga to saga. The process is typical in the way one person lays claim to someone else's property. For example, in *Sturlu saga* (ch. 28), a wellborn and wealthy man, Birningr Steinarsson, owns a valuable farm, Heinaberg, in the West Fjords. He is divorced. After he remarries, Einarr Þorgilsson, an aggressive broker, approaches Birningr's daughter by his first marriage and buys her claim to inheritance from Birningr. This purchase gives Einarr a hold on Heinaberg, to which he held no previous claim. Einarr, planning Birningr's downfall, asserts that Birningr's second marriage is unlawful and demands that Birningr move his family and goods to Einarr's own estate. Birningr refuses. In the fall Einarr sends men to steal some of Birningr's wethers, which are then slaughtered. Birningr turns to his kinsman, the broker Hvamm-Sturla (Sturla Þórðarson). Both men are members of the Snorrungar family, which traces its ancestry back several generations to Snorri goði, the cunning chieftain who appears frequently in the family sagas. Birningr makes an agreement by *handsal* to convey his property to Sturla. The fact that Einarr has this purchased claim causes Birningr's life to be disrupted and puts him on the defensive.

Goading.—Inciting friends, betters, or kin to carry out blood vengeance or to seek recompense for an insult is another way of gaining support. This situation usually arises when a conflict has been settled, not in terms of honor, but only in terms of the law. In such cases women often incited men to act, especially to seek vengeance for sons or husbands. In *Vápnfirðinga saga*, Bjarni Brodd-Helgason is goaded by his stepmother, Þorgerðr silfra, to avenge the death of his father Brodd-Helgi, killed by Geitir. In *Laxdœla saga* (ch. 48), Guðrún incites first her brothers and then her husband Bolli to act against Kjartan, who has previously insulted their family. Bolli later kills Kjartan (ch. 49).

As noted in the example from *Víga-Glúms saga* (ch. 8), Víga-Glúmr's mother, Ástríðr, by goading her son into killing Sigmundr for encroaching on her land, starts Glúmr on his way to becoming a famous chieftain. In *Njáls saga* (ch. 116), Hildigunnr Starkaðardóttir goads her uncle Flosi into action after her husband, Hǫskuldr Hvítanessgoði, is killed by the Njálssons. Rúnólfr Úlfsson counsels Flosi to settle peacefully and Flosi has asked him to go to the thing (ch. 115). Hildigunnr weeps and says Hǫskuldr should be avenged, but Flosi remains firm. Hildigunnr then throws her husband's bloodstained cloak on Flosi and calls on him to avenge all of Hǫskuldr's wounds. Flosi, throwing off the cloak, responds: "You are most monstrous; you want us to take the course that will bring all of us the most harm. But cold are the counsels of women." ("Þú ert it mesta forað ok vildir, at vér tœkim þat upp, er ǫllum oss gegnir verst, ok eru kǫld kvenna ráð.")

In *Laxdœla saga* (chs. 59–61), Guðrún sends for Snorri goði to get advice on how to avenge her husband Bolli's death. Snorri suggests that they ask Þorsteinn svarti and Lambi Þorbjarnarson to join their side, even though these men were in the party that attacked Bolli. Snorri hopes to gain their help by proposing that only Helgi Harðbeinsson, who struck a blow against Bolli and insulted Guðrún by wiping the bloody spear on her shawl, be killed. Snorri, acting as Guðrún's broker, has Þorgils Hǫlluson, the foster father of Bolli's son Þorleikr, lead the party. Þorgils will help Guðrún only if she marries him, but Snorri helps her deceive him into thinking she has promised herself to him. When Þorgils comes to visit, Guðrún shows her sons their father's bloody clothes. They begin to think of vengeance and, with Þorgils leading them, set off to seek support in their plan to kill Helgi. When Þorgils approaches Þorsteinn svarti with the plan to kill his brother-in-law Helgi, Þorsteinn first offers to pay to keep the peace, but then he gives in and agrees to Snorri's plan. Lambi also agrees to follow Þorgils so long as his relatives, the Óláfssons, are left alone.

Information passing.—The following are a few examples of this very common form of advocacy. In *Laxdœla saga* (ch. 47), Þórhalla in málga (the gossip) travels to Tunga and asks Kjartan Ólafsson which way he is riding. That same evening Þórhalla goes to Laugar and informs Bolli and the Ósvífrssons of Kjartan's movements. This information results in Kjartan's being ambushed and killed. In *Vápnfirðinga saga*, Brodd-Helgi learns of the stealing of his family's sheep from a shepherd. This results in Helgi's killing of the thief whom he had earlier outlawed. In *Hrafnkels saga Freysgoða* the washerwoman's information about the whereabouts of the brother of Hrafnkell's enemy results in a killing. In many cases of this type of advocacy, information spurs someone into a conflict or a resolution.

Appendix D

Examples of Resolution

THE feudeme of resolution falls into three major categories, with variations in each: (1) arbitrated settlement, whether in or out of court; (2) direct settlement between the concerned parties, whether violent or peaceful; (3) the rejection of an offer of resolution.

Resolution of conflict was not always final, unless it was a direct, amicable compromise between two feudists, which usually took place outside the court system. Even then, if one of the interested parties was abroad or was left out of the negotiations, compromise could be inconclusive. So it is with Skúta Áskelsson in *Reykdœla saga*. He is abroad when the settlement for the killing of Áskell is reached (ch. 16); when he returns, he carries out blood vengeance.

Often part or all of a resolution remained unfulfilled, thus leading to continued feud. Perhaps payment was not made or completed; someone might not have respected the decision of outlawry and might then have challenged the holding of the *féránsdómr* or might simply have stayed in the district. For example, in *Njáls saga*, Gunnarr does not leave Iceland for his three years of outlawry and thus precipitates the fight that costs him his life (see chap. 6). In *Droplaugarsona saga*, Helgi Droplaugarson ignores his outlawry by Helgi Ásbjarnarson for killing Hallsteinn, Droplaug's husband. He and Droplaug had put Hallsteinn's thrall up to killing Hallsteinn and then killed the thrall (chs. 7–8). Helgi Droplaugarson continues to go to the thing and to take people's cases. He is later killed when Helgi Ásbjarnarson attacks him.

Arbitration

Resolutions brought about by arbitration often included a balancing of killings and property, accomplished by fines, outlawry, or equalizing the status of the victims. Because arbitration was the most common type of resolution, the apparatus set up to carry it out functioned quickly and well. The courts met often enough to make peer judgments readily available. At times on-the-spot arbitrations were arranged by the disputants themselves, who chose arbitrators. A third possibility was the intervention of *góðviljamenn* or *góðgjarnir menn*. An arbitration, like a compromise, was a way to stabilize conflict, especially feud, by involving the society in decision making. Dependable means of settlement were necessary since, as noted earlier, there was no policing mechanism to enforce a resolution.

After the burning of Blund-Ketill in *Hœnsa-Þóris saga*, a fight between Tungu-Oddr's men and Þórðr gellir's (representing the ill Hersteinn Blund-Ketilsson) is stopped by *góðgjarnir menn*, and arbitration follows (ch. 14). After the settlement, however, Hersteinn kills Hœnsa-Þórir and the feud continues (ch. 15). When, in *Fóstbrœðra saga*, Helgi Snorrason and Þorsteinn Egilsson fight over a meadow that

Þorsteinn wants to buy and Helgi refuses to sell, *góðgjarnir menn* step in and arbitrate. Þorsteinn buys the meadow and pays for Helgi's wounds (ch. 12).

In *Ljósvetninga saga* (chs. 2−4), Þorgeirr goði and his sons are disputing over the outlawed Sǫlmundr Víðarsson. Sǫlmundr was banished but while in Norway became a favorite of that country's ruler, Hákon jarl. Hákon sends gifts to Þorgeirr goði and Guðmundr inn ríki in order to insure their support for Sǫlmundr's return to Iceland. Þorgeirr's sons object to the gifts, and Hǫskuldr Þorgeirsson kills Sǫlmundr when he returns. The Þorgeirssons wanted Sǫlmundr to be regarded as having fallen outside the law (*óheilagr*); they also wanted their father's share of the jointly owned *goðorð*. At the Fjósatunga thing, Snorri Eyvindarson Hlíðarmannagoði says he sees two possibilities in the case: either Hǫskuldr is allowed to judge it, in which instance Þorgeirr might lose his *goðorð*, or the case is given to arbitrators who will arrange a settlement. He and many others believe less trouble will come from choosing the latter. Men are selected to arbitrate, and the case is settled in the court. Sǫlmundr falls *óheilagr* and a large sum is paid for Arnórr, killed in the fight against Sǫlmundr.

The feud in *Heiðarvíga saga* between Snorri goði and the Borgfirðingar, including Illugi inn svarti and Þorgísl Arason, begins when Snorri's father-in-law, Víga-Styrr, is killed by Gestr Þórhallason (ch. 9). Gestr's father had been killed by Styrr (ch. 7). Taken in by the Borgfirðingar, Gestr escapes to Norway (ch. 10), but the cases and blood vengeance continue. After a battle between the Borgfirðingar and Barði Guðmundarson (chs. 30−31), Þorgísl Arason is tricked by Snorri goði into taking a peace oath in Barði Guðmundarson's presence. Þorgísl is then bound to keep the oath. At the thing Snorri goði is the arbitrator for Barði and Guðmundr Eyjólfsson, and he is also himself a principal. Þorgísl Arason and Illugi inn svarti arbitrate for the Borgfirðingar (chs. 33−37).

The payment of valuables or money was often part of an

arbitrated settlement. In *Njáls saga*, Hallgerðr gets her
foster father Þjóstólfr to kill her first husband because he
has slapped her. She then sends her foster father to her
mother's brother, Svanr the sorcerer, for protection while
she herself goes to her own father, Hǫskuldr Dala-
Kollsson. After being sidetracked by Svanr's magic, Ósvífr,
the father of Hallgerðr's dead husband, goes to Hǫskuldr
to request compensation. Hǫskuldr's half brother, Hrútr,
arbitrates; he says he will set the fine and will not spare
Hǫskuldr. Hǫskuldr and Ósvífr agree by *handsal* to drop
the case, a settlement accepted by Ósvífr because he trusts
Hrútr. Hrútr decides Hǫskuldr must pay 200 silvers and
also give Ósvífr a cloak, and everybody is satisfied (chs.
11–12).

In *Valla-Ljóts saga*, Guðmundr inn ríki takes to the
Althing the case against Ljótr Ljótólfsson, a *goði*, for
killing Halli Sigurðarson. Halli, a friend of Guðmundr's,
had recently moved to Ljótr's district. When Ljótr divided
up the Hrólfssons' inheritance of lands near Halli's farm,
Halli was displeased. He gave Ljótr the choice of facing a
case for breach of holiness (the division was made on
Michaelmas), or paying 50 silvers. Ljótr paid the money,
but later he killed Halli. Trustworthy friends of Ljótr's
arbitrate and 100 silvers are awarded for Halli, but Ljótr
keeps 50 of them for injuries by Halli. Guðmundr, who is
displeased with the decision, holds the money for the family
(chs. 3–5). In the same saga, after Hrólfr Sigurðarson,
Halli's brother, kills Þorvarðr Þorgrímsson, a relative of
Ljótr's, Guðmundr inn ríki notifies Ljótr that he wants to
have the case settled because he disapproves of the killing.
At the district thing Skapti Þóroddsson, a friend of Ljótr's,
is chosen to arbitrate, with the help of others. The fine for
the killing, 200 silvers, is to be paid to Ljótr's party (ch. 5).

Hjalti Skeggjason asks Gunnarr, in *Njáls saga* (ch. 66),
to accept arbitration in the case against Gunnarr for the
killings in the battle with Starkaðr Barkarson. Gunnarr
agrees after Hjalti promises never to go against him. Njáll,

Ásgrímr Elliða-Grímsson, and Hjalti arbitrate. Gunnarr's friends give him money at the thing for immediate payment of the fines assessed against him by the arbitrators. In the same conflict, a bit later (chs. 69–70), Njáll breaks up an ambush prepared for Gunnarr by Þorgeirr Starkaðarson and Þorgeirr Otkelsson. Both Gunnarr and the two Þorgeirrs ask Njáll to arbitrate, which he says he will do, but only at the thing. Mǫrðr Valgarðsson, who is critical of the Þorgeirrs for putting the case in the hands of Njáll, Gunnarr's most loyal supporter, presents the side against Gunnarr at the Althing. At the court, Njáll names twelve arbitrators who decide that each member of the ambush party should pay 100 silvers and each of the Þorgeirrs 200 silvers to Gunnarr.

Outlawry, with or without the payment of money fines, was sometimes the punishment meted out by arbitrators. In *Brandkrossa þáttr* (ch. 1), Ótryggr, who is staying with Oddr sindri, insults Ósvífr Oddsson at some games. Oddr kills his lodger and Helgi Ásbjarnarson brings a case against Oddr. Men try to arrange a settlement, and Bersi inn spaki is chosen to arbitrate. The fines levied on Oddr are small, but he is outlawed from the district and must give up his home. Helgi Ásbjarnarson takes over Oddr's farm. In *Ljósvetninga saga* (ch. 1), Sǫlmundr Víðarsson buys goods from Sigurðr, a Norwegian. When Sigurðr demands payment, Sǫxólfr Víðarsson, Sǫlmundr's brother, kills him. Arnórr, father of Sigurðr's partner, and others prepare the case for the thing, where there is arbitration. Sǫxólfr is banished for life, and his brother, for three years.

In *Hœnsa-Þóris saga* (ch. 15), at the thing, men are named to pronounce judgment toward the end of the long feud chain which began with the burning of Blund-Ketill. Hœnsa-Þórir, who originally perpetrated the killing, has already been killed by Blund-Ketill's son, Hersteinn. In the settlement Arngrímr goði, together with others present at the burning, is outlawed, and Þorvaldr Oddsson, who originally supported Hœnsa-Þórir, is banished for three years.

Þorvaldr is the son of a powerful chieftain, Tungu-Oddr. In *Vatnsdœla saga* (chs. 18–20), Hrolleifr Arnaldsson, the aggressive nephew of Sæmundr inn suðreyski, asks the farmer Uni for the hand of his daughter Hróðný. When he is refused, he declares he will make Hróðný his concubine, thus initiating a conflict with Uni and his son Oddr. Oddr ambushes Hrolleifr and his company; he kills one of Hrolleifr's followers and wounds Hrolleifr in the foot. Hrolleifr kills Oddr and one of his men. Uni seeks out the farmer Hǫfða-Þórðr and points out that Þórðr's reputation will suffer if he allows Hrolleifr free rein in the area. Together they approach Sæmundr and ask him to settle the case. At the arbitration Hrolleifr's land is awarded to Uni, and Hrolleifr is outlawed from the district.

In *Guðmundar saga dýra* (ch. 15), Jón Loftsson agrees to try to bring about a peace settlement in a dangerous feud between Guðmundr dýri and Sæmundr Jónsson over the burning to death of Ǫnundr Þorkelsson. Both sides accept, agreeing under oath that Jón alone shall make all settlements. Jón assesses fines for the burning of Ǫnundr and other men and sentences some of the burners to three years' outlawry and others to banishment for life. He takes into consideration that some men who were burned would have fallen *óheilagr* and that Gálmr had refused money to come out. Although feeling remains high, peace is maintained for some time after this settlement.

In *Njáls saga* (ch. 74), Njáll arranges arbitration at the thing in the case against Gunnarr for the killing of Þorgeirr Otkelsson. By killing Þorgeirr, Gunnarr has killed twice in the same family, thus going against Njáll's interdiction. A court of twelve assesses fines against Gunnarr and banishes Gunnarr and his brother Kolskeggr for three years. If they do not leave within a specified time, the banishment will become full outlawry. In the same saga (ch. 145), a twelve-man court, headed by Snorri goði, is named to settle the dispute between Flosi and Kári. In addition to fines, Flosi is banished for three years and the other burners are outlawed forever. In *Víga-Glúms saga* (ch. 19), Vigfúss Glúmsson and several Norwegians kill Bárðr Hallason, who killed Vigfúss's foster father for stealing sheep. The case goes to the thing for arbitration. Vigfúss is fined and banished for three years and the Norwegians are outlawed for life. Money is given for Vigfúss's journey.

At times marriage was also part of an arbitrated settlement. After the main feud in *Hœnsa-Þóris saga* (ch. 17), Tungu-Oddr wants to claim Ǫrnólfsdalr, the home of Hersteinn Blund-Ketilsson's father-in-law, Gunnarr Hlífarson. Tungu-Oddr's son Þóroddr, who is in love with Gunnarr's daughter Jófríðr, wants to end the long feud. Þóroddr takes the side of Gunnarr, his father's long-standing enemy, to prevent Tungu-Oddr from taking over the farm. When Tungu-Oddr comes to burn Gunnarr in his house, Þóroddr declares that Oddr will have to deal with him first, but men come between them and prevent a fight. The settlement includes Þóroddr's marriage to Jófríðr Gunnarsdóttir. In *Víga-Glúms saga* the men in the district arbitrate the dispute between Glúmr and the Esphœlingar; they agree that Glúmr shall arrange a marriage between Herþrúðr Gizurardóttir and Þorgrímr Þórisson (ch. 11). This conflict between Glúmr and the Esphœlingar came about when Glúmr arranged a marriage between Þórdís Gizurardóttir and a relative of his, a match that had been refused to Þorgrímr Þórisson. In *Njáls saga* (ch. 159), in the final settlement, Kári Sǫlmundarson marries Flosi's niece Hildigunnr, Hǫskuldr Hvítanessgoði's widow.

Direct Resolution

This type of resolution could come either in the midst of a feud or at the end of one. In *Laxdœla saga* (ch. 16), Hǫskuldr Dala-Kollsson is approached by a farmer, Þórðr goddi, for protection in a divorce suit. Hǫskuldr, who is well liked and well respected, does not intend to support

the farmer without compensation. After obtaining the
management of all the farmer's wealth by *handsal* and
getting the farmer to foster his favorite, but illegitimate,
son Óláfr pái, Hǫskuldr deals with the powerful family of
the farmer's wife. He settles the suit by giving the family
generous gifts and convincing them that they have no case.

Hólmganga was a way of directly resolving a dispute by a
one-to-one fight or duel. It was eventually outlawed in
Iceland (as noted in *Gunnlaugs saga ormstungu*, ch. 11). In
Reykdœla saga (ch. 1), Þorsteinn bolstǫng challenges Eysteinn Mánason to a *hólmganga* after Eysteinn refuses to
pay for linen sold to him by Þorsteinn. He wounds Eysteinn
in the foot and collects three marks of silver. In *Ljósvetninga saga*, Hrólfr Þorkelsson, in possession of the Ljós-
vetning *goðorð*, goes to the thing to settle with Eyjólfr
Guðmundarson over killings in a long-standing feud between Eyjólfr and Hrólfr's cousin, Þorvarðr Hǫskuldsson.
Eyjólfr states he is not certain he will want to pay. Hrólfr
asks support at the thing and, after being turned down by
Þorkell Geitisson, who will not go against Eyjólfr, tells
Skegg-Broddi that he will challenge Eyjólfr to a *hólmganga*, should Eyjólfr's men prevent him from proceeding
with his case. Skegg-Broddi is prepared to support him in
this decision. Eyjólfr, finally permitting Gellir Þorkelsson
to arbitrate, pays the fines (A, ch. 20; C, ch. 30). At the
beginning of *Eyrbyggja saga* (ch. 8), Þórólfr bægifótr successfully challenges an old, childless man to a *hólmganga* in
order to acquire his land. In *Njáls saga*, Hrútr Herjólfsson
challenges Mǫrðr gígja when they fail to settle the disposition of Unnr Marðardóttir's dowry after Unnr declares
herself divorced from Hrútr. Mǫrðr, who is an old man,
refuses to fight. The conflict over the divorce settlement
continues, and Hrútr tries to break the case on a legal
technicality. Gunnarr challenges Hrútr to a *hólmganga* and
Hrútr pays (chs. 8, 24).

Gunnarr is again the challenger in a later case over an
inheritance (ch. 60). When the case is about to end on a

legal technicality, Gunnarr challenges Úlfr Uggason on behalf of Ásgrímr Elliða-Grímsson. Also, in the case against Otkell mentioned earlier, Gunnarr is advised by Hrútr Herjólfsson to challenge Gizurr hvíti to a *hólmganga*, to have his brother Kolskeggr challenge Geirr goði, and to have men ready to attack Otkell and his men, but Gizurr comes to Gunnarr first with the offer of *sjálfdœmi* (ch. 51). Gunnlaugr ormstunga, in his saga, challenges Hrafn Qnundarson to a *hólmganga* at the thing, because they have recently exchanged insulting verses. Conflict between them over Hrafn's wife, Helga Þorsteinsdóttir, once promised to Gunnlaugr, has been long-standing. The two men's fathers and several other men part them, but no settlement is reached (ch. 11).

Blood vengeance is a form of violent direct resolution that is found widely in the sagas. In *Hávarðar saga Ísfirðings*, when Hávarðr takes to his bed for a year after the death of his son Ólafr, his wife Bjargey goads him into seeking retribution from Þorbjǫrn Þjóðreksson (chs. 5.– 9). When his attempts are unsuccessful, Hávarðr goes back to bed for another year. Again Bjargey arouses him, this time to seek atonement at the thing. Hávarðr refuses the settlement when Þorbjǫrn throws Ólafr's teeth at him. Although he has gained the support of Steinþórr, a powerful chieftain, Hávarðr again goes to bed for a year. After winning the support of her brothers, Bjargey makes a final attempt to induce her husband to act. This time a rejuvenated Hávarðr kills Þorbjǫrn and his brother Ljótr.

In *Valla-Ljóts saga* (ch. 9), Hrólfr Sigurðarson wants to pursue blood vengeance for the killing of his brother Bǫðvarr. Bǫðvarr, a merchant, has been killed on his return to Iceland in an act of blood vengeance for the killing of a relative of Valla-Ljóts's (ch. 7). This relative was killed by Hrólfr Sigurðarson (ch. 5) in blood vengeance for his other brother Halli, killed by Valla-Ljótr (ch. 4). Hrólfr is then advised against this policy by Þrándr from Grímsey because there has already been a settlement in the killing, although Hrólfr was not present at the settlement, and the chieftains' full enmity will be aroused if he goes against their settlement. Prándr tells him it is a bad habit to settle first and kill afterward. Hrólfr threatens to kill one more time and when Prándr asks him if he will take money, Hrólfr says he will accept *sjálfdœmi*. It is given reluctantly, and he awards himself 200 silvers.

Blood vengeance, as is clear from the above examples, is a legitimate but violent means of direct resolution. It often occurs after a legal settlement has directed compensation be paid to the injured family and fines or outlawry be assessed against the perpetrators. Humor often colors the process of blood vengeance.

Porsteins saga hvíta includes a number of acts of blood vengeance resulting from thefts by Einarr Pórisson and from his marrying of Helga, the betrothed of his partner, Porsteinn fagri. When the injured partner is refused compensation, he kills Einarr (ch. 6). Einarr's father gathers men to seek vengeance. He attacks and kills Porsteinn fagri's brother. Also killed is Einarr's brother-in-law Porgils, son of Porsteinn hvíti. Porsteinn fagri is outlawed and returns after five years. Upon his return Porsteinn fagri offers *sjálfdœmi* to Porsteinn hvíti for his killing of Porgils, his son. At first Porsteinn hvíti does not accept the offer, although Porsteinn fagri sets the payment at the highest level. Porsteinn fagri then makes the gesture of giving up his life by laying his head on the knee of Porsteinn hvíti, who invites him to move to his farm and manage it. Porsteinn fagri agrees to this settlement. The situation remains peaceful for eight years, during which time Porsteinn marries Helga. Porsteinn hvíti realizes that his grandson, Brodd-Helgi, is getting old enough to think about revenge. In order to avoid an additional killing, Porsteinn hvíti recommends that Porsteinn fagri go to Norway. Porsteinn fagri leaves and peace is maintained (ch. 7).

Sjálfdœmi is the procedure by which one party to a feud, usually the injured party, names his own award. In *Víga-*

Glúms saga (chs. 17–18), Bárðr Hallason, an *ójafnaðar-maðr*, and his blind father have a case against Hallvarðr, the foster father of Vigfúss Glúmsson, for stealing sheep. Glúmr voids the case. When a pig so fat it can hardly stand up disappears, Bárðr goes to summon Hallvarðr again. "And when he finds Hallvarðr, he brings the case to a speedy end by cutting off Hallvarðr's head." Bárðr's father goes to Glúmr and offers *sjálfdœmi*. Glúmr settles in a reasonable way, but later the case leads to blood vengeance.

In *Fóstbrœðra saga* the widow Sigrfljóð gives Vermundr 300 silvers after she has his thingmen, Ingólfr and his son Þorbrandr, killed (ch. 5). Later in the saga Bjarni Skúfsson takes Þorgeirr Hávarsson's horse to herd sheep while Þorgeirr is asleep. When Bjarni returns, he refuses to relinquish the animal before he reaches his house and a fight ensues. Bjarni's father's shepherd joins in and both he and Bjarni are killed. Illugi and Þorgils Arason, his cousins, offer Skúfr *sjálfdœmi* immediately and he accepts it (ch. 8). Both these resolutions are final.

In *Ljósvetninga saga*, after Guðmundr inn ríki has finally killed Þorkell hákr in the series of incidents following the insults against Guðmundr, he and his men travel to Guð-mundr's foster father, Einarr Konálsson. They announce the killing, and Einarr gives Guðmundr the money he is holding from Guðmundr's previous cases, telling him to offer compensation to those people, the Ljósvetningar, who hold the right to vengeance. Guðmundr meets with two of them, Tjǫrvi and Hǫskuldr Þorgeirsson, and the parties agree to settle (A, ch. 9; C, ch. 19).

In *Þorgils saga ok Hafliða*, Hafliði Másson finds himself making amends for his rude and unruly nephew Már. At one point Már kills the captain of a boat belonging to the farmer Hneitir. Már goes to Hafliði and tells him of the killing. Then Hneitir goes to Hafliði, his chieftain, who immediately offers to compensate his nephew's action in silver or else to take over the household and dependants of the dead man. This arrangement settles the matter. Soon after this incident the saga tells of the killing of Hneitir by Már (chs. 5–6).

In the same saga, Hafliði is to settle between himself and Þorgils Oddason, whom Hafliði has outlawed (ch. 18). Trusting in his strength as a *goði*, Þorgils has refused to leave, although reconciliation has failed. Hafliði finally gets *sjálfdœmi* with the condition that Þorgils not be outlawed or lose his rights to his *goðorð* and farm. All conditions are carried out; after the settlement is specified, many men contribute toward its payment. The settlement is final and both sides hold to it. Þorgils sends Hafliði generous gifts and afterward they side together in legal cases (chs. 28–32).

In *Íslendinga saga*, Sturla Sighvatsson has a case against the Hrafnssons because they are harboring their relative Aron Hjǫrleifsson, whom Sturla has outlawed. Acting on behalf of the Hrafnssons, Staðar-Bǫðvarr (Bǫðvarr Þórðarson of Staðr) settles with his cousin Sturla by paying ten hundreds on behalf of the Hrafnssons at the thing (ch. 55). Later in the same saga Óláfr Þórðarson and his brother Sturla with sixty men take livestock from Hólar, a farm belonging to Órækja Snorrason, their cousin. As the feud continues, Órækja plunders in the district and finally, in an effort to get *sjálfdœmi*, seizes Óláfr's ship and men. With Bǫðvarr Þórðarson acting to settle the dispute, Óláfr gives Órækja *sjálfdœmi*. Órækja then drops the case for the sake of *vinátta* (chs. 101–103).

Njáls saga has a number of familiar examples. The disputes settled by *sjálfdœmi* between Njáll and Gunnarr, which grew from an argument between their wives, have already been discussed. Earlier in the saga Hrútr Herjólfsson and his half brother Hǫskuldr Dala-Kollsson, in order to compensate for the slaying of Glúmr, the second husband of Hǫskuldr's daughter, Hallgerðr, present gifts to Glúmr's surviving brother. These gifts are offered and accepted only after Hallgerðr's foster father, Þjóstólfr, is killed. Þjóstólfr himself killed both Hallgerðr's first husband and Glúmr. As the second killing was contrary to Hallgerðr's wishes, she sends the foster father to her uncle Hrútr to be killed (ch. 17).

Later in the saga, Gizurr hvíti goes to Gunnarr and offers him *sjálfdœmi* against Otkell Skarfsson. Gunnarr has previously offered Otkell *sjálfdœmi* in the case of Otkell's accusation against Hallgerðr for stealing cheese. Otkell says that although the offer of *sjálfdœmi* is a good one, he would rather put the case in the hands of Geirr goði and Gizurr hvíti. He sends his friend Skammkell to the two chieftains to get their advice. On his return, Skammkell lies to Otkell, reporting that the chieftains wish to summon Gunnarr and continue the fight. Later on, when Gizurr discovers Skammkell's lie at the thing, he approaches Gunnarr. After some hesitation, Gunnarr accepts *sjálfdœmi*, pays for the damages caused Otkell by Hallgerðr, forces Otkell to take back the treacherous thrall he had previously sold Gunnarr, and awards himself a fine from Otkell for the summoning (chs. 49–51).

The killing of an *ójafnaðarmaðr* often became a necessity when his behavior threatened others in the community. Usually in these instances the disruptive party avoided the normal channels of negotiation. At times the immoderate character did not submit to arbitration because he was too powerful, because he was bent upon carrying out blood vengeance, or because he wanted to have his opponent outlawed. The society could stand the stress of unresolved conflict only for a reasonable period. When one man continually refused to participate in the resolution of a dispute, especially if he acted without regard for the balance of power, he might be killed by another chieftain who had the support of his peers. If a farmer killed an overbearing, disruptive person, chieftains often helped him to flee abroad to safety.

In *Hávarðar saga Ísfirðings* (ch. 11), Hávarðr kills Þorbjǫrn Þjóðreksson goði from Ísafjǫrðr, who killed Hávarðr's son Óláfr. At the thing no fine is imposed, as Þorbjǫrn was an *ójafnaðarmaðr* (ch. 22). Víga-Styrr is killed by Gestr, the son of Þórhalli, in *Heiðarvíga saga* (ch. 9). Styrr had harassed and finally ambushed and killed Þórhalli for taking in Einarr, against whom Styrr had many cases (ch. 7). As the settlements offered Gestr by Styrr were insulting (ch. 8) and Styrr was overbearing, Gestr is protected after the killing by various chieftains and passage to Norway is procured for him (ch. 10). In *Svínfellinga saga* (ch. 11), Qgmundr Helgason ambushes and kills Sæmundr Ormsson and his brother Guðmundr in a long-running conflict. Qgmundr is a powerful and popular farmer, whereas Sæmundr is an extremely overbearing *goði*. Qgmundr lets Abbot Brandr decide the case (ch. 14). A fine is levied on Qgmundr, and he must either go into the monastery at Þykkvabær or leave the district of Síða, both relatively light punishments for killing a chieftain. He chooses to leave the district.

Rejected Resolution

Settlements were refused, in most cases, when the feud had reached such proportions that one party wanted to inflict extreme harm on the other rather than gain something from the resolution. *Droplaugarsona saga* narrates a long feud between Helgi, son of the widow Droplaug, and Helgi, son of Ásbjǫrn. At one point Helgi and his mother Droplaug have Droplaug's second husband Hallsteinn killed. Helgi Ásbjarnarson takes up the case for this killing against his enemy, Helgi Droplaugarson, who is fined and banished for three years. Helgi Droplaugarson refuses to abide by the settlement and, although legally an outlaw, he continues to conduct his legal affairs as though nothing has happened. The two Helgis fight and Helgi Droplaugarson is killed. His brother, Grímr, survives and kills Helgi Ásbjarnarson, whose nephew, Hrafnkell goði Þórisson, then takes up the case and refuses Þorkell Geitisson's offer to pay on Grímr's behalf. Grímr, declared an outlaw (chs. 7–14), eventually dies abroad (ch. 15).

Reykdœla saga narrates a long feud between Vémundr kǫgurr Þórisson (Fjǫrleifarson) and Steingrímr Ǫrnólfsson. Many of the conflicts are arbitrated by Áskell Eyvindarson. In one case (ch. 12), Vémundr talks an idiot, Þorgeirr, into throwing a sheep's head at Steingrímr. Þorgeirr is killed by Steingrímr. Áskell Eyvindarson tries to maintain the peace by giving Steingrímr three good gifts to compensate for the insult, but Steingrímr refuses them. Steingrímr waits two years and then kills Vémundr's brother (ch. 13). In the same saga (ch. 15), Vémundr Fjǫrleifarson refuses two marks of silver which his uncle, the chieftain Áskell, offers him to settle the case against Steingrímr Ǫrnólfsson. Saying he does not want Áskell's money, Vémundr drops the case. The feud continues until Steingrímr's and Áskell's deaths balance each other out (ch. 16).

In *Hœnsa-Þóris saga* (ch. 9), when his house is being burned, Blund-Ketill offers again to settle the dispute over the hay Hœnsa-Þórir claims was stolen from him, but the offer is refused by Hœnsa-Þórir. Blund-Ketill is then burned.

In *Ljósvetninga saga* (A, ch. 6; C, ch. 14), Guðmundr inn ríki, who has been grievously insulted by Þórir Helgason and Þorkell hákr, plans his revenge. He finds an opportunity when Þórir is found to possess some goats that should have been included in a *féránsdómr* conducted by Guðmundr. Þórir offers Guðmundr a compromise in the case of the goats but the offer is refused (C) because Guðmundr prefers to have Þórir outlawed. In the same conflict, Guðmundr's brother Einarr wants Guðmundr and Þórir to compromise, but Guðmundr again refuses. Later on (A, ch. 6; C, ch. 15), Einarr again tries to persuade Guðmundr to settle. Instead of reaching a compromise, however, Guðmundr wants Þórir to give him all his possessions. In a dramatic gesture, Einarr throws a cloak on the

ground as an insulting gift and the brothers part on bad
terms. At the thing, Þorkell Geitisson makes a plea for
arbitration but Guðmundr once more refuses (A). Guðmundr's repeated rejections of a settlement are all part of
his plan to cause the downfall of the two men.

A persistent refusal to settle sometimes resulted in wearing down the opposition and obtaining the terms desired.
In *Ljósvetninga saga* (A, chs. 15–17; C, chs. 25–27), as a
result of a dispute between them, Eyjólfr Guðmundarson
and Þorvarðr Hǫskuldsson ride to the thing. Skegg-Broddi
approaches Eyjólfr and asks if he is ready to settle. When
Eyjólfr refuses, Skegg-Broddi talks to Eyjólfr's friend
Gellir Þorkelsson, who says that Eyjólfr will not settle
unless Brandr, Hǫskuldr, Þorkell, and Hallr, all Þorvarðr's
men, are outlawed. For his part Skegg-Broddi knows that
Þorvarðr will agree only to allow Hallr to be outlawed.
Again Skegg-Broddi asks Eyjólfr to settle, but he refuses a
second time. At the court Skegg-Broddi and Gellir make
another attempt. They also ask Þorvarðr to settle. Finally it
is agreed that Gellir is to arbitrate. Hallr is banished for life;
800 silvers are assessed for Koðrán Guðmundarson's
death; and Þorkell, Brandr, and Hǫskuldr are banished for
three years.

In *Hrafns saga Sveinbjarnarsonar*, Hrafn's thingman
steals part of a beached whale which Þorvaldr Snorrason
has bought. Hrafn offers to settle with Þorvaldr, but Þorvaldr prefers to steal from the one who stole from him. He
harasses Hrafn's thingmen (ch. 12). Later in the same saga
(ch. 19), when Þorvaldr, after further conflicts, attacks
Hrafn and sets fire to his house, Hrafn offers to settle.
Þorvaldr makes no response. From the burning house
Hrafn then offers to leave Iceland, but Þorvaldr refuses to
accept the compromise. Þorvaldr agrees to let all the others
out of the house, if Hrafn will let Þorvaldr do with him as he
wishes. Þorvaldr then seizes Hrafn, his nephew, and
another man. Hrafn is beheaded and the other two are
maimed.

In *Njáls saga* (ch. 49), Otkell Skarfsson refuses Gunnarr's offer of money and of *sjálfdœmi* in the case of Hallgerðr's stealing of cheese. In the same saga Njáll offers Flosi a settlement when Flosi and his men surround Njáll's farm and set fire to his house, but Flosi refuses (ch. 129). He is willing to let Njáll, the women, children, and servants out, but not Njáll's sons or his son-in-law Kári. Earlier in the saga Snorri goði heads a court of twelve arbitrators in the case of Hǫskuldr Hvítanessgoði's killing (ch. 123). After everything is arranged, Flosi and Skarpheðinn exchange insults and Flosi refuses to touch the money. Later, after Flosi's burning of Njáll, Hallr Þorsteinsson asks Kári to settle by compromise after he stops the fighting between Flosi and Kári and their supporters (ch. 145). Kári refuses and carries out blood vengeance.

Index

Actions, bringing of, 6
Advice, x, 12, 21, 71, 75, 88, 89, 103, 172, 194, 241, 242, 243, 247
Advocacy, x, xi, 37–38, 39, 40, 41, 42, 45–46, 51, 57, 64, 74–97, 114–141 passim, 152–154 passim, 161, 163, 168–179 passim, 180, 183–189 passim, 195, 203, 206, 223, 245–258 passim. *See also* Brokerage; Feudeme; Goading; Information passing; Kinship and kinship bonds; Self-advocacy
Advocacy, feudeme of, x, xi, xii, 37–38, 39, 40, 41, 42, 45–46, 57, 64, 74–97 passim, 115, 116, 117, 127, 155, 161, 163, 180, 195, 203, 206, 223, 245–258 passim. *See also* Arbitration; Brokerage, Goading; Information passing; Self-advocacy
aðalból, 148n, 149
Afanas'ev, Aleksandr, 47
Agriculture, 33–34
Agulandus, king, 197, 200
Alexander the Great, 3
Álfheiðr Þorvaldsdóttir, 16
Álfr Ǫrnólfsson, 254
Allegiance, 82, 214
Allen, Richard, 7n, 54–55
Alliance, 26, 66, 90, 104, 134, 189, 202, 213, 217, 245
Allodial-type holdings, 148, 149
Álptafjǫrðr, 104, 108, 171

Althing, xiii, 16, 27, 30, 37, 60, 63, 81, 90, 189–190, 210–216 passim, 250–253
Añabrekka, 139
Andersson, Theodore M., 49–53, 66n, 182
Án trúðr from Gunnlaugarstaðir, 234
Aptrgangr. See Revenant
Arbitration, 30, 42, 76, 92–93, 101, 102–106, 112, 120, 125, 127–128, 150, 159, 196, 197, 202, 223, 224, 229, 237, 239, 240, 242, 247, 249, 259–265, 273, 274, 275. *See also* Advocacy; *góðgjarn maðr*; *góðviljamaðr*; Resolution
árborinn maðr, 80
arfskot [fraud in inheritance matters], 150, 151, 152, 217
Ari inn fróði Þorgilsson, 143
Arngerðr Ásólfsdóttir, 237
Arngrímr goði Helgason, 118, 248, 263
Arngrímr Þorgrímsson, 19, 140
Arnkell goði Þórólfsson, 19, 70, 89–90, 109, 116, 120, 131–134, 148, 150, 153–154, 224, 229, 238, 244, 253
Arnórr rauðkinnr Steinólfsson, 16–18, 136–140
Arnórr Þorgrímsson, 261, 263
Aron Hjǫrleifsson, 270
Ásgeirr austmannaskelfir, 126

Ásgrímr Elliða-Grímsson, 167, 172, 175, 176, 178, 179, 226, 247, 263, 267
Ásgrímr Ketilsson, 252
Ásgrímr Þorvaldsson, 16
Áskell Eyvindarson, 177, 228, 229, 230, 231, 240, 247, 253, 255, 259, 273
Ásný knarrarbringa, sister of Þorsteinn tittlingr, 237
Assemblies, locations of, vi (map 1), 76. *See also* Althing; *várþing*; *leið*
Ástríðr Vigfúsdóttir, 225, 256
Ásvǫr Þórisdóttir, 171
Atli, a farmhand, 184, 185
Atli Hásteinsson, 124–125, 127, 151
Auðr, wife of Þórarinn svarti, 241, 244
Auðr, wife of Þórðr Ingunnarson, 254
Austfirðinga sǫgur, xv
áverkamál [legal action for blow], 89

Baltic lands, 196
Bandamanna saga, xiv, xv, 61, 229, 232, 234, 235, 239, 251
Barð in Fljót, 135
Barði Guðmundarsson, 238, 261
Bárðr Álfsson, 254
Bárðr Hallason, 249, 265, 269
Barter, 33, 34, 76
Basín, 199
Beck, Heinrich, xix, 24, 90–91
Beitivellir, 175, 176
Bekker-Nielsen, Hans, 122n
Benediktsson, Jakob, xiii
Beowulf, 3
Bergþóra Skarpheðinsdóttir, 65, 70, 95, 162, 180, 182, 183, 184–190 passim, 239
Bergþórshváll, 184, 186, 189
Bernarður of Averna, 201
Bersastaðir, 169
berserkr, 252
Bersi inn spaki Ǫzurarson, 263
Berufjǫrðr, 168
Birningr Steinarsson, 61, 93, 227, 231, 256
Bishops, 32, 91, 100, 155, 211, 212

biskupa sǫgur [bishops' sagas], 4, 5n, 32n
Bjargey Valbrandsdóttir, 267
Bjarni Brodd-Helgason, 51, 61, 108, 117, 131, 165, 167, 169, 171, 176, 178, 256
Bjarni Skúfsson, 269
Bjǫrn, from Snotrunes, 236
Bjǫrn, relative of Fjǫrleifarsons, 231
Bjǫrn hattarmaðr [pseudonym for Vémundr Þórisson]
Blood brotherhood, 41
Blood, rain of, 128
Blood vengeance, 67, 98, 107, 108, 110, 112, 115, 117, 134, 148, 181–182, 245, 267–268, 271
Blund-Ketill Geirsson, 22, 59, 70, 118, 228, 248, 260, 262, 273
Bolli Þorleiksson, 14, 15, 69, 70, 93, 145, 147, 222, 223–224, 238, 239, 248, 256, 257, 258
Bólstaðr, Arnkell's farm, 88, 89, 153
bóndi, pl. *bœndr* [farmer], xi, 22, 28, 29, 31, 78, 79–83, 90, 101, 128, 135, 181, 210, 211, 212, 213, 214, 215, 217. See also *þingfararkaupsbóndi*
Bookprosists, school of, 7, 9, 142, 190
Borgarfjǫrðr, xiii, xiv (map 2)
Borgfirðingar, 261
Borgfirðinga sǫgur, xiii
Brandkrossa þáttr, 263
Brandr Gunnsteinsson, 73, 250, 274
Brandr Jónsson, abbot, 272
Brandr Jónsson, bishop, 233
Brandr Sæmundarson, bishop, 103, 158
Breiðafjarðardalir, 146
Breiðafjǫrðr, xiv (map 2), 15, 105, 146
Breiðdalsheiðr, 169
Brennu-Njáls saga, x–xii, xiv (map 2), xv, xvi, 45, 54, 59, 61, 62, 65, 70, 71, 94, 100, 101, 107, 111–112, 117, 121, 147, 161–190 passim, 194, 200, 226, 227, 232, 234, 237–239, 243, 247, 248, 250, 254, 257, 260, 262, 264, 265, 267, 270, 275
Bribery, 177, 178, 234, 251

Brodd-Helgi Þorgilsson, 21, 30, 69, 71, 72, 108, 109, 148, 165, 193, 222, 227, 232, 246, 253, 268

Broddi Bjarnason, 229, 253

Brokerage, x, 41–44, 45, 74–83, 90, 92, 103, 140, 141, 145, 150, 172, 181, 192, 193, 194, 196, 197, 199, 202, 204, 223, 245–254. *See also* Advocacy

Brynjólfr rósta [the ruffian], 185, 186, 187

Burners, 117, 173, 175, 179, 264; committed by oath, 165; prosecution of, 174

Burning, xii, 13, 22, 45, 59, 107, 110, 111, 128, 153, 162, 169, 173, 182, 223, 228, 229, 244, 252, 253, 260, 263, 264, 265, 273, 274

Byzantium, 202

Bægifótshǫfði, 133

Bø, Olav, 107n

Candlemas, 13, 129

Chansons de geste, 4, 198

Character traits, 66

Charlemagne, 4. *See also* Karlamagnús

Cheating, 43, 67, 69, 70, 226, 232, 233, 240, 242

Chieftain. See *goði*

Chieftaincy. See *goðorð*

Chivalric romance, 4

Christianity, 9, 30, 35, 200, 211

Church, 31–35 passim

Clergy, 35, 91, 110, 155, 212

Climax theory, 50–53

Clover, Carol, 55–56

Cluster. *See* Feud cluster

Cluster, nuclear, 115, 116–117

Compensation, 19, 42, 43, 72, 75, 92, 99, 103, 112, 133, 139, 165, 183, 184, 185, 186, 187, 189, 202, 234, 235, 236, 238, 242, 243, 247, 265, 268, 269, 273

Compromise, 98, 102, 106, 109–110, 111, 119, 158, 179, 180, 181, 201, 249, 260, 273–274, 275

Conflict, x, xi, 39, 42, 44, 45, 51, 57, 63–74 passim, 111, 114–141 passim, 152–154 passim, 170, 174–175, 178, 183–188 passim, 201, 203, 206, 214, 222–244 passim, 260. *See also* Conflict, feudeme of; Dowry; Feudeme; Inheritance; Insult; Land; Seduction

Conflict, feudeme of, x, xi, xii, 2, 5, 39, 42, 44, 51, 57, 63–74 passim, 104, 111, 114–115, 116–117, 118, 120, 127, 155–162, 180, 181, 189, 194, 203, 206, 214, 222–224, 258, 260, 271

Confrontation, 40, 45, 97, 105, 115, 242

Cook, Robert, 74

Cottage Industry, 34

Court system, 214–217 passim

Cú Chulainn, 3

Cultural continuity, Iceland's, 26

Curse, in saga, 15, 193

Death, order of, in inheritance cases, 155–159

Deildartungumál [Tunga affair], 155

Dennis, Andrew, xix, 113n

Dirtskerry, in *Eyrbyggja saga*, 105

Dishonor, 12, 18, 19, 134

Disloyalty, knightly, 198

Dispute(s), 5, 12, 16, 20, 24, 40, 42, 43, 46, 69, 71, 115, 196, 208, 216, 273, 274

Divorce, 61, 71, 72, 228, 248, 249, 254, 256, 265, 267

dómr [court], 13. *See also duradómr; fjórðungsdómr*

Dowry, 2, 61, 68, 69, 71, 107, 128, 217, 227, 228, 248, 267

Drápuhlíð, Vigfúss' farm, 87, 121

Dreams, 167, 170

Droplaugarsona saga, xi, xiv, xv, 38–46 passim, 62, 72, 103, 116, 227, 231, 234, 236, 238, 241, 246, 254, 260, 272

Droplaug Þorgrímsdóttir, 39, 241, 260, 272

dróttinn [lord, master], 147

Duels, 79, 98, 107

Dundes, Alan, 48–49
duradómr [door court], 12, 13, 129, 130
Dynhagi, home of *Gálmr* Grímsson, 111
Dýrafjǫrðr, 230

Egill Skalla-Grímsson, 3, 11–12, 67, 75, 109, 196
Egill Skúlason, 251
Egils saga Skalla-Grímssonar, xiii, xiv, xv, 4, 69, 109, 196, 197, 251
Einarr Helgason, 231, 237
Einarr Konálsson, 241, 249, 269, 273
Einarr's Harbor, 125
Einarr Teitsson, goði, 12, 25, 75, 197, 251
Einarr Þorgilsson, 93, 118, 151, 227, 231, 237, 254, 256
Einarr Þórisson, 240, 268
Einarr Þveræingr Eyjólfsson, 249, 250, 269, 273
einvígi [single combat], 52, 107. *See* Duels
Eiríkr of Goðdalir, 171
Eiríkr Þorsteinsson, 237
Eiríkr ǫrðigskeggi [bristle-beard], 171
Eiss, 199
Eldjárn, Kristján, xvi
Elements, substitution of, in saga narrative, 206
England, 196
Epic heroes, 2, 192, 203
Epics, xxi, 4, 9, 49, 68, 196, 197, 199
Erlendr Brandsson, 239
Esphœlingar [the people of Espihóll], 19, 139, 225, 226, 265
Espihóll, 135, 136, 138
Ethics: chivalric, 202; Christian, 203
Exile. *See* Banishment
Eyfirðinga sǫgur, xv
Eyjafell, 65, 187
Eyjafjǫrðr, xii, 6, 64, 83, 84 (map 3) 100
Eyjólfr Bǫlverksson, 176, 178
Eyjólfr Einarsson, 240, 246
Eyjólfr Guðmundarson, 72, 250, 267, 274

Eyjólfr Hallsson, 119, 151
Eyjólfr Valgerðarson, 136, 229
Eyrbyggja saga, xiii, xiv, xv, 19, 43, 61, 69, 70, 72, 74, 87, 95, 104, 107, 109, 116, 120, 121, 128–134, 148, 150, 151, 152, 224, 228, 229, 238, 241, 244, 253, 266
Eyrr, 88
Eysteinn Mánason, 229, 231, 253, 266
Eyvaldr Øxna-Þórisson, 171
Eyvindr Bjarnason, 95
Eyvindr Þorkelsson, 177

Family sagas [*Íslendinga sǫgur*], xi–xv, xiv (map 2), 1, 4, 5, 7, 38, 143, 155, 161, 196, 198, 201, 203, 256
Famine, 34–35
Farmer. *See bóndi*
féránsdómr [court of confiscation], 103, 118, 220, 232, 242, 260, 273
Fetch, 186
Feud chain, 8, 44, 46, 58, 111–112, 114–142 passim, 161–190 passim, 183–189 passim, 206, 207
Feud clusters, xi, 8, 58, 114–142 passim, 123, 127, 140, 162–163, 183, 191–192, 194, 195, 196, 203, 206, 207, 224, 226, 245, 255; clusters, closing of, 97
Feudeme, active unit of saga feud, introduced, 57–62. *See also* Advocacy; Conflict; Resolution
Feudemic substitution and closure, 62, 96–97
Fictitious kinship bonds, 75, 247–248
Fifth court. *See fimtardómr*
fimtardómr [fifth court, the court of appeals], 81, 215
Fines, 33, 44, 102, 113n, 263
Finnbogason, Magnús, xvi
Fishing, 33
fjórðungsdómr [quarter court], vi (map 1), 214, 215
fjǫrbaugsgarðr [sanctuary], 219
fjǫrbaugsmaðr [lesser outlaw], 219. *See* Outlawry
fjǫrráðamál [lawsuit for conspiracy against one's life], 89

Flattery, 164, 177

Fljótamannagoðorð, 103

Fljótsdalr, 171

Fljótshlíð, 175, 188

Fljótshlíðingar [people of Fljótshlíð], 61

Flosi the priest, 239

Flosi Þórðarson, xii, 45, 53, 59, 64, 94, 112, 117, 162, 164, 167, 169, 171, 172, 174, 175, 176, 178, 180, 189, 192, 200, 250, 257, 264, 265, 275

Folkloristic element in *Hrafnkels saga*, 201, 203

Folktales, 1, 48

Foote, Peter, xix, 9, 113n

formlose Gewalt [formless power], 6

fornaldar sǫgur [sagas of antiquity], 4

Forni Sǫxólfsson, 16

Fornungar, 16

Fóstbrœðra saga, xiii, xiv, xv, 121, 224, 230, 238, 260, 269

Fosterage, 40, 41, 71, 75, 90, 104, 159, 160, 233, 240, 245, 247, 248, 266

Freeprosists (school), 7, 9

Free State, vi (map 1), 24, 29, 32, 37–38, 76–83, 101, 110, 207, 210, 211, 216

Freyfaxi, 201

Freyr, 201

Freysteinn bófi, 154

Friðgerðr Kjarvalsdóttir, 250

Fróðá on Snæfellsnes, 12, 14, 72, 74, 128, 129–131, 244

Gásar, ship landing, 17, 138

Geirmundar þáttr heljarskinns, xiv, xv, 78

Geirmundr heljarskinn, 78

Geitir Lýtingsson, 21, 30, 69–71, 75, 108, 109, 222, 227, 232, 246, 253

Gellir Þorkelsson, 251, 252, 267, 274

Genealogies, x, 52, 60, 62, 66, 87, 207

Geoffrey of Monmouth, 123

Geographical terms, xv

Germany, 212

Gestr Oddleifsson, 241, 251, 254

Gestr Þórhallason, 261

Ghosts, 12, 14, 72, 208, 244

Gifts, 9, 42, 75, 238, 239, 240, 248, 261, 266, 270, 273

Gils Þormóðarson, 237

Gísla saga Súrssonar, xiii, xiv (map 2), xv, 15, 61, 192, 249, 253

Gísli Markússon, 231

Gísli Súrsson, 61, 64, 75, 141, 192, 193, 194, 249, 253

Gizurr Hallsson, 16

Gizurr hvíti Teitsson, 12, 129, 172, 173, 176, 178, 267, 271

Gizurr Ísleifsson, bishop, 100, 212

Gizurr Kaðalsson, 17, 19, 58, 102, 139

Gizurr Þorvarðarson, 31

Glúmr. *See* Víga-Glúmr

Goading, 43, 52, 89, 92–95, 147, 153–154, 164, 177, 185–186, 188, 200, 203, 241, 244, 256–257, 267; priests subject to, 81

Goddastaðir, 108

góðgjarn maðr, pl. *góðgjarnir menn* [benevolent man], 90, 102, 260–261. See also *góðviljamaðr*

goði, pl. *goðar* [chieftain], xi, 6, 28, 31, 76, 79, 80–86, 90, 92, 99, 102, 103, 109, 117, 147, 150, 159, 169, 172, 209–211, 213, 215–217, 219, 220, 229

goðorð [chieftaincy], 16, 29, 39, 72, 80, 95, 178, 203, 210, 211, 215, 223, 234, 235, 245, 246, 248, 251–252, 261, 267, 270

góðviljamaðr, pl. *-menn* [man of good will], 102, 128, 218, 224, 260. See also *góðgjarn maðr*

Grágás, law compilation, 26, 44, 113, 145, 148, 151, 210, 212, 213

Graut-Atli [Gruel-Atli], 171

Grettir Ásmundarson, 3, 141, 192, 194, 244

Grettis saga Ásmundarsonar, xiv (map 2), xv, 3

Grímr Droplaugarson, 238, 241, 272–273

Grímr eyrarleggr Gunnsteinsson, 134

Grímr Tófuson, 124

Grímsey, 230

Gróa Gizurardóttir, 100

Guðbjǫrg Álfsdóttir, 227
Guðbrandr Þorsteinsson, 235–236
Guðbrandr Þorvarðsson, 250
Guðmundar saga dýra, xii, xv, 83,
    103, 110, 119, 151, 237, 239, 252,
    264
Guðmundarstaðir, 21
Guðmundr, witness to drownings, 155
Guðmundr Arason, bishop, 32, 91
Guðmundr inn dýri Þorvaldsson [the
    worthy], xii, 16, 75, 83, 103, 110,
    119, 192, 239, 252, 264
Guðmundr Eyjólfsson, 261
Guðmundr Grímsson, 99–100
Guðmundr Hallsson, 231
Guðmundr Ormsson, 272
Guðmundr inn ríki Eyjólfsson [the
    powerful], 31, 61, 93, 106, 169, 179,
    192, 229, 232, 241, 247, 249, 254,
    261, 262, 269, 273–274
Guðný Brandsdóttir, 231
Guðríðr Þorsteinsdóttir, 226
Guðrún Ósvífrsdóttir, 14, 15, 95, 145,
    147, 239, 254, 257
Guðrún Þórðardóttir, 239
Gunnarr Hámundarson of Hlíðar-
    endi, 52–53, 65, 107, 112, 113, 147,
    180, 182–189, 194, 226, 227, 232,
    237–238, 243, 245, 254, 260, 262,
    264, 267, 270, 271, 275
Gunnarr Hlífarson, 21, 75, 265
Gunnarsstaðir, 23
Gunnlaugr ormstunga Illugason
    svarta, 195, 267
Gunnlaugs saga ormstungu, xiii, xiv
    (map 2), xv, 195, 196, 266
Gunnsteinn Eysteinsson from Lón,
    134
Gurevich, Aaron Ya., 7n, 15, 149n
Gvitalín, 197, 199

Hafliði Másson, 31, 91, 99, 101,
    269–270
hagiography, influence of, 4
Hákon jarl, 261
Hákon, king of Norway, 227
Hákon Þórðarson, 239
Halla Lýtingsdóttir, 71, 171, 227

Hallberg, Peter, 5n, 6n
Hallbjǫrn inn sterki [the strong], 168
Halldóra Gunnsteinsdóttir, 134–135
Halldórr Óláfsson, 238
Halldórr Sturluson, 233
Halldórsson, Óskar, 9n
Hallfreðar saga, xv, 195
Hallfreðr Óttarsson, 195
Hallgerðr Hǫskuldsdóttir langbrók,
    65, 70, 95, 162, 180, 182–188, 190,
    232, 239, 262, 270–271, 275
Halli Sigurðarson, 238, 240, 262, 267
Halli Þorbjarnarson, 249
Hallr, brother of Ingjaldr, 242
Hallr Gizurarson, priest, abbot, and
    lawspeaker, 230, 252
Hallr of Síða, 168, 172, 175, 180
Hallr Ótryggsson, 274
Hallr Þorsteinsson, 275
Hallsteinn goði, of Hallsteinsnes, 244
Hallsteinn, of Víðivellir, 260, 272
Hallvarðr, foster father of Vigfúss,
    269
Hallveig Þorviðardóttir, 124
Háls Þórisson, 231
Halvorsen, Eyvind, 199n
handlag [handclasp to indicate formal
    agreement], 90. See *handsal*
handsal, verb *at handsala*, [formal
    handshake or handslap], 20, 71, 75,
    124, 127, 146, 151, 154, 177, 217,
    224, 227, 235, 255, 262, 266
Hánefr, of Óþveginstunga, 70,
    247–248
Haraldr inn hárfagri, king of Norway,
    77
Hárekr, from Áss, 250
Hásteinn Atlason, 125
Haugafjǫrðr, 125
Haukdœlir, 31
Haukr, man of Snorri goði, 224, 238
Hauksbók, version of *Landnámabók*,
    124
Hauldr, 80
Haunting, 14, 72, 128–134, 244
Hávarðar saga Ísfirðings, xiii–xv, 70,
    109, 224, 238, 240, 246, 250, 253,
    267, 271

Hávarðr inn halti Ísfirðingr, 70, 109, 224, 238, 240, 246, 253, 267, 271–272

Hávarðr Þórisson, 229

Heiðarvíga saga, xiii–xv, 61, 116, 121, 242, 261, 272

Heinaberg, 151, 256

Helgafell, 12, 20, 104, 129

Helga Krakadóttir, 268

Helgason, Jón, 7n

Helgastaðir, 16, 103, 119

Helga Þorsteinsdóttir, 267

Helgi Arngrímsson, 248

Helgi Ásbjarnarson, 39, 41, 42–46, 62, 72, 116, 228, 231, 234, 236, 238, 241, 246, 254, 260, 263, 272

Helgi Droplaugarson, 39, 41, 43, 44, 46, 62, 116, 228, 231, 234, 236, 241, 246, 254, 260, 272

Helgi Harðbeinsson, 257

Helgi Njálsson, 174, 181

Helgi Snorrason, 224, 260

héraðshǫfðingi [district leader], 20

Herjólfr Þórisson, 240, 246

Hermoen, messenger of Karlamagnús, 199

Hermundr Ávaldason, 236

hersir [regional military commander in Norway], 77

Hersteinn Blund-Ketilsson, 21, 75, 104, 260, 263, 265

Herþrúðr Gizurardóttir, 19, 135, 139, 265

Heusler, Andreas, 5, 6, 37, 49

Heydalir in Breiðdalr, 168

Hieatt, Constance, 199n

Hierarchy, lack of, 37–38, 42, 76–87

Hildigunnr Starkaðardóttir, 180, 257, 265

Hjalti Skeggjason, 176, 178, 262–263,

Hjarðarholt, 146

Hlenni the old, 135

Hlíðarendi, 52, 66, 185, 187, 188, 227

Hlíf, wife of Gunnsteinn, 134

Hneitir, from Ávík, 269

Hof, 21, 51, 170, 176

hóf [moderation], 30, 108, 218

Hólar, bishop's seat in northern Iceland, 32, 91, 212

Hólar, farm, 270

hólmganga [duel]. See also *einvígi*, 107, 194, 218, 227, 266–267

Hólmgǫngu-Ljótr, 224, 250

Hólmsteinn Bersason, 246

Hólmsteinn Spak-Bersason, 169, 171

Homespun. See *vaðmál*

Honor, 15, 18, 43, 45, 72, 73, 100, 110, 134

Hornafjǫrðr, 65

Horsefighting, 72, 110, 243

Hrafnagil, 18, 138

Hrafn, at Lundarbrekka, 70

Hrafn Brandsson, 239

Hrafnkell Freysgoði, 96, 169, 201, 203, 258

Hrafnkell goði Þórisson, 72, 168, 234, 246, 202, 272

Hrafnkels saga Freysgoða, xiv, xvi, 7n, 9, 95, 141–142, 191, 201–204, 258; folkloristic elements in, 201, 203

Hrafnkelsstaðir, 39, 169

Hrafn, son of Þorviðr, 125, 128

Hrafns saga Sveinbjarnarsonar, xiv (map 2), xv, xvi, 223, 231, 236, 274

Hrafnssons, 242, 252, 270

Hrafn Sveinbjarnarson, 223, 230

Hrafn Þorkelsson, 250

Hrafn Ǫnundarson, 267

Hreiðarr Refsson, 21

Hróaldr Eiríksson, 171

Hróarr Hámundarson, 165

Hróðný Unadóttir, 264

Hrólfr Sigurðarson, 98, 262, 267

Hrólfr Þorkelsson, 267

Hrólfssons, 262

Hrolleifr Arnaldsson, 249, 264

Hrútr Herjólfsson, 61, 71, 107, 227, 254, 262, 267, 270, 271

Humor, 106–107, 268

Hvammr in Dalir, 91, 156

Hvammr in Hvammssveit, 22

Hvammr in Þórsárdalr, 108, 131

Hvamm-Sturla. See Sturla Þórðarson

Hæringr Þorgrímsson, 126

Hœnsa-Þórir, 59, 118, 228, 248, 260,

263, 273
Hoensa-Þóris saga, xiii, xiv (map 2), xv, 21, 30, 59, 70, 75, 104, 118, 248, 260, 263, 265, 273
Hǫfða-Þórðr, 264
hǫfðingi [leader], 105
hǫfuðból, 148–149n
Hǫskuldr Dala-Kollsson, 71, 146, 200, 227, 248, 262, 265, 270
Hǫskuldr Þráinsson Hvítanessgoði, 111–112, 180, 188, 200, 238–239, 240, 247, 248, 257, 265, 275
Hǫskuldr Þorgeirsson, 261, 269, 274

Icelandic Commonwealth. *See* Free State
Illugi Arason, 269
Illugi inn svarti, 228, 261
Immigrant society, 26–27
Immunity, 113n
Information, nonactive unit of saga feud, 45, 58, 63–65, 67, 161, 206, 207
Information passing, 39–40, 58, 92, 93, 116, 128, 178, 180, 183, 187, 188, 257–258
Ingimundr Þorsteinsson, 249
Ingjaldr Hallsson, 232
Ingjaldr Helgason, 16, 136
Ingjaldr Hrólfsson, 240
Ingjaldr Hǫskuldsson, from Keldur, 165
Ingjaldr Sauðeyjargoði, 242
Ingólfr sviðinn, 238, 269
Ingólfr Þorsteinsson, 68, 72, 235, 252
Ingólfr Þorvaldsson, 243
Inheritance, 2, 42, 67, 69, 105, 118, 231, 256, 262, 266
Insult, 2, 39, 70, 73, 112, 115, 165, 167, 170, 178, 180, 183, 186, 194, 195, 216n, 222, 223, 228, 232, 234, 235, 239–242, 246, 253, 255, 256, 263, 267, 272, 273–274, 275. *See also* Verse, insulting
Interdiction, religious, 142
Irish monks, 210
Ísleifr Gizurarson, 212
Íslendingabók [the Book of the Ice-

landers], xii, xiii, 26
Íslendinga saga, xiv, xv, 61, 242, 252, 270
Íslendinga sǫgur. See Family sagas
Íslenzk fornrit, xii–xvi
Ísólfr at Tjǫrnes, 72, 250

jafnaðardómr [case before an umpire], 102
Jófríðr Gunnarsdóttir, 265
Jóhannesson, Jón, xv, xvi, 144n
Jón Ketilsson, 252
Jón Loftsson, 31–32, 61, 156, 158, 264
Jónsson, Guðni, xiii, xv
Jón Þorsteinsson, 236
Journey, 4, 12, 15, 18, 45, 54, 88, 118, 162, 163–179, 180, 253, 265
Judges, 92, 104, 215, 234
Judgment, 263
Judicial system, vi (map 1), 76, 214–216
Jury, of neighbors, 179. See also *kviðr*
Jǫkulsfirðir, 238

Kaðall, father of Gizurr, 135
Kálfafell in Lón, 168
Kálfr, from Stokkahlaða, 243
Kári Hrútsson, 244
Kári Sǫlmundarson, xii, 64, 94, 117, 162, 164, 167, 172, 173, 178. 180, 189, 192, 200, 239, 264, 265, 275
Karlamagnús, 197
Karlamagnús saga, 4, 198–201
Karlsson, Gunnar, 10
Katla of Holt, 72, 244
Ker, W. P., xviii, xix, 49, 63
Ketilbjǫrn inn gamli Ketilsson, 126
Ketill Sigfússon, 240
Ketill Þorsteinsson, 99–100
Ketill þrymr Þiðrandason, 45, 170
Killing, and arbitration, 58, 66, 98, 102, 106, 109, 115, 182, 212, 237, 238–239, 244, 260, 264, 267
Kinship and kinship bonds, 17–19, 22, 41, 42, 53, 66, 67, 75, 87, 90, 104, 134–140, 164, 169, 172, 180, 190, 196, 212, 215, 217, 234, 245,

247–249, 265
Kjalleklingar, kinsmen of Vigfúss
  Bjarnarson, 88–89, 105
Kjartan at Fróðá, 12, 14, 74, 129
Kjartan Óláfsson, 14, 15, 70, 72, 93,
  145–148, 195, 222, 223–224, 238,
  239, 256, 258
Kjartan Þorvaldsson, 254
Klemet Karlsefnisson, 254
Knappavǫllr, 167
Knútr, brother of Auðr, 254
Koðrán Guðmundarson, 274
Kolbeinn Tumason, 111
Kolfinna Ávaldadóttir, 236
Koll-Oddr vegandi, 91
Kolr, a foreman, 184
Kolr Víga-Skútuson, 177
Kolskeggr Hámundarson, 232, 243,
  264, 267
Konáll Ketilsson of Einarsstaðir, 229
Konunga sǫgur [Kings' sagas], 4
Konungsbók [private lawbook], 210.
  See also *Grágás*
Kormákr Ǫgmundarson, 140, 195
Kormáks saga, xv, 196
Kotkell, a Hebridean, 244, 251, 254
Krákunes, a valuable forest, 20, 154,
  224
Kristjánsson, Jónas, xv
Krossavík, 171
kviðr [jury of neighbors], 216

Lagarfljót, 170
Lambasons, 165
Lambi Sigurðarson, 232
Lambi Þorbjarnarson, 257
Land, x, 2, 14–15, 20–21, 31–33,
  34–35, 42, 66, 69–70, 77–79, 109,
  118, 143–159 passim, 217, 223–
  227. See also Produce of the land
Landnámabók [the Book of Settle-
  ments], xii, xiii, 15, 26, 78, 121, 123,
  124, 127, 143, 144, 151, 152
landnámatíð (*landnámsǫld*) [the time
  of settlement], 26, 77–79, 210
landnámsmaðr, pl. *landnámsmenn*
  [settler], 77, 78, 79, 80, 104, 122,
  124, 143

Lárusson, Magnús Már, 148n
Latin, 36–37
Laugaland, 119
Laugar, 14, 15, 145, 146, 258
Laugarvatn, 175
Law, orally preserved, 216
Law Council, 113n
Lawmaking, 211. See also *lǫgrétta*
Law Rock, 158
Law system, development of, 210
Laxdœla saga, xiii–xv, 14, 61, 68–
  72, 93, 116, 121, 145, 146, 150, 155,
  195, 222, 223, 226, 227, 238, 239,
  242, 244, 249, 251, 254, 256, 257,
  265
Laxdœlir [the men of Lax River
  dale], 61
Learning, in Iceland, 36–37
leið [fall assembly], 214
leiðangr [Old Norwegian levy], 77
Leiðólfr, from Leiðólfsstaðir, 125
Líndal, Sigurður, 148n
Literacy, passage into, 36
Livestock, 33, 34, 42, 70, 116, 228,
  231–233, 269
Ljósvetningar, 177, 269
Ljósvetninga saga, xiv, xv, 61, 72, 93,
  103, 106, 172, 231, 232, 238, 241,
  249, 250, 254, 261–263, 267, 269,
  272, 274
Ljótr Þjóðreksson, 267
Ljúfini, priest, 231
Loftr Markússson, 223, 231
Lón in Hǫrgárdalr, 134
Lord, Albert, 56–57
Lotman, Y., xix, 114
Love, unrequited, 195. See also Poets'
  sagas
Loyalty, 189, 198; to the king, 196
Lundarbrekka, 70
lygi sǫgur [lying sagas], 4
Lýtingr, of Sámsstaðir, 247
Lǫgberg [lawrock], 212–215
lǫgeyrir, pl. *lǫgaurar* [law ounce], 230
lǫgmaðr, pl. *lǫgmenn* [legal advisors
  to the lawspeaker], 216
lǫgrétta [the national legislature or
  law council], 81, 211, 215, 219

Lǫg-Skapti. *See* Skapti Þóroddsson
lǫgsǫgumaðr, pl. lǫgsǫgumenn [law-
speaker], 216
Lönnroth, Lars, 53−54, 163n, 164n

Magic, 15, 248, 262
Magnús berfœttr, king of Norway,
160
Máni of Grímsey, 230
Már Bergþórsson, 269
Már, follower of Snorri goði, 89−90
Margrét Oddsdóttir, 237
Marriage, 17−19, 21, 41, 42, 53,75,
104, 106, 134−140, 180, 196, 217,
248−249, 265, 268. *See also* Kinship
and kinship bonds
Melkólfr, the slave, 232
Memorization, 8
Memory, collective, 59−60
Michaelmas, 238, 262
Móeiðarhváll, 243
Monastery, 272
Mosfell, 173
Motif, 48,
Motifeme, 48−49
Musset,Lucien, xix, 24
Mýlaugr, 229
Mýnes, 241
Mýrar, 223
Mǫðrufell, 19, 140
Mǫðruvellingar, 179
Mǫðruvellir, 136, 169
Mǫrðr gígja Sighvatsson [the fiddle],
61, 71, 227
Mǫrðr Valgarðsson, 62, 172, 174, 176,
178, 200, 232, 237, 238, 243, 263

Narrative: strategy, xi, 5, 5n, 8, 46−
57, 111, 112, 115−117, 120−121,
127, 133−134, 173, 183, 203−204,
206
Njáll Þorgeirsson, xii, 45, 52, 65, 101,
112, 117, 147, 162, 164, 172, 174,
180, 182, 184−189, 194, 200, 234,
237, 240, 245, 247, 248, 262−264,
270, 275
Njáls saga, See *Brennu-Njáls saga*
Njálssons, 53, 172, 180, 187, 194, 200,

238, 239, 247, 257
Njarðvík, 45, 170
Nordal, Sigurðr, xiii, 7, 9, 142, 190
Norway, 4, 5, 24, 30, 32, 77, 80, 160,
193, 212, 225, 232, 237, 240, 261,
268, 272
Norwegian, 228, 265
Nôtre Dame, 160. *See also* Sæmundr
inn fróði

Obligation, x, 6, 22, 25, 40, 41−45,
75, 79, 88, 104, 164−165, 171, 177,
178, 189, 190, 192, 197, 202, 205,
212, 244, 247, 248
Oddaverjar, 31, 160
Oddi, 157, 159
Oddkatla from Þjórsárdalr, 135
Oddkell from Þjórsárdalr, 135
Oddný Brodd-Helgadóttir, 168
Oddr Kǫtluson, 244
Oddr Ófeigsson, 72, 232, 234, 235,
239, 251, 252
Oddr sindri, 263
Oddr Unason, 264
Odysseus, 3
óðal [allodial property], 148
Óðinn, xii, 156
Ófeigr Járngerðarson, 106
Ófeigr Skíðason, 251, 252
óheilagr [unprotected by the law],
105, 220, 236, 261, 264
óhelgi [state of being *óheilagr*], 220
ójafnaðarfullr. See *ójafnaðr*
ójafnaðarmaðr, pl. *ójafnaðarmenn*
[unjust or overbearing man], 30,
82, 98, 107, 108−110, 116, 117, 147,
187, 213, 217−218, 224, 229, 232,
238, 243, 250, 269, 271, 272
ójafnaðr [injustice, unfairness], 17,
21, 67, 109, 137, 146; full of *ójafnaðr*, 152
Óláfr Hávarðsson, 70, 238, 241, 246,
253, 267, 272
Óláfr Hǫskuldsson, 254
Óláfr pái, 91, 146, 147, 195, 200, 227,
248, 266
Óláfr Þórðarson, 270
Óláfssons, 257

Ólason, Vésteinn, 10, 50n
Old Icelandic Commonwealth. *See* Free State
Old Norse, pronunciation of, xii
Olgeirsson, Einar, 37
Ólsen, Björn M., xx, 114
Opponents, paying off of, 251
Ordeal: by iron, 237; trial by, 226
Order, addressed more than justice, 101
Orrostudalr, 125
Órækja Snorrason, 270
Óspakr Glúmsson, 72, 232, 235, 239, 251
Ósvífr, Hallgerðr's father-in-law, 262
Ósvífr Helgason, 14, 145, 146
Ósvífr Oddsson, 263
Ósvífrssons, 258
Otkell Skarfsson, 232, 267, 271, 275
Ótryggr, 263
Óttar at Grímstungur, 72, 235
Outlaw, 72, 191, 220, 235, 242, 270, 272
Outlaw sagas, xiii, 4, 192, 195, 197
Outlawry, 3, 12, 71, 91, 100, 102, 112, 113, 113n, 118, 119, 193, 197, 203, 219, 223, 225–226, 228–233, 236–238, 240, 242, 247, 249–251, 253, 254, 258–261, 263–265, 268, 270, 271, 273, 274
Overbearing man. *See ójafnaðarmaðr*
óvinfengi [enmity], 17, 137
Óþveginstunga, 70

Páll Sǫlvason, priest, 156–159
Pálsson, Hermann, xix
Parable, 99
Pattern, narrative, 147–148
Payment, 15, 33, 42–43, 46, 103, 112, 173, 177, 194, 224, 238, 240, 242, 243, 245, 247, 259, 261, 262, 263, 266, 267, 268, 269, 270, 271, 274
Perkins, Richard, xix, 113n
Pike, Kenneth, 48
Place names, 66
Plausibility, 121
Poets, attitude toward feud, 141
Poets' sagas, xiii, 4, 72, 140, 195, 197

Political system, 76–87. *See also* Free State
Portents, x, 66, 67, 167, 187, 207
Power, 42, 72, 73, 75, 77, 80, 82, 83, 92, 102, 148, 190, 196, 216, 217, 218, 222, 234, 271, 272
Prestssaga Guðmundar góða, xv, 91
Priests, 12, 14, 110, 129, 130
Produce of the land, 223, 228–231
Productivity, 34–35
Prophecy, 58, 187, 189
Propp, Vladimir, 47–50

Quarter Court. *See fjórðungsdómr*
Quarter divisions, boundaries of, vi (map 1)

Rafnsson, Sveinbjörn, 10, 123n, 149
Ragnheiðr Gellisdóttir, 252
Rannveig, wife of Þorgrímr skinnhúfa, 228, 254
Rannveig Þorgeirsdóttir, 171
Realism, 5, 10, 26, 226
Reciprocity, 90, 164, 247
Refr Gestsson, 135
Refr inn rauði Steinbjarnarson, 21
Reinfrei, 199
rekspegn, 80
Repetition, 10, 67, 121, 163, 180, 182, 189
Resolution, x, xi, 39, 40, 41, 42, 46, 51, 57, 68, 75, 97, 98–113 passim, 114–141 passim, 153, 158, 159, 161, 184–189 passim, 200, 201, 203, 206, 217, 223, 232, 233, 235, 240, 242, 247, 259–275 passim. *See also* Arbitration; Blood vengeance; Feudeme; Vengeance
Revenant(s) [*aptrgangr* or *aptrganga*], 3, 12, 75, 128–131, 244. *See also* Haunting
Revenge, 96, 203, 267, 268, 273
Reykdœla saga ok Víga-Skútu, xiv (map 2), xv, 61, 70, 93, 228, 229, 230, 231, 240, 246, 247, 253, 255, 259, 266, 273
Reykir in Byskupstunga, 176
Reykjaholt, 156

Richgiver [*Stakksmýrr*] field, 223
riddara sǫgur [knights' sagas], 4
rímur, 57
Rollant [Roland], 11, 197, 199, 201
Rumors, 234
Rúnólfr Kaðalsson, 136
Rúnólfr Nikulássson, 110
Rúnólfr Úlfsson, 257

Saldís, wife of Gizurr Kaðalsson, 19, 135, 140
Sámr Bjarnason, 95, 96, 97, 202, 203
sáttarmaðr [arbitrator], 219
Scovazzi, Maco, 7n, 190
Seduction, 72–73, 193, 234, 235–238
Self-advocacy, 92–93, 108–109, 118, 254–256
Self-judgment. See *sjálfdœmi*
Settlement of disputes. See Resolution
Settlement period. See *landnámatíð*
Settlers, original. See *landnámsmaðr*
Síða, 272
Sigfússon, Björn, xv, 10, 31
Sigfússons, 165, 172, 175, 182
Sighvatr Hallsteinsson, 96
Sighvatr Sturluson, 223
Sigmundr Lambason, 65, 186–189
Sigmundr Þorkelsson, 109, 225, 226, 229, 256
Sigrfljóð, widow from Jǫkulsfirðir, 238, 269
Sigurðr, Norwegian merchant, 233
Sigurðr Fáfnisbani, 4
Sigurðr hrísa, son of Haraldr hárfagri, 124
Sigurðr kerlingarnef, from Laugar, 237
Silver, 33, 42, 220
Símon Bjarnason, 236
Single combat, 187, 226, 227. See also *hólmganga*; *einvígi*
sjálfdœmi self-judgment, 46, 98, 102, 107, 108–109, 157, 159, 184, 185, 186, 187, 218, 225, 232, 234, 242, 247, 249, 252, 267, 268, 269, 270, 271, 275
Skálaholt (Skálholt) [bishop's seat],

32, 211
Skálavað, 96
Skammkell from Hof, 271
skapraun, 63
Skapti Þóroddsson, lawspeaker, 178, 216, 229, 262
Skapti Þorsteinsson, 179
Skarpheðinn Njálsson, 112, 147, 177, 184, 186, 188, 194–195, 239, 247, 248, 275
Skegg-Broddi Bjarnason, 250, 254, 267, 274
Skjǫldr, Sigmundr Lambason's Swedish companion, 65, 186, 188
skógarmaðr [full outlaw], 219. See also Outlawry
skreið [stockfish], 33–34n
Skriðudale River, 39
Skúta Áskelsson, 259
Slaves, 20, 151, 217, 225, 228, 229, 260, 271; payment or compensation for, 183, 184, 185
Slay, Desmond, xix
Snorri Eyvindarson, Hlíðarmannagoði, 261
Snorri goði, 12, 20, 61, 72, 74, 87, 88, 91, 106, 109, 112, 116, 120, 128, 150, 154, 167, 178, 179, 192, 200, 224, 229, 238, 253, 256, 257, 261, 264, 275
Snorri Hallsteinsson, 96
Snorri Sturluson, 159
Snorrunga family, 256
Snæfells Peninsula, 152
Sorcerer, 251
Sorcery, 234, 244, 254, 262
Spá Gils, a seer, 241
Spak-Bersi Qzurarson, 169
Springtime thing. See *várþing*
Staðar-Bǫðvarr Þórðarson, 270
Staðarhóll, 231
Staðarhólsbók, private lawbook, 210. See also *Grágás*
Starkaðr Barkarson, 243, 254, 262
Stealing. See Theft
Steinarr Qnundarson, 11, 69, 75, 109, 196, 251
Steingrímr Qrnólfsson, 70, 71, 228,

230, 240, 246, 255, 273
Steinn Refsson, 21
Steinn Þorbjarnarson, 230
Steinólfr Arnórsson, 19, 140
Steinólfr Ingjaldsson, 16, 136
Steinvǫr Hallsdóttir, Flosi's wife, 168
Steinþórr, from Eyrr, 88, 224, 250, 253, 267
Stórhǫfðingjar [magnates], 29, 198
Sturla Sighvatsson, 242, 252, 270
Sturla Þórðarson (Hvamm-Sturla), 31, 91, 108, 156–159, 227, 231, 233, 237, 254, 256, 270
Sturlubók, version of *Landnámabók*, 123
Sturlunga saga(s), xii, xiv (map 2), xv, 1, 4, 5, 36, 87, 110, 143, 161, 198, 223
Sturlungar, 29, 156
Sturlu saga, xiv (map 2), xv, 61, 93, 108, 118, 151, 154, 155, 227, 231, 233, 237, 254, 256
Styrr. *See* Víga-Styrr
Summoning, 72, 129, 174, 271
Support, x, 13, 28, 44, 71, 75, 76, 79, 100, 101, 104, 106, 109, 117, 153, 154, 164, 168, 169, 179, 224, 226, 248, 249, 250, 252, 253, 254, 256, 265–266, 267, 271, 275; seeking of, 15, 41, 117, 118, 157, 161, 162, 165, 167, 169, 172, 178, 179, 189, 192, 194, 196, 202, 245, 246, 249, 253, 257
Sure-giver, *Vitazgjafi* field, 70, 225, 226, 243
Svanr the sorcerer, uncle of Hall-gerðr, 262
Svarfdœla saga, xiv (map 2), xv
Svartr, farmhand, 183, 184
Svartr, a Hebridean, 236
Svartr, Vémundr's slave, 229
Sveinn Sturluson, 233
Sveinsson, Einar Ól., xiii, xv, xvi, xix, 47
Svið, 110
Sviðinhornadalr, 171
Svínafell, 168, 172
Svínfellinga saga, xv, xiv, 272

Syntagmatic patterns, 46–57
Sæmundr inn fróði Sigfússon, 32, 160
Sæmundr inn suðreyski, 249, 264
Sæmundr Jónsson, 264
Sæmundr Ormsson, 272
Sǫlmundr Víðarsson, 232, 261, 263
Sǫrli Brodd-Helgason, 167, 168, 169, 171
Sǫxólfr Víðarsson, 232, 263
Sørensen, Preben Meulengracht, 9, 10, 149–150n

Temple, pagan, 106
Theft, 39, 44, 46, 69, 70, 71, 109, 116, 118, 124, 181, 183, 225, 228, 229, 230, 231, 232, 238, 239, 241, 242, 248, 254, 256, 258, 265, 268, 269, 270, 271, 273, 274, 275
Thing districts, 214
Thingman [*þingmaðr*], 16, 82–86, 110, 212, 213, 214, 269
Thing tax. *See* þingfararkaup
Thrall. *See* slave
Threat, 118, 174, 235, 271
Timber, dispute over, 228–229
Tithe, 31, 233
Tjarnir, farm in Eyjafjarðardalr, 135
Tjǫrvi, from Guðmundarstaðir, 21
Tjǫrvi Þorgeirsson, 269
Todorov, Tzvetan, xx, 191
tólftarkviðr [panel of twelve], 216n
Tomasson, Richard, xx, 27n, 143
Torfi, of Torfufell, 240
Trade, 33–34
Travel (nonactive unit of saga feud), x, 63–66, 161, 206
Tunga affair, 155, 158
Tunga in Sælingsdalr, 14, 145, 146, 257
Tunguland [the Tongue Lands], 155–159
Tungu-Oddr Ǫnundarson, 12, 30, 75, 197, 251, 260, 264, 265

Úlfarr kappi, 108
Úlfarr, Þorbrandr's freedman, 108, 152, 153, 224, 229
Úlfarsfell, 108, 133, 151, 152

Úlfr Uggason, 226, 267
Uni from Unadalr, 264
Units of travel and information. *See* Information; Travel
Unnr Marðardóttir (daughter of Morðr gígja), 61, 71, 107, 227, 267
Uppsalir, 19, 140
Uspensky, B. A., xix, 114
útlagi [outlaw], 220. *See also* Outlawry

vaðmál [homespun], 33, 39, 220
Valgerðr Óttarsdóttir, 68, 235
Valgerðr Rúnólfsdóttir, 136
Váli, relative of Oddr Ófeigsson, 232, 239, 251
Valla-Ljótr Ljótólfsson, 267
Valla-Ljóts saga, xiv, xv, 98, 238, 240, 262, 267
Valþjófsstaðir, 169
Vápnafjorðr, 168, 169, 170
Vápnfirðinga saga, x, xiv, xv, 21, 30, 43, 61, 69, 70, 71, 75, 108, 109, 116, 117, 148, 165, 193, 222, 227, 232, 246, 253, 256
varnaðarmaðr [protector], 153
várþing [spring assembly], 16, 44, 81, 197, 212, 214, 215, 216, 221
Vatnsdœla saga, xiv, xv, 68, 73, 234, 235, 248, 249, 252, 264
Vémundr kogurr Þórisson (Fjorleifarson), 70, 71, 93, 228, 230, 240, 246, 247, 248, 255, 273
Vengeance, 95, 133, 182, 257, 269. *See also* Blood vengeance
Vermundr inn mjóvi Þorgrímsson, 88, 89, 238, 269
Verse, insulting, 141, 188, 267
Vestfirðinga sogur, xiii
Víðines, 135
Víðivellir, 96
Víðiwood, 124–125
Víga-Glúmr, xii, 75, 109, 192, 240, 243, 256
Víga-Glúms saga, xii, xiv, xv, 16, 58, 61, 70, 72, 109, 134, 135, 224, 243, 249, 250, 256, 265, 268–269
Víga-Hrappr Orgumleiðason, 240

Víga-Skúta Áskelsson, 177
Víga-Styrr Þorgrímsson, 61, 88, 116, 242, 261, 272
Vigdís Ingjaldsdóttir, 68, 242, 249
Vigdís Þorvaldsdóttir, 16
Vigfúss Bjarnarson, 87, 89, 121
Vigfúss Glúmsson, 249, 265, 269
Vigfúss Onundarson, 110
Vigfússon, Guðbrandur, 32n
vinátta [friendship], 42, 174, 177, 248, 270. *See also* *vinfengi*
vinfengi [friendship], 17, 42, 75, 95, 134, 137, 217, 245, 249. *See also* *vinátta*
Violence, xxi, 42, 53, 101, 106, 112, 113, 117, 120, 207
Voting rules, 211
vætti (also *váttr*) [witness], 216. *See also* Witnesses

Whales, 69, 70, 229–231
Wilson, David, 9n
Witching, 72, 244
Witnesses, 14, 18, 152, 216, 226, 233
Women, treated as possessions, 72, 235
Writing in medieval Iceland, 36–37

Yngvildr Þorgilsdóttir, 237
Yngvildr Þorkelsdóttir, 170

þáttr pl. *þættir*, [short story], 51, 61, 196
þingfararkaup [thing tax], 213
þingfararkaupsbóndi pl. *þingfararkaupsbændr*, 28n, 79, 80, 212, 213
þinglagseyrir [standardized ounce], 220–221
þingmaðr. *See* Thingman
Þingvollr [the thing plain], xii, 211. *See also* Althing
Þjórs River, 124, 175
Þjórsárdalr, 135
Þjóstarr, 203
Þjóstólfr, fosterfather of Hallgerðr langbrók Hoskuldsdóttir, 262, 270, 271
Þóra, daughter of King Magnús, 160

Þórarinn, father of Grímr Tófuson, 124

Þórarinn, man from Breiðafjǫrðr, 226

Þórarinn moldoxi, 227, 254

Þórarinn svarti, 241

Þórarinn Þórisson, 135, 249

Þorbjǫrg, wife of Páll Sǫlvason, 156, 157

Þorbjǫrn, at Árskógr, 230

Þorbjǫrn, at Eyrr, 224, 250

Þorbjǫrn digri, 241

Þorbjǫrn Þjóðreksson, 70, 109, 238, 241, 253, 267, 271

Þorbjǫrn Qzurarson, 124

Þorbrandr Ingólfsson, 238, 269

Þorbrandr Þorfinnsson in Álptafjǫrðr, 108, 120, 132, 154

Þorbrandssons, 95, 154, 244, 253

Þórdís Gizurardóttir, 17, 58, 135, 136

Þórdís Guðmundardóttir, 169

Þórdís Súrsdóttir, 61

Þórdís, wife of Þorsteinn at Desjarmýrr, 236

Þórðarson, Matthías, xiii

Þórðr, at Vǫðlar, 255

Þórðr enn dofni Atlason, 125–126

Þórðr, farmhand at Hof, 243

Þórðr, from Hǫfði, 135

Þórðr, from Tunga, 21

Þórðr, of Geirólfseyrr, 39, 40, 41, 44, 45

Þórðr gellir, goði, 21, 22, 30, 61, 71, 75, 104, 105, 248, 260

Þórðr goddi, 242, 248, 249, 265

Þórðr Ingunnarson, 254

Þórðr Kárason, 248

Þórðr kausi Snorrason goða, 12, 129

Þórðr leysingjason, 65, 186, 187

Þórðr Þórarinsson, 16, 237, 239

Þorgeirr, at Hrafnkelsstaðir, 41, 42, 43, 45, 116, 231

Þorgeirr Eiríksson, 171

Þorgeirr Hávarsson, 230, 238, 269

Þorgeirr Ljósvetningagoði, 261

Þorgeirr Otkelsson, 237, 262, 264

Þorgeirr skorargeirr Þórisson, 173, 174, 176, 178

Þorgeirr smjǫrhringr, 273

Þorgeirr Starkaðarson, 237, 243, 254, 262

Þorgeirssons, 261

Þorgerðr silfra Þorvaldsdóttir, 95

Þorgerðr Þorbeinisdóttir, wife of Vigfúss, 87–90, 121

Þorgerðr Þorvaldsdóttir, 135

Þorgestlingar family, 88

Þorgils Arason, 269

Þorgils Hǫlluson, 248, 257

Þorgils Másson, 230

Þorgils Oddason, 99, 101, 270

Þorgils saga ok Hafliða, xv, 99, 158, 269

Þorgils Þórðarson, 126

Þorgils Þorsteinsson, 171, 268

Þorgísl Arason, 261

Þorgríma galdrakinn, 13, 130

Þorgrímr, freedman, 241

Þorgrímr goði Kjallaksson, 104, 106, 228

Þorgrímr Hallormsson, 248

Þorgrímr Hlífarson, 134

Þorgrímr kampi Qzurarson, 124, 125

Þorgrímr nef, 15

Þorgrímr skinnhúfa, 227, 254

Þorgrímr Þórisson, 17, 18, 19, 58, 72, 138–140, 265

Þorgrímr ørrabeinn, 126

Þórgunna, Hebridean woman, 12, 128, 129

Þórhalla in málga, 257, 258

Þórhalli at Jǫrvi, 272

Þórhallr Ásgrímsson, 172, 173, 175, 248

Þórhallr, relative of Hávarðr Ísfirðingr, 246

Þórhildr Þorkelsdóttir, 106

Þórir Akraskeggr (also called Þorgils Akrakarl), 232, 242, 248

Þórir inn auðgi Þorsteinsson [the wealthy], 155, 157

Þórir, farmer at Mýnes, 241

Þórir from Espihóll, 18, 136, 138

Þórir goði Helgason, 232, 233, 241, 249, 255, 273

Þórir Hrafnkelsson, 169

Þórir viðleggr Arnarson, 13, 129, 130

Þórir þiðrandi, 170, 171
Þorkatla Oddkelsdóttir, 135
Þorkatla Vémundardóttir, 247
Þorkell fullspakr Ketilsson, 170
Þorkell Geitisson, 39, 45, 61, 108, 117, 171, 176, 267, 273, 274
Þorkell hákr Þorgeirsson, 241, 253, 255, 269, 273
Þorkell Hallgilsson, 274
Þorkell hvelpr, 254
Þorkell inn hávi, 225, 226
Þorkell krafla Þorgrímsson, 236, 248
Þorkell lǫgmaðr, 70
Þorkell meinakr, 106
Þorkell silfri, 248
Þorkell trefill, 155, 226
Þorkell leppr Þjóstarsson, 202
Þorlákr Þórhallsson, bishop, 32, 155
Þorlaug Pálsdóttir, 155–156
Þorleifr, of Sogn, 124
Þorleikr Bollason, 248
Þorleikr Hǫskuldsson, 244, 248, 251, 254
Þormóðr Bersason, 238
Þormóðr Steinbjarnarson, 21, 75, 222
Þóroddr skattkaupandi, farmer at Fróðá, 13, 130
Þóroddr Tungu-Oddsson, 265
Þóroddr Þorbrandsson, 132–133
Þórólfr, a man from Breiðafjǫrðr, 242
Þórólfr bægifótr [lamefoot], 19, 74, 107, 108, 134, 150, 152, 154, 224, 229, 244, 266
Þórólfr Mostrarskegg Ǫrnólfsson, 104
Þórólfr sleggja, 234
Þórólfsfell, 65, 184, 185, 187
Þórólfsson, Björn K., xiii
Þórr, 105
Þórsárdalr, 132
Þórsnes, 104, 105
Þórsnesingar [the men of Þórsnes], 104–106
Þórsnessþing [Þórsnes thing], 104–106
Þorsteinn, at Desjarmýrr, 236
Þorsteinn Ásbjarnarson, 237
Þorsteinn bolstǫng, 266
Þorsteinn drettingr Bjarnason, 233

Þorsteinn Egilsson, 11, 69, 75, 196, 224, 251, 260
Þorsteinn Eyjólfsson, 225
Þorsteinn fagri Þorfinnsson, 240, 268
Þorsteinn holmuðr Skaptason, 179
Þorsteinn Ingimundarson, 234, 252
Þorsteinn inn hvíti Ǫlvisson, 171, 268
Þorsteinn Síðu-Hallsson, 253
Þorsteinn stangarhǫgg Þórarinsson, 51, 95, 243
Þorsteinn surtr inn spaki Hallsteinsson, 226
Þorsteinn svarti, 155, 257
Þorsteinn tittlingr, 237
Þorsteinn þorskabítr Þórólfsson, 104, 105
Þorsteins saga hvíta, xv, 240, 268
Þorsteins þáttr stangarhǫggs, xv, xvi, 51, 61, 95, 243
Þorsteinsson, Björn, xviii, xxi, 10, 148
Þórunn Ásgeirsdóttir, 126
Þorvaldr, father of Kjartan, 254
Þorvaldr Ketilsson þryms, 170
Þorvaldr krókr Þórisson, 250
Þorvaldr krókr from Grund, 135
Þorvaldr Oddsson, 228, 263, 264
Þorvaldr Snorrason, 223, 230, 252
Þorvarðr from Eskigrasey, 233
Þorvarðr Hǫskuldsson, 72, 250, 266, 274
Þorvarðr inn auðgi Ásgrímsson, 16
Þorvarðr Þorgeirsson, 119, 237
Þorvarðr Þorgrímsson, 262
Þorviðr Úlfarsson, 124, 125
Þráinn Sigfússon, 66, 187, 232, 240, 247
Þuríðr Barkardóttir, mistress at Fróðá, 13, 14, 129, 130, 132
Þuríðr Þórðardóttir, 135
Þrándr from Grímsey, 98, 267
þriðjungsþing [three-chieftain assembly], 212
Þváttá [Þvátt River], 168, 172
Þverá, 17, 137

Ǫgmundr Helgason, 272
Ǫgmundr Þorvarðsson sneis, 237, 252
Ǫlfysingar, 178

Ǫlkofra þáttr, xiv, xv, 61, 229, 253
Ǫlkofri (Þórhallr ǫlkofri), 229, 253, 254
Ǫlvir, 171
Ǫnundr bíldr, 125, 128
Ǫnundr sjóni Ánason, 11, 69, 75, 109
Ǫnundr Þorkelsson, 16, 110, 119, 197, 252, 264
Ǫrn of Vælugerði, 124
Ǫrnólfr rella, 228, 255

Ǫrnólfr tǫskubak, 135
Ǫrnólfsdalr, 265
Ǫzurr hvíti Þorleifsson, 124, 126, 127, 148, 151

Ørlygr, Þorbrandr's freedman, 108
Ørlygsstaðir, 108, 151
Øxfirðingar [people of Axe Fjord], 177
Øxna-Þórir, 171

This index was prepared with the help of Björn Ellertsson, Mary Jennings, and Geoffrey Lindsey.

Printed in the United Kingdom
by Lightning Source UK Ltd.
9569300001B